Saving Capitalism

JAMES S. OLSON

Saving Capitalism

The Reconstruction Finance
Corporation and the New Deal,
1933–1940

PRINCETON UNIVERSITY PRESS

PRINCETON, NEW JERSEY

Copyright © 1988 by Princeton University Press

Published by Princeton University Press, 41 William Street,
Princeton, New Jersey 08540
In the United Kingdom: Princeton University Press,
Guildford, Surrey

Library of Congress Cataloging in Publication Data will be
found on the last printed page of this book

ISBN 0-691-04749-9

This book has been composed in Linotron Sabon type

Clothbound editions of Princeton University Press books are
printed on acid-free paper, and binding materials are chosen for
strength and durability. Paperbacks, although satisfactory
for personal collections, are not usually suitable
for library rebinding

Printed in the United States of America by Princeton
University Press, Princeton, New Jersey

TO DAVID BURNER

who believed in me long before anyone else

Contents

Acknowledgments

OVER THE YEARS I have accumulated a variety of debts in writing this book. I am, of course, indebted to a host of professional librarians and archivists for their unfailing courtesy and expertise, particularly those individuals at the Library of Congress, the National Archives, the Herbert Hoover Presidential Library, the Franklin D. Roosevelt Presidential Library, and the Newton Gresham Library at Sam Houston State University. David Burner, my friend and mentor at the State University of New York, Stony Brook, has been a kind and consistent critic over the years. No student could have asked for a more dedicated teacher. I am also grateful to the Research Council of Sam Houston State University for the summer grant which financed my final research trip on this project. Finally, my wife Judy has been, to say the least, a good sport about the book. She has lived with me for twenty-one years, and with the RFC for twenty of them. Surely any court of the land would see that as cruel and unusual punishment.

Abbreviations Used in Notes

COHR	Columbia University Oral History Research Office
EHFA	Electric Home and Farm Authority
EIB	Export-Import Bank
FDIC	Federal Deposit Insurance Corporation
FDRPL	Franklin D. Roosevelt Presidential Library, Hyde Park, New York
FHA	Federal Housing Administration
FNMA	Federal National Mortgage Association
HHPL	Herbert Hoover Presidential Library, West Branch, Iowa
HOLC	Home Owners' Loan Corporation
ICC	Interstate Commerce Commission
NA	National Archives, Washington, D.C.
NRA	National Recovery Administration
OF	Official File—Franklin D. Roosevelt Presidential Library
OH	Oral History Section—Herbert Hoover Presidential Library
PP	Presidential Papers—Herbert Hoover Presidential Library
PPF	President's Personal File—Franklin D. Roosevelt Presidential Library
PPP	Post-Presidential Papers—Herbert Hoover Presidential Library
PWA	Public Works Administration
REA	Rural Electrification Administration
RFC	Reconstruction Finance Corporation
RG	Records Group in National Archives
SF	Subject File—Herbert Hoover Presidential Library
TVA	Tennessee Valley Authority
WPA	Works Progress Administration

Saving Capitalism

The Origins of the Reconstruction Finance Corporation

ON THE EVE of the Great Depression, no sector of the U.S. economy was weaker than the money markets. After World War I the U.S. financial system was a haphazard collection of 50,000 financial institutions. More than 30,000 were commercial banks; the rest were savings banks, building and loan associations, industrial banks, credit unions, and finance companies. Their numbers far exceeded demand.[1] State banking authorities had been too liberal with bank charters, and banks were often grossly undercapitalized. Urbanization was depopulating rural areas just when automobiles were drawing people into the banks of larger cities. Chain stores and mail-order houses hurt rural banks by driving country stores into bankruptcy. Rural banks were slowly losing clientele.[2] Finally, the farm depression of the 1920s ruined thousands of small banks. Many had made enormous loans for acreage expansion during World War I, only to have the revival of European agriculture destroy commodity prices and land values after 1918. Between 1921 and 1929 more than 5,000, or one-quarter of small-town banks failed.[3]

Rural banks were not the only weak link in the financial chain. Business profits rose during the 1920s, but much of the money found its way into the booming securities and real es-

[1] *New York Times*, April 27 and May 23, 1930; Jack Dublin, *Credit Unions: Theory and Practice* (Detroit, 1966), p. 149; Gerald Fischer, *The American Banking Structure* (New York, 1968), p. 110; Raymond J. Saulnier, *Industrial Banking Companies and Their Credit Practices* (New York, 1940), p. 2; Josephine Ewalt, *The Savings and Loan Story, 1930–1960* (Chicago, 1962), p. 26.

[2] Fischer, *American Banking Structure*, p. 201.

[3] Paul Trescott, *Financing American Enterprise: The Story of Commercial Banking* (New York, 1963), p. 5.

tate markets. Speculation was so intense that even weak securities with little dividends potential were in demand. Between 1925 and 1928 the *New York Times* industrial index went from 134 to 311, and the number of investment trusts and holding companies from less than 300 to more than 750. Brokers' assets went from $4 billion in 1922 to $10 billion in 1929.[4] Seduced by the lure of big profits, thousands of financial institutions liquidated government bonds and poured money into speculative ventures. Federal borrowing declined substantially in the 1920s, and government bond yields were less than 4 percent. Higher returns on stocks, corporate bonds, and mortgages were irresistible.

During the 1920s, government bonds fell from 18 to only 2 percent of life insurance company assets, while real estate and urban mortgages went from 25 to 45 percent. Building and loan associations increased their assets by $6 billion in the 1920s, most of it in real estate mortgages. Mutual savings bank portfolios went from 44 percent to 55 percent in real estate and mortgages, while government bonds dropped from 18 to 11 percent. Credit unions had more than 40 percent of their assets in real estate by 1930.[5] Less liquid than ever before, the money market was vulnerable to declines in the construction industry or securities values. Changes in corporate finance had also weakened commercial banks. Corporate profits mounted in the 1920s and dependency on commercial banks for equity and working capital declined. It was easier to float stocks and bonds than secure bank loans. The volume of commercial pa-

---

[4] John Kenneth Galbraith, *The Great Crash, 1929* (Boston, 1954), pp. 53–54, 183–84; Hugh Bullock, *The Story of Investment Companies* (New York, 1959), pp. 40–42; Benjamin Beckhart, *The New York Money Market*, vol. 3. *Uses of Funds* (New York, 1932), pp. 181–85.

[5] John Lintner, *Mutual Savings Banks in the Savings and Mortgage Markets* (Boston, 1948), pp. 216–22; J. Carroll Moody and Gilbert C. Fite, *The Credit Union Movement: Origins and Development, 1850-1970* (Lincoln, Nebr., 1971), p. 128; Shephard Clough, *A Century of American Life Insurance* (New York, 1946), pp. 306–8; Raymond J. Saulnier, *Urban Mortgage Lending by Life Insurance Companies* (New York, 1950), pp. 12–13; Ewalt, *The Savings and Loan Story* pp. 6–9; and American Bankers' Association, *The Earning Power of Banks* (New York, 1939), pp. 242–45.

per dropped from \$2.5 billion in 1923 to \$1 billion in 1929. With demand down for commercial loans, banks turned to the real estate and investment markets. Commercial loans constituted 71 percent of bank loans in 1923, but only 53 percent in 1929.[6] During the same period, real estate loans grew from \$1.4 to \$4.5 billion—from 5 to 13 percent of bank loan assets. Collateral loans to stock brokers increased from 23 to 33 percent of assets.[7] Between 1920 and 1930, bank holdings of corporate and foreign bonds increased by \$3 billion and local government bonds by \$1 billion. Yields were higher than on federal government bonds. Federal bonds declined from 35 percent of commercial bank assets in 1923 to only 28 percent in 1929.[8]

Banks were in deep trouble by 1929. In 1918, self-liquidating, short-term commercial paper had comprised the bulk of bank assets, but by 1929 those assets were loans and investments whose liquidity depended on general capital values.[9] During times of economic growth, stocks, bonds, and real estate were liquid because they could readily be sold on the booming exchanges. But if panic replaced optimism, bank assets would quickly freeze. Forced to sell at highly deflated prices, banks would see their capital disappear overnight. Unable to supply depositors with cash, they would have to default.[10] It seemed an unlikely scenario in the 1920s, and bankers ignored prudent warnings, but after 1929 the nightmare came true.

Government fiscal policies made the problem worse. During the 1920s, Secretary of the Treasury Andrew Mellon kept interest rates low because they reduced debt service costs and

---

[6] American Bankers' Association, *Changes in Bank Earning Assets* (New York, 1936), p. 18; Beckhart, *New York Money Market*, vol. 3, pp. 242–45.

[7] American Bankers' Association, *Changes in Bank Earning Assets*, p. 12; George Soule, *Prosperity Decade: From War to Depression, 1917–1929* (New York, 1947), p. 155; Beckhart, *New York Money Market*, vol. 3, pp. 128–34; Robert Sobel, *The Great Bull Market: Wall Street in the 1920s* (New York, 1968), pp. 115–16.

[8] Beckhart, *New York Money Market*, vol. 3, pp. 128–34.

[9] American Bankers' Association, *Changes in Bank Earning Assets*, p. 14.

[10] Ibid., pp. 14–15.

made it easier to float new Treasury securities. He helped reduce corporate and personal income taxes, releasing more disposable income into the securities markets. Tax reductions on capital gains shifted investment funds away from tax-free municipal and state government bonds and into the stock market, inflating securities prices even more. Mellon's goal of eliminating the national debt destroyed an important market for private funds. Because federal spending was less than 4 percent of the gross national product, fiscal policy was only a minor factor in the boom, but it contributed nonetheless.[11]

Federal Reserve Board policies fueled the boom. The board could have sold government bonds on the open market and raised discount rates, but it seemed a difficult choice. Discouraging the investment boom required higher interest rates, which would only attract more foreign capital to the United States. The United States already held more than 40 percent of the world's gold supply, and most economists believed that international financial stability would not return until Europe reestablished the gold standard. Low interest rates would stimulate investment abroad and assist the return of the gold standard, but they would also magnify the investment mania in the United States. Economists also worried that discouraging speculation might inhibit legitimate business expansion. Throughout the 1920s, the Federal Reserve Board pursued ambiguous policies.[12] To stem the speculative tide, the board raised the discount rate from 3.5 to 5 percent between 1925 and 1928, but at the same time, to stimulate "legitimate" economic growth, Federal Reserve banks purchased bankers' acceptances.[13]

[11] Marcus Nadler, Sipa Heller, and Samuel Shipman, *The Money Market and Its Institutions* (New York, 1955), pp. 181–82; Benjamin Beckhart, James G. Smith, and William Brown, *The New York Money Market*, vol. 4. *External and Internal Relations* (New York, 1932), p. 390; Sobel, *The Great Bull Market*, pp. 51–54; Cedric B. Cowing, *Populists, Plungers, and Progressives: A Social History of Stock and Commodity Speculation, 1890–1936* (Princeton, 1965), p. 187.

[12] Elmus R. Wicker, *Federal Reserve Monetary Policy, 1917–1933* (New York, 1966), pp. 85–86, 102, 107, 126; and Lester V. Chandler, *American Monetary Policy, 1928–1941* (New York, 1971), pp. 83–89.

[13] Margaret Myers, *Financial History of the United States* (New York,

Federal Reserve officials incorrectly assumed that the method of expanding the money supply guaranteed the uses of the funds. They thought they could discourage speculation with high discount rates while stimulating economic growth through heavy purchases of bankers' acceptances. But the purchase of bankers' acceptances increased the excess reserves flowing into the securities markets. With new Federal Reserve funds, most bankers increased reserves and reduced their Federal Reserve bank debt, wiping out the impact of the discount rate. Stock prices soared until 1929, when the board decided that the call loan rate, fluctuating between 7 and 12 percent, was high enough and speculation intense enough to make discount rate changes futile.[14]

High discount rates then attracted nonbank lenders into the market. Thousands of corporations, convinced that stock market yields made it more fruitful to speculate with surplus funds than reinvest, put cash in the call loan market. Because the Federal Reserve Board did not concern itself with the destination of nonbank investment funds, it had little control over the boom in securities markets in 1928 and 1929. Narrow vision eliminated much of the board's influence and contributed substantially to the collapse of the stock market in 1929 and 1930.[15]

The stock market crash threatened the money markets because of steep declines in commodity prices, land values, and securities. Thousands of marginal financial institutions verged on disaster. Rural banks, with assets tied up in agricultural mortgages, could not convert them to cash and pay off frightened depositors. With assets frozen, thousands of rural banks closed.[16] It had a chain reaction affect on larger, urban banks.

1970), pp. 301–5; Wicker, *Federal Reserve Monetary Policy*, pp. 118, 123, 127–28, 140.

[14] Galbraith, *The Great Crash*, pp. 34–36; Wicker, *Federal Reserve Monetary Policy*, pp. 129, 135–36, 143; David Elliott, "The Federal Reserve System, 1914–1929," in Herbert V. Prochnow, *The Federal Reserve System* (New York, 1960), pp. 310–15.

[15] Wicker, *Federal Reserve Monetary Policy*, pp. 142–43.

[16] Charles Collins, *Rural Banking Reform* (New York, 1931), pp. 67–68; *Commercial & Financial Chronicle*, November 27, 1930.

Many city banks had made emergency loans to rural banks or were linked to them through correspondent relationships. The stock market crash had severely eroded the value of their own assets. Rural bank failures frightened depositors, who began withdrawing money, so bankers were forced to sell prime securities. With thousands of banks trying to convert securities into cash, the stock market slumped even more. It was a vicious cycle.[17] Finally, business activity was down as well, reducing loan repayments.[18]

Railroad problems also threatened the money market. Throughout the 1920s railroad freight volume had declined because of competition from truck and airline carriers; freight rates and profits were down. After 1929, revenues declined even more, and a number of Class A lines defaulted on dividends. Railroad bond values fell sharply. For years railroad bonds were blue chip investments for banks, savings banks, and life insurance companies. Once the most prized investment in the country, railroad bonds had become unmarketable, and bank asset values reflected the collapse. The money market was facing financial catastrophe.[19]

The situation steadily deteriorated in 1930 and 1931. Whereas more than 5,000 commercial banks had failed between 1921 and 1929, including 641 failures in 1929, the position was even worse in 1930. The collapse of the National Bank of Kentucky in October triggered a brief regional banking panic, as did the failure of New York City's Bank of the United States in December. When the financial dust cleared for

[17] Lynn Muchmore, "The Banking Crisis of 1933: Some Iowa Evidence," *Journal of Economic History*, 30 (September 1970), 627–40; J. M. Daiger, "Confidence, Credit, and Cash," *Harper's*, 166 (May 1933), 279–92.

[18] Trescott, *Financing American Enterprise*, pp. 199–203.

[19] Mark W. Potter, "The Railway Situation," April 23, 1931, unpublished manuscript, NA, RG 40, Department of Commerce; Franklin Snow, "The Railroads Again Become a Problem," *Commerce and Finance*, 20 (January 14, 1931), 58; Samuel O. Dunn, "Railroads Still in Dump," *Forbes*, 28 (September 1, 1931), 45; *New York Times*, January 7, 1932; Grenville Clark, "Memorandum as to the Proposed President's Committee on the Transportation System," October 13, 1931, unpublished manuscript, NA, RG 40, Department of Commerce.

1930, more than 1,350 commercial banks had closed. It was the worst year in United States financial history.[20]

Foreign banking troubles then complicated things. In May 1931, the Kredit-Anstalt, Austria's largest private bank, closed, spreading fear throughout Central Europe. Several important German banks failed in July, and liquidity crises developed in France, the Netherlands, and Belgium in August. Worried about the stream of bad news from home and abroad, American depositors, between January and September, withdrew nearly $3 billion in deposits. More than 1,000 commercial banks went under. In Britain, fears of a worsening depression inspired British investors to demand hard currency for paper pounds, which the Bank of England could not meet. And so Britain decided to abandon the gold standard in September. Then the rest of Europe, afraid the United States was about to do the same, began converting dollar reserves to cash, drawing down the American gold supply by $275 million in just two weeks. In September, another 450 American commercial banks failed.[21]

Weakness in the money market reverberated throughout the rest of the economy. Consumers began to postpone major purchases, and personal consumption dropped from $77 billion in 1929 to $60 billion in 1931. Bankers converted assets to cash and reduced credit. Pessimistic about the economic future, businessmen postponed investment. Between 1929 and 1931, investment spending dropped from $16 billion down to only $5.6 billion. The economy was caught in a deflationary spiral. With inventories accumulating, businessmen reduced orders from manufacturers who, in turn, had to lay off workers. Consumer spending declined more.[22] Facing an economic disaster, bankers and businessmen alike abandoned the rhetoric of laissez-faire and began demanding government action.

Worried about the long-range consequences of government

[20] *Commercial & Financial Chronicle*, November 22, 1930; Milton S. Friedman and Anna Jacobsen Schwartz, *The Great Contraction, 1929–1933* (Princeton, 1967), pp. 12–19.

[21] Friedman and Schwartz, *The Great Contraction*, pp. 19–20.

[22] Lewis C. Solmon, *Economics* (New York, 1972), inside cover.

intervention, President Herbert Hoover preferred a private solution. He turned to the banking community, hoping his faith in voluntarism would be vindicated. At an October conference in Andrew Mellon's New York apartment, Hoover had prominent bankers organize the National Credit Corporation. With subscriptions totaling $500 million from commercial banks all over the country, the NCC was supposed to make low-interest loans to troubled banks. But the NCC was too cautious, loaning only $10 million in October and November, hardly enough to ease the monetary crisis. NCC directors were unwilling to risk assets in weak banks.[23]

With the economy collapsing around him and a presidential election looming on the horizon, Hoover looked back to World War I for an answer. It was hardly an unexpected step. For Hoover, the Great War and the Great Depression were related phenomena. In his view, the depression was simply the last phase of World War I. Hoover remarked in 1931 that "I believe you will all agree with me that the destruction of life and property, the great tax burdens, and the social and political instability which resulted from the Great War have had large responsibility in its [the depression's] origins."[24] Hoover also saw the war and the depression as similar crises. Both had brought drains on national resources, and both had become in their own time the country's most important priority. Dealing with the depression, Hoover remarked early in 1932, was "like a great war, in that it is not a battle on a single front but upon many fronts."[25] To fight his own battle, Hoover turned to the wartime administration of Woodrow Wilson.

President Woodrow Wilson and Congress, under extraordinary pressure to supply the Allied powers with unlimited materiel and worried about interest group rivalries and destructive competition in the economy, had established a host of new government agencies. The World War I bureaucracy was

[23] James S. Olson, "Herbert Hoover and the National Credit Corporation," *Annals of Iowa*, 41 (Fall 1972), 1104–13.

[24] William S. Myers, ed., *The State Papers and Other Public Writings of Herbert Hoover* (New York, 1934), vol. I, p. 559.

[25] *New York Times*, January 6, 1932.

the country's first experience with state capitalism on a massive scale. The direction the government took in marshalling the country's economic resources illustrated the depth of faith most Americans still had in the workings of the private market. Although the government intervened directly in the economy with a variety of regulations and subsidies, it did not assume ownership of the means of production and distribution, allowing profits to accumulate and be paid out to stockholders. In a time of economic crisis, the United States turned not to socialism but to state capitalism—placing the resources of the federal government behind the private economic establishment, determining priorities, and arbitrating interest-group conflicts, but not fundamentally altering the nature of the social and economic order.

Early in September 1916, as part of the preparedness campaign sweeping through the United States, Congress authorized Wilson to establish the U.S. Shipping Board, a five-person group charged with organizing an Emergency Fleet Corporation to construct, purchase, lease, and refit merchant vessels. In case of war, the need for supplies in Europe would be immediate, but the lead time for constructing new vessels in government shipyards was too long (the first new vessel delivered from the government shipyard in Philadelphia was not ready until after the war). When war did break out, the U.S. Shipping Board created a new merchant marine fleet by purchasing private vessels and refitting seized German and Dutch transports. By the end of the war, the U.S. Shipping Board owned one of the largest merchant fleets in the world, second only to Great Britain.[26]

The United States declared war in April 1917, and in July the Wilson administration established the War Industries Board to coordinate war production. Less than a year later, Wilson placed Bernard Baruch at the head of the WIB and gave the board new power to establish production priorities, suspend antitrust laws, fix prices, purchase supplies for the Allied

[26] John B. Hutchins, "The American Shipping Industry since 1914," *Business History Review*, 28 (June 1954), 109–11.

powers, convert existing factory facilities to a war footing, and dictate to corporate management production levels and the sources of their supplies and raw materials. Enjoying almost autocratic powers, Bernard Baruch became an economic potentate and the War Industries Board an ambitious attempt at industrial coordination. Although it frequently suffered from gross inefficiency as well as the competitive instincts of private business, it nevertheless contributed to the enormous productive outburst of the American economy during World War I.[27]

A month after creation of the War Industries Board, Congress passed the Lever act which, among other provisions, established a Food Administration and a Fuel Administration. Both agencies were to help maximize the production of food, fiber, coal, and petroleum, and to conserve and control their distribution throughout the country. Herbert Hoover was named to head the Food Administration and Harry A. Garfield the Fuel Administration. Both agencies implemented voluntary and occasionally mandatory rationing of food and fuel so that the American Expeditionary Force in Europe would have the supplies it needed. Hoover prided himself on the crusades he launched for "victory" gardens, meatless days, wheatless days, and fiber conservation. Although the Food and Fuel Administrations often became bogged down in bureaucratic red tape, corporate competition, and the conflicting demands of producers and consumers, they did assist in reallocating precious resources to the war effort.[28]

Late in 1917, with the economy apparently out of control, widespread demand appeared for drastic government action to coordinate the transportation system. Shippers wanted federal coordination to help reduce freight rates, labor unions thought it would bring the eight-hour day and higher wages,

[27] For a history of the War Industries Board, see Robert D. Cuff, *The War Industries Board. Business-Government Relations during World War I* (Baltimore, 1973). An excellent biography is Jordan A. Schwarz, *The Speculator. Bernard M. Baruch in Washington, 1917–1965* (Chapel Hill, 1981).

[28] Schwarz, *The Speculator*, pp. 86–87; Ellis W. Hawley, *The Great War and the Search for a Modern Order. A History of the American People and Their Institutions, 1917–1933* (New York, 1979), pp. 23–25.

and government bureaucrats thought it would eliminate duplicated services and increase freight volume. On December 26, 1917, Wilson created the U.S. Railroad Administration, which took control of the country's transportation system. He named William Gibbs McAdoo to head the new agency, and McAdoo quickly moved to pool equipment and facilities, establish route assignments, and improve service. The Railroad Control Act of March 21, 1918, gave the new agency legislative backing, limiting government control to a twenty-one-month period and appropriating $500 million to finance federal operations. Over the next year the Railroad Administration forced the railroads to share cars, locomotives, yards, depots, and engine houses; move freight by permit in order to reduce congestion; pay fines for loading and unloading delays; consolidate small shipments to avoid waste; and reduce advertising and passenger service.[29]

The most successful of the new agencies was the War Finance Corporation, created by an act of Congress on April 5, 1918, to augment capital investment markets and make loans to war industries. William Gibbs McAdoo was put in charge of the WFC. By the end of the year the WFC had made direct loans totaling $71.3 million, most of them to public utilities, banks, and building and loan associations. By the end of 1919, that total was up to $306.5 million, with more than two-thirds of the money loaned to railroads under the control of the Railroad Administration, and $46 million to exporters. Worried about the postwar adjustment of the economy, Congress had authorized the WFC in March 1919 to make export loans as a means of boosting domestic production. Along with the U.S. Shipping Board, the WFC became an important tool in expanding American exports after World War I.[30]

Congress continued to find the WFC useful after the war. The Agricultural Credits Act of 1921 gave the WFC $300 million to

[29] Ari and Olive Hoogenboom, *A History of the ICC. From Panacea to Palliative* (New York, 1976), pp. 84–90.

[30] *First Annual Report of the War Finance Corporation* (Washington, D.C., 1919), pp. 9–10; *Second Annual Report of the War Finance Corporation* (Washington, D.C., 1920), pp. 10–13.

loan to farmers needing intermediate credit, and in 1924 the
Federal Intermediate Credit Bank system assumed those responsibilities. The government began liquidating the WFC in
1924, a process which took six years. By 1931, while Hoover
was organizing the NCC, prominent private bankers as well as
Eugene Meyer, chairman of the Federal Reserve Board and a
former member of the WFC board of directors, were urging him
to revive the War Finance Corporation. When the failure of the
National Credit Corporation became obvious in December
1931, Hoover did just that, calling on Congress to establish a
Reconstruction Finance Corporation.[31]

For Hoover, the depression was a crisis of confidence; the
economy would not revive until private bankers increased
business loans. He assumed there were thousands of frustrated
businessmen clamoring for credit, just as there had been during World War I, and thousands of frightened bankers unwilling to make loans because of the rash of bank failures. With up
to $2 billion in capital, the RFC was to make low-interest loans
to commercial banks, savings banks, savings and loan associations, insurance companies, mortgage companies, credit
unions, and railroads. Railroad loans were especially important because of heavy financial investments in railroad bonds.
Through loans to railroads and financial institutions, the RFC
would restore banker confidence and stimulate an increase in
commercial credit. Recovery would then ensue.

Congress responded quickly and Hoover signed the bill into
law on January 22, 1932. He named Eugene Meyer, former
member of the WFC board, as chairman of the RFC board, and
Charles Dawes, former vice-president of the United States, as
president. Secretary of the Treasury Ogden Mills was an ex-officio member, as was H. Paul Bestor, head of the Federal Farm
Loan board. All four were Republicans. As Democrats on the
board, Hoover appointed railroad expert Harvey Couch of
Arkansas, Houston banker Jesse Jones, and Utah banker Wilson McCarthy. They hired lawyers, accountants, bank exam-

[31] James S. Olson, *Herbert Hoover and the Reconstruction Finance Corporation, 1931–1933*, (Ames, Iowa, 1977), pp. 12–13, 24–27, 41–43.

iners, and secretaries, rented space in the Department of Commerce's old building at the corner of Pennsylvania Avenue and 19th Street, and went into business.[32]

The RFC was a direct descendent of the War Finance Corporation. Like the WFC, it had eight divisions: auditing, legal, treasury, secretarial, agency, examining, statistical, and railroad.[33] Like the WFC, the RFC had thirty-three local offices to evaluate loan applications. Eugene Meyer recruited WFC people to staff the RFC. George Cooksey, former director of the WFC, became the first secretary of the RFC. Meyer picked Morton G. Bogue, formerly special legal counsel to the WFC, as RFC general counsel. Leo Paulger, George Holmberg, and George Brennan, all bankers with the WFC, staffed the RFC examining division. Paulger drew up a list of bankers who had assisted him with the WFC in the 1920s and recruited many of them to staff local RFC offices.[34] Finally, both the WFC and RFC viewed themselves as temporary institutions of state capitalism hoping to rejuvenate private money markets with injections of government money. Revival of normal credit channels would stimulate business production and employment.[35]

Despite the similarities, however, the RFC was a startling departure in peacetime public policy. Senator George Norris, a progressive Republican from Nebraska, commented that he could have never imagined "putting the government into busi-

[32] Eugene Meyer, COHR, pp. 627–29; New York Times, January 23–31 and February 1–7, 1932; Jesse H. Jones, Fifty Billion Dollars (New York, 1951), p. 514.

[33] Working Papers, Interoffice Communication No. 22, February 2, 1944, and "Functional Organization Charts," March 18, 1932, NA, RG 234, RFC, Secretarial Division.

[34] First Annual Report of the WFC, p. 1; New York Times, February 3, 1932; RFC, Minutes, 1 (February 9, 1932), 62; RFC, Quarterly Report for February 2 to March 31, 1932 (Washington, D.C., 1932), pp. 1–2; Fourth Annual Report of the War Finance Corporation (Washington, D.C., 1922), p. 2; "RFC Loan Agencies and Managers," February 7, 1932, unpublished manuscript, Jones Papers.

[35] Washington Post, January 16, 1932; Third Annual Report of the War Finance Corporation (Washington, D.C., 1921), p. 1; George Cooksey to Ogden Mills, March 11, 1932, Mills Papers.

ness as far as this bill would put it."[36] Hoover felt the same way. The very idea of so thoroughly subsidizing the private money markets violated his personal philosophy. The RFC was also independent of Congress, the director of the budget, and the public. It could sell its notes and obligations privately, and loan repayments would provide a revolving fund for future transactions. Managed properly, the RFC could function indefinitely without further congressional appropriations. Although it had to issue monthly and quarterly reports, the RFC did not have to reveal the names of its borrowers or the amounts of its loans.[37] Hoover knew his actions were unprecedented, but he had little choice. In a radio address to the nation, he said:

> As I have stated before, in the shifting battle against depression, we shall need to adopt new measures and new tactics as the battle moves on. The essential thing is that we should build soundly and solidly for the future.[38]

By July 1932 the RFC had loaned more than $1 billion to 4,000 banks, railroads, credit unions, and mortgage loan companies. Although bank failures declined to only eighty-five in August, the RFC had not helped increase the total supply of credit, a goal the administration considered critically important.[39] Thousands of bankers had accepted RFC loans, but huge volumes of excess reserves were accumulating at Federal Reserve banks and bank loans were still declining. Between 1929 and 1932, Federal Reserve member bank loans had dropped from more than $23 billion to $11 billion as bankers turned to liquid government securities. Bankers explained they were just prudent and the RFC was exaggerating the number of eligible borrowers and their demand for credit.[40]

[36] *Congressional Record*, 75 (January 11, 1932), 1703.

[37] *Washington Post*, January 23, 1932.

[38] Myers, *State Papers*, vol. II, p. 317.

[39] RFC, *Quarterly Report for March 1–June 30, 1932* (Washington, D.C., 1932), Table 13.

[40] American Bankers' Association, *Changes in Bank Earning Assets*, pp. 7–8, 13–14, 36–38.

Convinced the credit crisis was prolonging the depression, Hoover tried to increase commercial loans. In a July 1932 meeting with Atlee Pomerene, soon to be the new RFC chairman, Hoover said that

> many of the banks were failing to perform their duties to their clientele and to aid industry and that, if we could not bring about a change for the better in the next four or five months, the country would be a financial loss.[41]

To prevent that, Hoover sponsored a meeting of the Federal Reserve Banking and Industrial Committees in late August to discuss the credit situation. A parade of administration officials argued that the federal government had restored financial stability, and that the burden of responsibility had shifted to private business. Bankers should suppress liquidity fears and increase business loans.[42] In a speech to the National Radio Forum on August 29, Jesse Jones, an RFC board member, said:

> There has been too much reluctance on the part of banks, trust companies, etc., to borrow for the purpose of relending, not alone from the RFC but from any source. Most banks have been endeavoring to get as liquid as possible . . . too much for the public good.[43]

It was frustrating for the Hoover administration. Despite unprecedented efforts on behalf of the private economy, the RFC had not revived commercial credit, business investment, production, or employment. Not only were banks refusing to increase commercial loans despite huge volumes of excess reserves, the administration was not even sure the RFC was really strengthening the banking system. In June, the Central Republic Bank of Chicago had asked for assistance. Suffering from

---

[41] See unpublished personal recollection by Atlee Pomerene, July 25, 1932, Pomerene Papers.

[42] "Confidential History of the National Conference of Banking and Industrial Committees," unpublished manuscript, July 27–28, 1932, HHPL, PP, SF, Cabinet, Commerce; Charles Hamlin Diary, August 31, 1932, Hamlin Papers.

[43] "Speech by Jesse Jones to the National Radio Forum," August 29, 1932, HHPL, PP, SF, RFC, History, p. 174.

deflated assets and the collapse of the Insull utilities empire, the bank was on the brink of failure. To prevent a massive banking panic in the Midwest, the RFC extended a $90 million loan to the Central Republic Bank. The administration had to publicize the loan widely to reassure the public. Although the bank failed two months later, its liquidation took place without fanfare.[44]

Small bankers also complained the RFC ignored them. RFC officials explained that more than 70 percent of its loans had gone to banks located in towns with fewer than 5,000 people and that only 2 percent had gone to banks in cities of more than one million people. Critics countered that more than 40 percent of RFC funds had gone to banks located in cities with more than 200,000 people.[45] What critics failed to acknowledge was that 210 of the largest banks in the country accounted for more than 40 percent of all assets. The entire banking system was weak in 1932—large as well as small banks were in trouble. Banks with massive deposits were often burdened with massive volumes of frozen assets. They needed large RFC loans. In 1932 the RFC loaned $950 million to banks and trust companies, and $330 million went to only twenty-six banks. But this was certainly not inconsistent in a financial system where 210 banks controlled 40 percent of deposits.[46]

Because of the persistence of the depression, Hoover changed course in the summer of 1932. He had long opposed federal relief programs because he believed the RFC would

[44] *Chicago Tribune,* June 7, 1932; Charles Hamlin Diary, March 1 and June 18, 1932, Hamlin Papers; Jackson Reynolds, COHR, p. 97; Herbert Hoover, *The Memoirs of Herbert Hoover* (New York, 1952), vol. 3, pp. 170–71; *Wall Street Journal,* June 8, 1932; *Federal Reserve Bulletin,* 29 (December 1933), 745; *Congressional Record,* 75 (January 28, 1932), 2877–79; RFC, Minutes, 5 (June 27, 1932), 1017–26; Henry Stimson Diary, June 27, 1932, Stimson Papers; *Commercial & Financial Chronicle,* July 2, 1932.

[45] RFC, *Quarterly Report for January 1 to March 31, 1933,* Table 7; *Congressional Record,* 75 (July 7, 1932), 14799.

[46] *Financial Age,* 65 (January 16, 1932), 45–57. These figures were compiled by comparing the 210 largest banks listed in *Financial Age* with the list of all individual RFC loans in 1932. See RFC, Index to Minutes, 1 (1932), 656–1246, NA, RG 234, RFC, Secretarial Division.

quickly stimulate a recovery. But by summer he could no longer resist the demands from liberal Democrats and progressive Republicans in Congress. Because of criticisms of the RFC, Hoover also decided that Eugene Meyer was expendable. The fact that Meyer also vigorously opposed any expansion of RFC authority into relief, welfare, and public works only made that decision easier.[47]

Although he did not like the idea of federal relief, Hoover knew there was no alternative as long as the economy lingered in its slump. At the end of May, he introduced a relief bill to Congress, and throughout June he battled Robert Wagner and John Nance Garner to prevent them from amending it. Wagner wanted the RFC to make relief grants totaling $500 million to states, and Garner wanted it to provide for loans to individuals as well as state, county, and city governments, and to force publication of all RFC loans. Although Hoover acquiesced on the last proposal after vetoing one version of the bill, he finally succeeded in pushing his version through the Congress and signing it on July 21, 1932. The Emergency Relief and Construction Act provided $300 million for RFC relief loans to states; $1.5 billion for loans on self-liquidating public works; $36 million for twelve regional agricultural credit corporations to make marketing loans; and required publication of the recipients of RFC loans. Because Hoover wanted to give the RFC fresh leadership, the bill also removed the chairman of the Federal Reserve Board and Federal Farm Loan commissioner as ex-officio members.[48]

Charles Dawes resigned from the RFC during the crisis over the Central Republic Bank, and with Eugene Meyer and

[47] Herbert Hoover to Henry Steagall, July 8, 1932, NA, RG 234, RFC, Administrative Subject File; Henry Stimson Diary, July 18, 1932, Stimson Papers; Herbert Hoover, *Memoirs*, vol. III, p. 168; Charles Hamlin Diary, July 6, 12, 19, and September 1, 1932, Hamlin Papers; *Wall Street Journal*, July 28, 1932.

[48] *Reconstruction Finance Corporation Act as Amended and Provisions of the Emergency Relief and Construction Act of 1932* (Washington, D.C., 1932), pp. 1–4. For a complete description of Hoover's role in the legislation, see Olson, *Herbert Hoover and the Reconstruction Finance Corporation*, pp. 62–75.

H. Paul Bestor also leaving, Hoover had three vacancies. To thwart liberal critics, he gave Democrats a majority. Atlee Pomerene, a progressive Democrat and former United States senator from Ohio, replaced Eugene Meyer as chairman of the RFC board, and Hoover named Charles A. Miller, head of the RFC New York loan agency and an advocate of federal relief, to replace Dawes. To fill Bestor's vacancy, Hoover selected Gardner Cowles of Iowa, a staunch Republican and former congressman. Democrats controlled the RFC board four votes to three: Atlee Pomerene, Wilson McCarthy, Jesse Jones, and Harvey Couch opposed to Ogden Mills, Charles Miller, and Gardner Cowles.[49]

With the presidential election looming ahead, Hoover hoped the RFC's new authority would blunt political criticism while its loans shored up the banking system and stimulated a business expansion. Neither hope was fulfilled. The RFC's relief and public works construction programs embroiled Hoover in more controversy, and RFC bank loans did little to stimulate commercial credit, business investment, and employment. In fact, by the end of the year the money markets were once again headed for collapse.

The RFC was inundated with requests for public works and relief loans. Pomerene established a Self-Liquidating Division to deal with public works and an Emergency Relief Division for relief. From the outset, the Self-Liquidating Division encountered serious problems. The administration hoped the $1.5 billion would provide tens of thousands of jobs in the winter of 1932–1933, but time-consuming delays were inherent in the self-liquidating approach. Projects capable of producing a revenue involved complex planning. Bridges, toll roads, hydroelectric plants, electric power distribution lines, slum clearance and low-income housing, and urban sewer systems required detailed engineering studies before actual construction could begin. The administration made sure all proj-

[49] *Wall Street Journal*, July 28, 1932; *Chicago Tribune*, June 24, 1932; Jones, *Fifty Billion Dollars*, p. 521; Discussion Notes, July 7, 1932, Harrison Papers.

ects would generate an income sufficient to pay operating and maintenance costs, interest assessments, and amortization. The public works program was delayed until 1933. When Hoover left office in March 1933, the RFC had approved ninety-two applications totaling $197 million, but disbursed only $20 million, hardly enough to carry the unemployed through the winter.[50]

The Emergency Relief Division faired little better. It managed to loan its $300 million, but the political controversy it generated was a disaster for Hoover. It became immediately apparent in August 1932 that $300 million was completely inadequate. On the first day of the month five states requested more than $200 million, and the RFC began rationing money. In the process Hoover appeared cold, apathetic, and stingy, willing to loan billions to banks while millions of people starved. The RFC had cumbersome application procedures, insisted that states increase their own tax revenues to the limit, and extended money only for short periods.[51] Governor Gifford Pinchot of Pennsylvania, enraged when the RFC denied several requests on procedural grounds, went public with his criticisms of the administration in September and October.[52] The RFC, so generous with the banks but so cautious with the unemployed, appeared to be an instrument of big business, completely oblivious to the real disaster engulfing the nation. The negative publicity contributed to Hoover's overwhelming election defeat.

RFC agricultural loans also failed. In August 1933 the RFC established a Regional Agricultural Credit Corporation in each of the twelve Federal Land Bank districts and loaned each district $3 million. The Credit Corporations were designed to

[50] U.S. Congress, Senate, Committee on Banking and Currency, *Hearings on S. 5336: Further Unemployment Relief through the* RFC, 72d Cong., 2d Sess., 1933, pp. 105–12.

[51] B. M. Miller to George Cooksey, July 29, 1932, NA, RG 234, RFC, Emergency Relief; *New York Times*, July 31, 1932.

[52] For the controversy between Pinchot and Hoover, see James S. Olson, "Gifford Pinchot and the Politics of Hunger, 1932–1933," *Pennsylvania Magazine of History and Biography*, 96 (October 1972), 508–21.

make loans to farmers for the cost of seed, cultivation, harvesting, and marketing. To avoid competition with private banks, interest rates were set at 7 percent.[53] The corporations could also make loans to banks, agricultural credit corporations, and livestock loan companies if they would reloan the money to marketing organizations selling commodities. The administration believed that commodity prices were low because distributors could not get loans to make their initial purchases from farmers. With that credit they could make the purchases, reviving demand for farm products and raising prices. The key to the farm problem was the same as that for industrial production: the supply of credit. Instead of having to sell recently harvested crops in glutted markets, farmers could sell them to marketing corporations which would wait for favorable conditions.[54]

But the RFC Agricultural Credit Division also ran into trouble. Farmers complained that 7 percent interest was exorbitant, far higher than market rates, and many refused to participate. The RFC never increased the capital of the Regional Agricultural Credit Corporations beyond the initial $36 million, and by the end of the year the Agricultural Credit Division had financed only $5 million in loans.[55]

Finally, even the economic logic of the RFC bank loan program came into disrepute in late 1932 and early 1933. In an election campaign speech, Ogden Mills reminded the public:

> Wouldn't things be much worse if every bank was closed and the savings of 40,000,000 depositors tied up and no credit facilities available? Wouldn't they be much worse if the assets of our great fiduciary institutions . . . were com-

---

[53] RFC, *Regional Agricultural Credit Corporation Bulletin No. 1* (Washington, D.C., 1932), p. 1; RFC, Minutes, 8 (September 8, 1932), 289–90; RFC, *Special Loan Agency Bulletin* (Washington, D.C., 1932), p. 1.

[54] See speech by Atlee Pomerene to the New England Council of Governors, November 17, 1932, Pomerene Papers. Atlee Pomerene to Charles McNary, October 18, 1932, in RFC, Minutes, 9 (October 18, 1932), 916–18; *Chicago Tribune*, November 4, 1932.

[55] RFC, *Quarterly Report for April 1 to June 30, 1934* (Washington, D.C., 1934), Table 6.

pletely frozen; if all values were temporarily frozen from lack of a market?[56]

Unfortunately, Mills was accurately predicting the future. In August a banking panic had spread from Boise throughout southern Idaho, and on November 1 the governor of Nevada declared a bank holiday when one of the state's major banks was about to fail.[57] In October, securities prices weakened and bank failures began to climb: 102 in October, 95 in November, and 100 in December. Applications for RFC loans began to increase dramatically, and during the last quarter of the year depositors removed more than $300 million from the banking system.[58]

By the end of the year, the RFC had authorized loans totaling $1,623,704,844 to thousands of financial institutions and railroads.[59] But the economy was no healthier. No amount of loan money could save the railroads. They had received more than $337 million from the RFC—$280 million to just fifteen lines. Ten eventually declared bankruptcy. Freight revenues did not sustain fixed costs. In the first seven months of 1932, railroads failed to meet $160 million in fixed charges. Fixed obligations for 1932 were $181 million, but would climb to $295 million in 1933 and $370 million in 1934. The composite value of the railroad bond index was thirty-seven in January 1932, fourteen in June, revived thirty-five in September, and twenty-six in December. RFC loans had not improved the railroad bond market; those bonds were frozen, unmarketable assets for thousands of banks.[60]

[56] See speech by Ogden Mills at Worcester, Massachusetts, October 28, 1932, Speech File, Mills Papers.

[57] James S. Olson, "Rehearsal for Disaster: Hoover, the RFC, and the Banking Crisis in Nevada, 1932–1933," *The Western Historical Quarterly*, 6 (April 1975), 149–62; "The Boise Banking Panic of 1932," *Idaho Yesterdays*, 18 (Winter 1974–1975), 25–28.

[58] *Federal Reserve Bulletin*, 21 (December 1935), 803 and 19 (December 1933), 745.

[59] RFC, *Quarterly Report for October 1 to December 31, 1932* (Washington, D.C., 1933), Table 13.

[60] RFC, "Weekly Report of Economic Conditions," September 17, 1932, NA,

The entire money market rested precariously on public opinion. When the weaknesses of a particular bank became widely known, runs on the bank, its affiliates, and neighboring institutions developed, sometimes threatening a regional economy. Any local breach in public confidence had the potential of creating a panic for the entire national banking system. Banks were not liquid or sound enough to deal with the crisis. Continuing declines in securities values had impaired bank assets and eroded their capital. When withdrawal pressures mounted, bankers liquidated assets at depressed values. Not until new investment restored their capital could they become really solvent and private investment was not forthcoming in 1932. The RFC had nearly loaned its total of $2 billion but the economy was in no better shape at the end of 1932 than it had been at the beginning. Economic catastrophe was just around the corner.

RG 234, RFC, Statistical Division; Interstate Commerce Commission, *Forty-Sixth Annual Report* (Washington, D.C., 1933), p. 5; Herbert Spero, *Reconstruction Finance Corporation Loans to Railroads, 1932–1937* (New York, 1939), 13–14, 140–43; *Commercial & Financial Chronicle*, January 28, 1933.

CHAPTER II

The Emergency Banking Act of 1933

THE FINAL CRISIS began for Herbert Hoover in December when Congress convened in lame-duck session. Still upset about stingy relief programs and worried about more evidence of economic decline, progressive Republicans and liberal Democrats mounted new attacks on the RFC. Senators Robert La Follette, Jr., of Wisconsin and James Couzens of Michigan held hearings of the Senate Manufactures Committee and scathingly criticized RFC relief policies.[1] Senator Robert Wagner, Democrat from New York, accused the RFC of negligence during the relief crisis and began writing legislation to force changes in the RFC.[2] Republican Congressman Hamilton Fish of New York demanded a congressional investigation of all businesses which had declared bankruptcy after receiving RFC loans.[3] Democratic Senator Cordell Hull of Tennessee wanted to investigate RFC agricultural loans and reduce RFC interest rates to 4 percent.[4] Just when the Association of Railway Executives was lobbying for unlimited RFC railroad loans, Senator Couzens wanted them to be eliminated.[5] The RFC was besieged from all sides.

At the same time the RFC was worrying about the supply of credit. Late in the summer of 1932, the RFC board decided the liquidity crisis was over, and the accumulation of excess re-

[1] *Washington Post*, January 8, 1933.

[2] *Washington Post*, January 10, 1933.

[3] *Washington Post*, December 23, 1932, and February 3, 1933.

[4] *Washington Post*, February 8, 1933.

[5] *Washington Post*, January 28, 1933; U.S. Congress, Senate, Committee on Banking and Currency, *Hearings on S.J. Res. 245: Joint Resolution to Suspend the Making of Loans to Railroads by the RFC*, 72d Cong., 2d Sess., 1933, p. 1; U.S. Congress, Senate, Committee on Interstate Commerce, *Hearings on S. 1580: A Bill to Relieve the Existing National Emergency to Interstate Railroad Transportation*, 73d Cong., 1st Sess., 1933, p. 39; RFC, Minutes, 7 (August 18, 1932), 856–57; *Wall Street Journal*, January 28, 1933.

serves strengthened Hoover's assumption that the banks were using RFC money to liquefy assets rather than increase credit.[6] Hoover was so frustrated with bankers that he threatened in November 1932 to compete directly with them through RFC business loans, a step toward state capitalism he could hardly have imagined a year earlier. By the end of the year confidence was turning into pessimism because of continuing instability in the money markets.[7] Instead of working directly to increase credit, the RFC staged a desperate and ultimately unsuccessful attempt to prevent a collapse of the entire banking system. The first strong evidence that the money markets were disintegrating came in Iowa. Late in December and early in January several major Iowa banks failed, including the American Trust Company of Davenport. To prevent a chain reaction of failures throughout the state, the governor declared a banking holiday on January 20, 1933.[8] Several other banks with RFC loans also failed. Late in January the Bank of America and Trust Company in Memphis, Tennessee, called on the RFC for a $13 million loan, and the state governor endorsed the request. The RFC consented and the bank survived.[9] But at the other end of the state, the RFC refused requests from the East Tennessee National Bank and the Fidelity Bankers Trust Company in Knoxville because their assets were too depleted. The RFC law had required that all loans be adequately secured, and the RFC board took that responsibility seriously. It had little choice. Putting RFC money into dangerously weak banks would quickly have depleted its resources. The RFC had no intention of underwriting the entire banking system. All it hoped to do was shore up the assets of reasonably strong institutions

[6] *New York Times*, October 5, 1932; Walter Newton to Atlee Pomerene, October 12, 1932, HHPL, PP, SF, RFC; see copy of speech, November 17, 1932, Pomerene Papers; *Wall Street Journal*, November 19, 1932.

[7] "Weekly Review of Economic Conditions," December 19, 1932, NA, RG 234, RFC, Statistical Division; *Washington Post*, February 1, 1933; Atlee Pomerene to Arthur W. Dean, January 28, 1933, Pomerene Papers; *Real America*, 1 (May 1933), 36.

[8] *Des Moines Tribune*, January 21, 1933.

[9] RFC, Minutes, 12 (January 24, 1933), 1321.

threatened by temporary circumstances. It provided liquidity, not solvency. Both Knoxville banks were insolvent.[10]

Financial instability in Iowa and Tennessee affected other regions of the country. On January 25 the Pioneer Trust Company of Kansas City closed and a banking panic spread quickly in Kansas and Missouri. When the city's largest bank, Fidelity National, lost $36 million in deposits between January 25 and January 30, the Federal Reserve Bank of Kansas City asked the RFC for an emergency loan of $7.5 million on behalf of the bank. The RFC agreed, but financial insecurity was sweeping across the country. In January more than 249 banks suspended operations, the highest monthly total in RFC history.[11]

More trouble came late in January when the Hibernia Bank and Trust Company of New Orleans experienced severe runs on deposits. Senator Huey Long appeared before the RFC board and requested an emergency loan of $20 million, saying the Hibernia had correspondent banks throughout Arkansas, Tennessee, and Texas. The board sent a team of bank examiners to New Orleans, but on February 4 the governor of Louisiana declared a banking holiday to stop the runs throughout the state. The RFC granted the loan, but deep concern about the state of the money markets was developing.[12] That apprehension became pessimism and ultimately helplessness.

In February the crisis became a catastrophe. Although there was no increase in the total volume of money in circulation in January, funds were shifting toward stronger money markets in New York and Chicago. People distrusted individual banks but not the entire financial system. Banks losing cash borrowed on their sound assets from the RFC, converted assets into cash at severely depressed prices, and drew on their balances at stronger banks. That weakened strong banks as well.[13] Massive sales of stocks and bonds, the calling in of

---

[10] *Nashville Tennessean*, January 22–23, 1933.

[11] RFC, Minutes, 13 (February 3, 1933), 185–90.

[12] RFC, Minutes, 13 (February 5, 1933), 347–60; "Review of Economic Conditions," March 3, 1933, NA, RG 234, RFC, Statistical Division; *New Orleans Times-Picayune*, January 28 and February 5, 1933.

[13] *Federal Reserve Bulletin*, 19 (April 1933), 209–10.

working capital loans, and collateral foreclosures and tax auctions only perpetuated the cycle. Asset values eroded more and public confidence dropped. The banking system could not stand another major regional liquidity crisis.

The crisis came sooner than anyone anticipated. In mid-February the two largest banks in Detroit closed. Dependent on the automobile industry, the Union Guardian Trust Company and the First National Bank of Detroit came on hard times when car sales dropped late in the 1920s. Both were heavily invested in the securities markets and sustained major losses after 1929. The Hoover administration was convinced that the failure of those banks would trigger an unprecedented national banking crisis. They were right. The RFC agreed to loan $65 million to the Union Guardian Trust Company if local businessmen like Edsel and Henry Ford would subordinate, i.e., allow other investors to have first claim on, some of the bank's assets. When Ford refused to cooperate, negotiations broke down. The First National Bank of Detroit then applied for a $100 million loan, but the RFC, convinced the bank could not be saved, refused. On February 13, both banks closed. Governor Comstock of Michigan declared a banking holiday the next day.[14]

The Michigan banking holiday was the last straw for the money markets. The transfer of funds from weak to strong banks increased as did direct withdrawals, especially in New York, Chicago, and Cleveland. In the first week following the Michigan holiday, the volume of money in circulation increased by $150 million. That was only a beginning. During the last week of February, it went up by $750 million. Since January, depositors had removed more than $1 billion from the banking system. The RFC could not replace what depositors were removing. Once it had become obvious that even the RFC could not cope with the panic, state after state imposed some form of holiday or banking restriction.[15]

[14] For an account of the Detroit banking crisis, see Olson, *Herbert Hoover and the Reconstruction Finance Corporation*, pp. 102–5.

[15] *Annual Report of the Federal Reserve Board* (Washington, D.C., 1932), p. 154; *Federal Reserve Bulletin* 20 (April 1934), 251.

During the last two weeks of the Hoover administration, the RFC tried to deal with an enormous variety of banking problems. In Cleveland, the Michigan crisis precipitated runs on the Cleveland Trust Company and the Union Trust Company, and while the RFC was trying to work out a rescue there, the situation in Detroit continued to deteriorate. The idea of using clearinghouse scrip instead of currency to deal with the local economy in Detroit and Cleveland gained more advocates. The Baltimore Trust Company came to the RFC for money, but on February 24 Governor Ritchie of Maryland declared a banking holiday.[16] The panic was out of control.

On February 23 Indianapolis banks restricted withdrawals to 5 percent. On February 27, the governor of Ohio declared a voluntary holiday and Arizona restricted withdrawals. And on March 1–2, Arizona, California, Idaho, Kentucky, Minnesota, Mississippi, Nevada, Oklahoma, Oregon, Tennessee, Texas, Utah, Washington, Wisconsin, Georgia, and New Mexico imposed holidays. Withdrawal limitations were mandated in Iowa, Nevada, Nebraska, New Jersey, Pennsylvania, Vermont, West Virginia, Colorado, and North Carolina.[17] By March 3 only the banks in the largest financial centers remained open without restrictions, but on the morning of Franklin D. Roosevelt's inauguration the governors of New York and Illinois closed the banks of New York City and Chicago.[18] The financial system had collapsed and Hoover's worst fears had come true. Despite nearly $2 billion of RFC loans in just over a year to thousands of financial institutions, railroads, state relief commissions, and farmers, the economy had ground to a halt by March 4, 1933. The RFC had failed.[19]

[16] Federal Reserve Board, Minutes, 20 (February 23–25, 1933), 232–43; RFC, Minutes, 12 (February 15, 18, and 21–27, 1933), 980, 1240, 1449, 1524, 1588, 1787, 1819, 1845.

[17] "Weekly Review of Economic Conditions," March 3, 1933, NA, RG 234, RFC, Statistical Division.

[18] Federal Reserve Bulletin, 19 (March 1933), 113–25; Arthur Ballantine, "When All the Banks Closed," Harvard Business Review, 26 (Autumn 1948), 138; RFC, Minutes, 14 (March 4, 1933), 425; Charles Hamlin Diary, March 3–4, 1933, Hamlin Papers.

[19] Eugene Meyer, COHR, pp. 678–80.

On March 6, two days after his inauguration, President Franklin D. Roosevelt declared a nationwide banking holiday and three days later sent the Emergency Banking Act to Congress where it passed in a matter of hours. The dramatic move to address the banking crisis institutionalized his reputation as a man of action and Hoover's as a hopeless conservative. What Roosevelt actually did was take a piece of legislation which officials in the Hoover administration had already drafted and present it to the Congress as his own.

The Emergency Banking Act had five separate titles. Three were especially important. Title I legalized the bank holiday Roosevelt had already declared. Title II permitted the comptroller of the currency to name a conservator with powers of receivership over national banks verging on insolvency. The conservator could subordinate depositor and stockholder interests in order to reorganize the banks. Title III authorized the RFC to purchase the preferred stock or capital notes of banks and trust companies to provide them with long-term investment funds and relieve them of short-term debts to the government. The first three were the substance of the bill. Title IV allowed Federal Reserve banks to discount previously ineligible assets and to issue new Federal Reserve notes on the basis of those assets as a means of ending currency shortages. It was of little use after the banking holiday because so much money flowed back into banks. Title V appropriated $2 million to implement the legislation.[20]

The ideas for the national banking holiday, the bank conservation procedures, and the RFC stock buying program all evolved during the last year of Hoover's presidency. But the idea of a national holiday had been circulating for years. As early as 1918 Milton Elliott, then legal counsel for the Federal Reserve Board, speculated about the future and expected that at some time the federal government might find it necessary to abandon the gold standard or at least embargo gold exports. He discussed his ideas with Walter Wyatt of the Federal Reserve Board staff, who suggested amending the Trading with

---

[20] *Washington Post*, March 10, 1933.

the Enemy Act of 1917 to authorize the president to impose an embargo during financial emergencies.[21] In January 1932, during the liquidity crisis preceding establishment of the RFC, Ogden Mills and President Hoover considered a national banking holiday to relieve the crisis. In June, during the Central Republic Bank of Chicago crisis, Mills again considered the idea and consulted with Adolph Miller, Walter Wyatt, and Eugene Meyer. Massive RFC loans made such extraordinary action unnecessary. In the fall of 1932, Mills approached Wyatt about the constitutionality of a national banking holiday, and Wyatt explained to him the amendments he had added to the Trading with the Enemy Act.[22]

As the inadequacy of the RFC loan program became clearer early in 1933, the administration again began toying with the idea of a national banking holiday. Something had to be done to calm the money markets. In mid-February, George Harrison of the Federal Reserve Bank of New York and Walter Wyatt urged Hoover to declare a holiday under the Trading with the Enemy Act.[23] Mills was confident a holiday would give the country a breathing spell and time to formulate new legislation. Hoover was not so desperate yet. He questioned the constitutionality of a banking moratorium and still hoped that less drastic steps, like more RFC loans, a federal guarantee of bank deposits, clearinghouse certificates, and aggressive Federal Reserve open market operations would make a holiday unnecessary. Hoover had a hard time seeing reality. None of the suggestions had any chance of success until the panic affecting millions of people could be controlled. He was out of touch with political reality. Any drastic measure to save the banking

[21] Francis G. Awalt, "Recollections of the Banking Crisis of 1933," *Business History Review*, 43 (Autumn 1969), 364–65; Presidential Logs, March 2, 1933, HHPL, PPP, Banking Crisis, "The Last Phase," pp. 25–26.

[22] Awalt, "Recollections," pp. 364–65; Charles Hamlin Diary, October 13, 1932, Hamlin Papers.

[23] *New York Herald Tribune*, August 23, 1944; Awalt, "Recollections," pp. 364–65; Charles Hamlin Diary, February 15 and 24 and March 1, 1933, Hamlin Papers; Raymond Moley, OH, HHPL, pp. 9–10.

system would require the cooperation of a Democratic Congress, and Hoover had little credibility among them.[24]

But none of the alternatives worked out. Senator Carter Glass of Virginia informed Hoover that federal legislation guaranteeing bank deposits would never get through Congress.[25] The Federal Reserve Board worried that clearinghouse certificates would undermine their own legitimacy and create more public uncertainty. Clearinghouse scrip looked like play money, hardly something to reassure people.[26] More RFC loans had little support either. By February the RFC was inundated by thousands of legitimate applications for massive loans it could not satisfy. Even the strongest, most solvent banks in the country needed help.[27] Finally, the administration was waging an unsuccessful battle with the Federal Reserve Board over open market operations. Ogden Mills and Herbert Hoover wanted Federal Reserve banks to purchase $100 million in government securities to liquefy the money markets, but Eugene Meyer refused to make the recommendation, arguing that it would do nothing to ease the crisis. By that time $100 million was only a drop in the bucket. Billions of dollars of assets were frozen solid and millions of depositors were clamoring for their money. As far as Meyer was concerned, open market operations had been neutralized by the dimensions of the crisis. Mills was certain the decision would terrify liquidity-conscious bankers throughout the country.[28]

The pressure of events forced Hoover to reconsider a national banking holiday. He wrote to the Federal Reserve Board on February 22 asking their advice, but Eugene Meyer wrote

[24] Presidential Logs, February 20, 1933, HHPL, PPP, Banking Crisis; Charles Hamlin Diary, February 15, 1933, Hamlin Papers; Federal Reserve Board, Minutes, 20 (March 1, 1933), 282–84; Raymond Moley, OH, HHPL, pp. 9–10, 15–16.

[25] Presidential Logs, February 15, 1933, HHPL, PPP, Banking Crisis.

[26] Presidential Logs, February 14–15, 1933, HHPL, PPP, Banking Crisis.

[27] RFC, Minutes, 13 (1933), NA, RG 234, RFC, Secretarial Division; Presidential Logs, February 23, 1933, HHPL, PPP, Banking Crisis.

[28] Raymond Moley, OH, HHPL, pp. 14–15; Charles Hamlin Diary, December 14, 1932 and January 26, 1933, Hamlin Papers; Federal Reserve Board, Minutes, 20 (February 27, 1933), 257–58.

back that the "Board does not desire to make any specific proposals for additional measures or authority, but it will continue to give all aspects of the situation its most careful consideration."[29] Hoover came back to them on February 28 asking about the usefulness of doing nothing, guaranteeing bank deposits, or issuing clearinghouse certificates, but the board refused to make any recommendation while opposing deposit guarantees and clearinghouse certificates. Hoover thought Meyer was criminally passive during the crisis, getting back at him now for choosing Mills instead of him as secretary of the treasury. Jesse Jones and the Democrats on the RFC board saw Meyer's intransigence as typical of the Wall Street establishment waiting to profit from other people's troubles. Meyer would not budge.[30]

On March 2 Hoover asked Attorney General DeWitt Mitchell about the constitutionality of a banking holiday. He doubted its legality unless president-elect Franklin D. Roosevelt would promise to convene Congress immediately in special session and ratify the declaration. Ogden Mills asked Hoover to get the opinion of the Federal Reserve Board.[31] Mills and Awalt met with the board later that day. At the meeting Mills announced that Hoover was prepared to impose a holiday between March 3 and March 5 if Roosevelt would concur. In the early morning hours of March 3, the board endorsed the proposal. Walter Wyatt drafted a holiday proclamation, gave one copy to Mills, and sent several others to the White House. Wyatt and Mitchell then wrote a holiday proclamation as a joint congressional resolution in case Congress would pass the bill before adjourning on March 3.[32]

[29] Federal Reserve Board, Minutes, 20 (February 25, 1933), 245–46.

[30] Federal Reserve Board, Minutes, 20 (March 1–2, 1933), 281–87; Charles Hamlin Diary, March 1, 1933, Hamlin Papers.

[31] Presidential Logs, March 2, 1933, HHPL, PPP, Banking Crisis, "The Last Phase," pp. 25–26; Federal Reserve Board, Minutes, 20 (March 2, 1933), 301–2; Charles Hamlin Diary, March 2, 1933, Hamlin Papers.

[32] Federal Reserve Board, Minutes, 20 (March 2, 1933), 299, 318–19; *New York Herald Tribune*, August 23, 1944; Charles Hamlin Diary, March 2–3, 1933, Hamlin Papers; Raymond Moley, OH, HHPL, pp. 15–16; Walter Wyatt,

All day March 3 and into the early morning of March 4 negotiations over the holiday continued between the two administrations. Mills was in constant touch with incoming Secretary of the Treasury William Woodin. Late on March 3 Adolph Miller of the Federal Reserve Board visited with Roosevelt and left him with several copies of the proclamation. Roosevelt argued that Hoover already had sufficient authority to declare the holiday. He offered to support a holiday lasting through noon on March 4 but not a three-day holiday or any emergency legislation. President Hoover decided not to declare a holiday unless Roosevelt reconsidered.[33]

Pressure mounted on Hoover to declare the holiday even without Roosevelt's support. Mills was adamant about the need for a moratorium. The Federal Reserve Board and the Federal Reserve banks of New York and Chicago demanded an immediate holiday. Frustrated with the vacillations of the Federal Reserve Board and the political motivations of the New Dealers, Hoover held his ground: no holiday unless Roosevelt publicly endorsed it. Hoover had been brought kicking and screaming to the point of declaring the holiday, but would not or emotionally could not take all the responsibility himself. It was such a drastic, unprecedented measure that he would not go it alone. Roosevelt was equally stubborn but for different reasons. He wanted to preserve all of his options, avoid being tainted with Hoover's "kiss of death" reputation, and even exploit the seriousness of the situation. Things could not

---

"Skeleton Outline," unpublished manuscript, Bank Holiday-1933-Gold, Goldenweisar Papers; Personal Notes, Federal Reserve Board meetings, March 2–3, 1933, Bank Holiday-1933-Gold, Goldenweisar Papers; Awalt, "Recollections," pp. 357–60; Ballantine, "When All the Banks Closed," p. 138; Eugene Meyer, COHR, p. 674; J.F.T. O'Connor Diary, May 11, 1933, O'Connor Papers.

[33] Ogden Mills to Herbert Hoover, March 2, 1933, HHPL, PP, SF, Franklin D. Roosevelt; Raymond Moley, OH, HHPL, pp. 9–10; *New York Herald Tribune*, August 23, 1944; Henry Stimson Diary, March 3–4, 1933, Stimson Papers; Awalt, "Recollections," pp. 357–58; Herbert Hoover to Eugene Meyer, March 4, 1933, Federal Reserve Board Records, Bank Holiday File; Presidential Logs, March 3, 1933, HHPL, PPP, Banking Crisis, "The Last Phase," pp. 27–34.

get any worse, only better, and he would reap credit for the inevitable improvement.[34]

With the holiday idea dead, Ogden Mills turned his attention to closing those financial centers still open, effectively creating a banking moratorium without actually declaring one. With the assistance of George Harrison in New York and Eugene M. Stearns, chairman of the Federal Reserve Bank of Chicago, Mills convinced the governors of Illinois, New York, Massachusetts, New Jersey, Iowa, and Pennsylvania to declare statewide holidays. By the time of Franklin D. Roosevelt's inauguration on March 4, the banking system of the United States had ceased to function.[35]

After the inaugural festivities on March 4, Roosevelt convened a series of conferences to discuss the banking emergency. On March 5, William Woodin invited several members of the Hoover administration to participate. Ogden Mills, Arthur Ballantine, and Francis Awalt attended and played important roles in developing reconstruction measures. Walter Wyatt retrieved his copy of the proclamation that he and former Attorney General DeWitt Mitchell had written and Hoover had approved. The new Attorney General Homer Cummings examined the document carefully, and on March 6, 1933, President Roosevelt signed it and formally declared the holiday. On March 9, Title I of the Emergency Banking Act legalized it.[36]

Title II of the Emergency Banking Act reorganized thousands of closed banks. The Hoover administration had long

[34] Presidential Logs, March 3–4, 1933, HHPL, PPP, Banking Crisis; Charles Hamlin Diary, March 3 and 8, 1933, Hamlin Papers. Also see the resolutions of the various Federal Reserve banks favoring declaration of a national banking holiday, Federal Reserve Board Papers, Bank Holiday File, March 3, 1933.

[35] Awalt, "Recollections," pp. 359–60; Charles Hamlin Diary, March 3 and 12, 1933, Hamlin Papers; Eugene M. Stearns to Charles Hamlin, August 11, 1933, and George Harrison to Charles Hamlin, August 15, 1933, Federal Reserve Board Papers, Bank Holiday File.

[36] Awalt, "Recollections," pp. 362–63; Ballantine, "When All the Banks Closed," p. 138; Raymond Moley, OH, HHPL, pp. 9–11; Henry Stimson Diary, March 5, 1933, Stimson Papers; Personal Notes, March 5, 1933, Bank Holiday-1933-Gold, Goldenweisar Papers.

been concerned about reorganization procedures. Throughout 1932 the comptroller of the currency had difficulty securing unanimous agreement from depositors and stockholders—a few depositors or stockholders could delay reorganization by refusing to subordinate their holdings. Delays left billions of dollars tied up in lengthy court battles. Those assets were just as frozen as money locked up in the poor investments of open banks. Mandatory control by the federal government over national bank depositors and stockholders had to be developed and the requirement of unanimous consent eliminated. Francis Awalt began to explore alternatives to traditional practices.[37]

At the same time, Ogden Mills and Eugene Meyer were trying to convince Hoover to abandon the idea of clearing-house scrip, claiming it circumvented the Federal Reserve system. They placed before Hoover an idea from Secretary of State Henry Stimson for the comptroller of the currency to isolate the free assets of any national bank. He could then force depositors and stockholders to subordinate the exact amount of any deficiency. The bank would issue a certificate of obligation to each depositor for his share of the deficiency, guaranteeing that the profits of the bank would be paid to depositors until losses were recovered.[38] Awalt liked the idea. In February 1933, Awalt and Wyatt drafted a bill permitting the comptroller to declare bankrupt any closed national bank and appoint a conservator to begin reorganization or liquidation. They sent the bill to Mills and he immediately sent it on to Hoover with his endorsement.[39]

As usual, Hoover was reluctant, primarily because he was convinced the Democratic Congress would not support the bill so close to the inauguration and because it seemed to interfere so directly with private property rights. His own fears were immobilizing him once again. Senators Carter Glass of Virginia and Joseph Robinson of Arkansas confirmed his fears. Hoover

[37] Awalt, "Recollections," p. 364.
[38] Presidential Logs, February 14–16, 1933, HHPL, PPP, Banking Crisis; Henry Stimson Diary, February 15, 17, and 21, 1933, Stimson Papers.
[39] Awalt, "Recollections," pp. 364–65; Charles Hamlin Diary, February 17 and 21, 1933, Hamlin Papers.

was also afraid that if Congress passed the bill it might lead to an even more severe financial crisis, particularly in New York and Chicago, where, the situation still seemed under control. Hoover refused to promote the Bank Conservation Act in the last two weeks of his administration.[40]

Hoover's thoughts about the Bank Conservation Act mirrored his ideas about the bank holiday. He waited and waited until disaster forced his hand, and by then it was too late. Early in March he realized the Bank Conservation Act was the only way of reorganizing thousands of closed banks. Hoover tied the bank holiday to the Bank Conservation Act. A national holiday without a sound reorganization plan would be foolish, while the Bank Conservation Act would fail unless a holiday protected the thousands of banks that were still solvent. Hoover and Mills asked Roosevelt to approve the holiday and call Congress into special session on March 6 to pass the bank conservation bill. Roosevelt refused to commit himself to a measure he had not developed or studied. The Bank Conservation Act became Title II of the Emergency Banking Act during the first two days of the New Deal.[41]

Title III of the Emergency Banking Act gave the RFC authority to invest government money in the preferred stock of troubled banks. It became obvious in 1932 that the real problem for many banks was not temporary liquidity but improved capital structures. Hoover and the RFC board knew that banks with serious financial difficulties had to raise more capital to offset the deflation of their assets. But banks were poor investments. People were afraid to put in deposits, let alone investment capital. During the Nevada, Chicago, Detroit, Kansas City, and New Orleans crises, RFC officials urged banks to raise enough new capital to match government loans. The

[40] Charles Hamlin Diary, February 21, 1933, Hamlin Papers; Presidential Logs, February 15, 1933, HHPL, PPP, Banking Crisis; Raymond Moley, OH, HHPL, pp. 9–13.

[41] Presidential Logs, March 1–3, 1933, HHPL, PPP, Banking Crisis. Also see the recollections by Atlee Pomerene of a 1937 meeting with Hoover in which Hoover praised the bank reconstruction program of the New Deal, Box 37, Pomerene Papers.

banks had tried but failed, and only the federal government could fill the gap. President Hoover resisted federal investment in private institutions because it resembled socialism. RFC loans and RFC relief programs had been bad enough; to make the federal government an owner of thousands of banks was worse.

Early in February 1932 Franklin W. Fort, former congressman from New Jersey and president of the Lincoln National Bank of Newark, urged Hoover to allow RFC purchases of the preferred stock of banks and trust companies. Hoover was skeptical, but he referred Fort to John W. Pole, then comptroller of the currency. Hoover opposed endowing the federal government with such authority as long as RFC loans appeared successful, but he wanted to keep the proposal available as an emergency measure. Fort consulted with Pole, but nothing happened in April and May because the administration felt that short-term RFC loans would restore stability.[42]

After the summer crisis in Chicago, talk of government investment in private banks became more urgent. During the spring and summer of 1932, George Harrison and Owen D. Young of the Federal Reserve Bank of New York started promoting the idea because so many banks had capital as well as liquidity problems. They wanted the RFC to make direct purchases of the preferred stock of troubled, private banks. Hoover was reluctant.[43] During the June crisis, however, the idea gained the cautious approval of Harvey Couch and Wilson McCarthy of the RFC board. Charles Dawes, Eugene Meyer, Jesse Jones, H. Paul Bestor, Charles Miller, Atlee Pomerene, and Gardner Cowles remained skeptical. It was too drastic a step, one to be taken only when regular RFC loans had failed. Hoover's opinion was gradually changing.[44] In August 1932 Hoover named Franklin Fort to head the newly established

[42] Awalt, "Recollections," pp. 364–65; Franklin W. Fort to Herbert Hoover, February 7, 1932, HHPL, PP, SF, Financial Matters; Franklin W. Fort to Eugene Meyer, March 29, 1933, HHPL, PP, SF, Federal Reserve Board.

[43] Discussion Notes, June 30, 1932, Harrison Papers.

[44] Discussion Notes, July 7, 11, and 14, 1932, Harrison Papers; Jones, *Fifty Billion Dollars*, p. 19; Winston P. Wilson, *Harvey Couch* (Nashville, 1947), p. 157.

Federal Home Loan Bank system, an important part of the recovery program.[45] Hoover's faith in Fort had grown immensely, and from that new post Fort advocated direct RFC investment in banks and trust companies.

An inverse relationship existed between the Reconstruction Finance Corporation and the government investment proposal. As traditional RFC policies appeared less effective, the idea of government investment became more imperative. In December Eugene Meyer came around to the idea, and he began arguing that either the RFC or Federal Reserve Banks invest in preferred stock. Francis G. Awalt, the new comptroller of the currency, enthusiastically endorsed the plan. Later in January Fort and Awalt convinced Charles Miller of the RFC board, and under the combined influence of Fort, Miller, Harrison, Young, Meyer, and Awalt, Hoover became more sympathetic. Mills, along with Jones, McCarthy, Couch, and Pomerene, was still skeptical. Hoover told Wyatt, Fort, and Awalt to draft legislation permitting the RFC to purchase the preferred stock of national banks.[46]

In February, Hoover called Melvin Traylor, a prominent Democrat and president of the First National Bank of Chicago, and asked for his opinion. He needed some Democratic support and he was not getting it from Congress or the RFC board. Traylor flew to Washington and enthusiastically endorsed the bill. He also agreed to meet with Senator Glass to discuss the possibilities of maneuvering the bill through Congress. Mills now favored the idea. Glass warned them that the proposal had as much chance as the national holiday measure and the Bank Conservation Act. He did not even want to introduce it. The idea stalled there. Awalt and Wyatt kept copies of the bill in their files.[47] The bill became Title III of the Emergency Banking Act.[48]

---

[45] *Washington Post*, August 7, 1932.

[46] Discussion Notes, November 7, 1932, Harrison Papers; Franklin W. Fort to Carter Glass, January 3, 1933, HHPL, PP, SF, Financial Matters; Eugene Meyer, COHR, pp. 619–23; Jones, *Fifty Billion Dollars*, p. 21; Awalt, "Recollections," pp. 364–66; Stanley Reed, OH, HHPL, p. 9.

[47] Awalt, "Recollections," pp. 364–65.

[48] Jones, *Fifty Billion Dollars*, p. 21.

During the first days of the new Roosevelt administration, some of Hoover's closest associates stayed on as advisers. They had written the legislation for the banking holiday, the bank reorganization procedures, and the preferred stock purchase program. William Woodin respected the abilities of Ogden Mills, Arthur Ballantine, and Francis G. Awalt.[49] They had all been partially responsible for the banking crisis and played decisive roles in formulating the reconstruction plan. Between March 4 and March 9 they worked closely with Roosevelt, Woodin, and Homer Cummings, as well as brain trusters Adolf Berle, Jr., and Raymond Moley. They had already developed three specific proposals and they impressed Woodin and Berle with their understanding of the crisis. They had also worked closely with Walter Wyatt, E. A. Goldenweisar, and Eugene Meyer of the Federal Reserve Board. Wyatt had drafted each bill. The power of the Federal Reserve system was solidly behind the proposals of Mills, Ballantine, and Awalt. On March 7, after several meetings with Woodin, Roosevelt, Goldenweisar, and Berle, the old Hoover associates specifically proposed the Emergency Banking Act as a follow-up to the banking holiday. Woodin asked Wyatt and Ballantine to draft an omnibus measure declaring a banking moratorium, creating a bank conservation program, and permitting the RFC to invest in the stock of banks and trust companies.[50]

Roosevelt brought Congress back in special session on March 9 and presented the Emergency Banking Act. Within hours the bill was law.[51] Its origins have been obscured over the years by political rhetoric, but behind this earliest New

[49] Raymond Moley, *The First New Deal* (New York, 1966), pp. 214–16.

[50] *New York Herald Tribune*, August 23, 1944; Raymond Moley, OH, HHPL, pp. 9–16; Charles Hamlin Diary, March 9, 15, and 19, 1933, Hamlin Papers; Personal Notes, March 4–6, 1933, Bank Holiday-1933-Gold, Goldenweisar Papers; Henry Stimson Diary, March 4, 5, and 28, 1933, Stimson Papers; Ballantine, "When All the Banks Closed," p. 138; Eugene Meyer, COHR, p. 674; Henry Bruere, COHR, pp. 159–60; Jackson Reynolds, COHR, pp. 170–72; Ogden Mills to George Dayton, September 15, 1933, Mills Papers; Awalt, "Recollections," pp. 366–71; Presidential Logs, March 5, 1933, HHPL, PPP, Banking Crisis.

[51] *New York Times*, March 10, 1933.

Deal drama, the Hoover administration had developed the economic tools which eventually restored stability to the money markets. Because of political problems with the lame-duck Congress, economic confusion about triggering a more serious banking panic, fears of delegating too much power to the federal government, and concern about the long-range implications of state capitalism, Hoover had postponed the three major proposals until it was too late. By the time he was willing to push the legislation aggressively, Hoover's presidency was over. As Secretary of State Henry Stimson recalled in his diary, Hoover was unwilling "to make the last days in office an admission of bankruptcy."[52] The first major achievement of the New Deal, the Emergency Banking Act, was also the last major proposal of the Hoover administration.

[52] Henry Stimson Diary, March 4, 1933, Stimson Papers.

CHAPTER III

Czar: Jesse Jones and His Empire

WITH THE INAUGURATION came changes on the Reconstruction Finance Corporation board. To replace Atlee Pomerene as RFC chairman, Roosevelt toyed with the idea of appointing Newton Baker or Amos Pinchot before finally deciding on Jesse Jones, the dominant figure among Democrats on the existing RFC board. Jones was a fiscal conservative, but only in the sense that he did not want government money wasted. Skillful use of even enormous amounts of money caused him few misgivings, as long as the primary role of government spending was underwriting capitalism. Jones brought what he called a "Democratic business" philosophy to Washington. Instead of being a tool of major corporations and Wall Street investment firms, the "new" RFC would provide liquidity and capital to as broad a business base as possible. While Herbert Hoover, Ogden Mills, and Eugene Meyer had viewed the RFC as a temporary agency designed to restore liquidity to the money markets, Jones was far more visionary. He felt the RFC could restore vitality to a moribund economy through massive infusions of credit. Blessed with an extraordinary ego and ability to match, Jones put his personal stamp on the RFC as few government officials ever do. Energetic and autocratic, Jones was the ultimate entrepreneur. He completely dominated the RFC and was the central figure in the New Deal promotion of state capitalism during the 1930s.[1]

The Emergency Banking Act of 1933 launched the RFC on an extraordinary odyssey, making it one of the most powerful agencies in the history of the federal government. Slowly, almost imperceptibly as it poured billions of dollars into the economy, the RFC evolved into a major New Deal agency in

[1] Jones, *Fifty Billion Dollars*, passim; Arthur M. Schlesinger, Jr., *The Age of Roosevelt*, vol. II. *The Coming of the New Deal* (Boston, 1958), pp. 425–26.

1933 and 1934. Confined at first to mopping up the unfinished banking business of the Hoover administration, the RFC quickly became much more than that—more than Franklin D. Roosevelt and most New Dealers could ever have imagined. Blessed with a huge supply of money and the authority to borrow much more, the RFC was uniquely independent, free for the most part from the annual Capitol Hill pilgrimages other agencies made to beg for appropriations. In recalling the way the RFC operated, longtime Secretary to the Federal Reserve Board Chester Morrill remarked:

> [I]t became apparent almost immediately, to many Congressmen and Senators, that here was a device which would enable them to provide for activities that they favored for which government funds would be required, but without any apparent increase in appropriations, and without passing an appropriations bill of any kind to accomplish its purposes. After they had done that, there need be no more appropriations and its activities could be enlarged indefinitely, as they were almost to fantastic proportions.[2]

Each day the RFC loaned millions, but each day it also received back millions in repayments. Jesse Jones bragged about the RFC's efficiency and balance sheet, and was proud that it managed to loan out billions and collect from borrowers with interest. Early in 1936, for example, he wrote to the president outlining RFC assets and liabilities and pointing out that in three years the RFC had handed out more than $8 billion in loans, received repayments totaling $3.2 billion, and had earned more than $294 million in interest.[3]

Its unique structure and political convenience made the RFC a favorite of congressmen and the president, who turned to it frequently for economic assistance. By the mid-1930s, the RFC was making loans to banks, savings banks, building and loan associations, credit unions, railroads, industrial banks, farm-

[2] Chester Morrill, COHR, p. 182.
[3] Jesse Jones to Franklin D. Roosevelt, January 24, 1936, NA, RG 234, RFC, White House Correspondence; Clifford Durr, COHR, pp. 36–39.

ers, commercial businesses, federal land banks, production credit associations, farm cooperatives, mortgage loan companies, insurance companies, school districts, joint stock land banks, federal intermediate credit banks, and livestock credit corporations. In early 1934, Congress extended the RFC's statutory authority and appropriated $850 million for its use, but after the bill passed there seemed some question about whether RFC spending was limited to the $850 million or whether it could also use the revolving funds it was receiving from banks. The president assured Jones that he could spend the appropriated $850 million as well as the incoming loan repayments. By 1935 the RFC had made more than 40,000 loans to borrowers in every congressional district, and it had become the most ubiquitous of the New Deal agencies. To one degree or another, every member of Congress ended up in Jones's debt.[4]

Because of its revolving credit fund and loan-making experience, the RFC became a convenient tool for Roosevelt in financing all the agencies. The Reconstruction Finance Corporation was the capital bank for the New Deal. Under the authority of the Emergency Relief and Construction Act of 1932, the RFC had created an Emergency Relief Division to loan $300 million to local and state relief agencies. Although a source of great controversy,[5] the Emergency Relief Division loaned out all the money in 1932 and early 1933. In May 1933, after the legislation long sponsored by Senators Robert Wagner of New York and Edward Costigan of Colorado made it through Congress, Roosevelt established the Federal Emergency Relief Administration and named Harry Hopkins to head it. Hopkins drew heavily on the personnel, office equipment, and social work studies the RFC Emergency Relief Division had already compiled. The RFC provided $1.5 billion between 1933 and 1935 to finance relief grants.[6]

[4] RFC, *Summary of the Activities of the Reconstruction Finance Corporation and its Condition as of December 31, 1935*, p. 5; Franklin D. Roosevelt to Jesse Jones, January 21, 1934, FDRPL, OF 643, RFC.

[5] Olson, "Gifford Pinchot and the Politics of Hunger, 1932–1933," 508–20.

[6] Olson, *Herbert Hoover and the Reconstruction Finance Corporation*, pp. 77–80.

The RFC also established a $1.5 billion Self-Liquidating Division under Hoover to finance large-scale public works. Because the economic lead time for large-scale engineering projects was so long, the Self-Liquidating Division of the RFC loaned only $20 million before Hoover left office in March 1933,[7] but when Roosevelt took over he had the new Public Works Administration take over all the RFC's construction files, projects, and personnel. Secretary of the Interior Harold Ickes was in charge of the PWA, and he worried about the liquidity of the bonds it acquired from local governments to finance the projects. The last thing Ickes wanted was for the PWA to become saddled with a huge volume of unmarketable assets. He complained to the president about the problem, and Roosevelt had the RFC assist the PWA by purchasing the bonds it accepted from local political agencies. By 1936 the RFC had purchased $700 million in PWA bonds.[8]

The Reconstruction Finance Corporation financed a host of other New Deal agencies because its huge reserves and fiscal independence gave Roosevelt the power to act without specific congressional authorization. The RFC supplied $200 million to the Home Owners' Loan Corporation; $40 million to the Farm Credit Administration; $44 million to the Regional Agricultural Credit Corporations; $125 million to the Federal Home Loan banks; $145 million to the Federal Farm Loan Commissioner; $55 million to the Federal Farm Mortgage Corporation; $83 million to the Federal Housing Administration; $246 million to the Rural Electrification Administration; and $175 million to the Resettlement Administration. When Congress passed the Emergency Relief Appropriation Act of 1935, which led directly to the establishment of the Works Progress Administration, the RFC provided the new agency with $1 billion so it could begin work immediately.[9]

At times Roosevelt found the RFC most convenient. In 1932,

[7] U.S. Congress, Senate, Committee on Banking and Currency, *Hearings on S. 5336, Further Unemployment Relief through the RFC*, 72d Cong., 2d Sess., 1933, pp. 105–12.

[8] RFC, *Quarterly Report for September 30 to December 31, 1940* (Washington, D.C., 1941), pp. 6–8.

[9] Ibid., pp. 6–8.

45

when the Central Republic Bank of Chicago applied for the $90 million loan, Mayor Anton Cermak of Chicago appealed to the Hoover administration for an RFC loan of $70 million, backed by tax anticipation warrants, to pay teachers' salaries. Hoover denied the request because he felt it was not within RFC authority, and the denial fueled a political firestorm in the Midwest—$90 million going to one bank while teachers starved.[10] Soon after his inauguration, Roosevelt had the RFC extend a loan of $22.3 million to the Chicago Board of Education.[11] When small businessmen in Los Angeles complained after the 1933 earthquake about the need for government assistance, Roosevelt got the RFC to make nearly $13 million in low-interest loans for rebuilding. When farm middlemen complained about the taxes they had to pay under provisions of the Agricultural Adjustment Act of 1933, the president had the RFC make short-term working capital loans until they had been able to pass on the costs.[12] The RFC mushroomed in size because it gave everyone—politicians and businessmen—enormous flexibility.

Its growth, however, was not simply the outcome of flexibility and financial resources. Government bureaucrats come and go, usually leaving behind no trace of their individual personalities, but Jesse Jones was an exception. Like few other government officials in American history, he built the RFC in his own image, transforming it from a large, impersonal agency to a personal fiefdom. Jones was a powerful, imposing man. Tall by the standards of the 1930s, his huge chest and larger belly, covered with double-breasted suits, seemed to fill whatever room he entered. He was always in command. The round face topped with fine, grey-white hair was almost grandfatherly in appearance, except for those out-of-place thick, black eyebrows. He had an instinct "for the jugglar" and a willingness, even enthusiasm, for cutting down to size anyone who threatened his hegemony in the New Deal. Bred

[10] *Chicago Tribune*, June 2, 3, 10, 12, 19, 20, 22, 1932.
[11] RFC, *Summary of the Activities of the Reconstruction Finance Corporation and its Condition as of December 31, 1935*, p. 7.
[12] Ibid., p. 5.

on a steady diet of Texas Democratic politics, Jones harbored few ideological assumptions. He was in love with money and power, nurtured an incorruptible sense of personal ethics, and gave no quarter to rivals. But at the same time, Jones had been raised in the tradition of the Southern "good old boy," and he prized loyalty as the greatest of virtues. Jones had neither liberal sympathies for the suffering of the poor nor conservative ones for the prerogatives of the rich. He was comfortable with the fundamental structure of the economy. He feared neither Wall Street nor Washington, and he equated success with money and money with boldness and innovation. Jones carried that philosophy with him to the RFC.[13]

Jones was born on April 22, 1874, in Robertson County, Tennessee. The family moved to Dallas, Texas, when he was still a boy, and he graduated from Hill's Business College there in 1891. After rising in his uncle's lumber company to general manager, Jones purchased his own firm, moved to Houston, and then began his climb to prominence. He entered real estate and construction in 1903, banking in 1905, and newspaper publishing in 1908. Eventually Jones became one of the largest real estate developers in the country, constructing and operating fifty major buildings in Houston, together with properties in other major cities, particularly New York. He became president of what later became the Texas Commerce Bank system in 1912, an original stockholder of the Humble Oil and Refining Company (later Exxon), and sole owner of the *Houston Chronicle* in 1926.

Like most Southerners before World War II, Jones was a loyal Democrat, conservative on most social issues but ideological about very few. He was a businessman in the entrepreneurial sense, anxious to make the system work on his behalf regardless of political philosophy. Throughout his life, Jones possessed an extraordinary, almost populistic resentment of the Wall Street financial establishment, which he viewed as

---

[13] For personal recollections of Jones, see Stanley Reed, COHR, pp. 82, 96, and 101; Jerome Frank, COHR, pp. 50–51; and William Clayton, COHR, p. 100.

narrow-minded, hopelessly conservative, and too committed to the tight-money policies which stifled business expansion in the South and West. He had no problem supporting President Roosevelt in his campaign for the Securities Act of 1933, the Securities Exchange Act of 1934, or the Public Utility Holding Company Act of 1935. The Banking Act of 1935, which transferred power from the Federal Reserve Bank of New York to the Board of Governors in Washington, delighted Jones.[14]

Jones became a political force in Houston before World War I, not only through his own entrepreneurial instincts but through construction of the ship channel, which made the city a major port on the Gulf Coast and attracted dozens of new industries to southeast Texas. Jones was active in Democratic politics, a firm believer in sound money, and had stubbornly supported Woodrow Wilson's presidential bid in 1912. The Texas delegation to the Baltimore nominating convention had stood by Wilson through forty-six ballots, and in return Wilson had offered Jones a number of posts—first assistant secretary of the treasury, ambassador to Belgium, or secretary of commerce—which he declined to accept. But in 1918, Wilson asked Jones to become director general of military relief for the American Red Cross. Working with Jones on the Red Cross was John W. Davis, solicitor general of the United States and later the Democratic presidential candidate in 1924. For several months in 1918 former President William Howard Taft lived with Jones in Washington, and Senator Warren Harding of Ohio was next door. Jones made dozens of important friends in Washington, D.C., in 1918 and 1919. John Davis had him direct fund-raising for his 1924 presidential bid, and in 1928 Jones managed to bring the Democratic nominating convention to Houston, after building a 25,000-seat convention center to hold it.[15]

A self-made multimillionaire, Jones had an instinctive per-

[14] Jesse Jones to the Texas Congressional Delegation, June 30, 1935, FDRPL, OF 643, RFC.

[15] There is no outstanding biography of Jesse Jones. For a journalistic account written by a personal friend, see Bascom N. Timmons, *Jesse H. Jones: The Man and the Statesman* (New York, 1956). In particular, see pp. 96–109.

sonality. He knew how to handle people and money, to see the future and assess economic trends, and look into a man's eyes to judge his character. Jones bragged about having read only one book in his entire life, a biography of Sam Houston, and had a disdain for education and elites, particularly those of Ivy League and Wall Street vintage. During the Hoover years, he could barely stand Eugene Meyer and Charles Dawes, both of whom were, in his opinion, up to their necks in the old money of the Northeast. Quick to judge and slow to forgive, Jones gave no mercy to his opponents and no end of support to his friends, and he jealously guarded RFC prerogatives. One of his favorite expressions to associates on the board of directors was his claim that "there's a shotgun in the corner to get legislation for the RFC to keep somebody else from getting it."[16]

But there was more to Jones's power in Washington than the force of his own personality. Although he never held elective office, Jones managed to become a major center of power in Washington, the Great Depression's version of what Bernard Baruch had been during World War I. Part of that power was simply a by-product of RFC loans. Throughout the 1930s, the RFC made thousands of loans in every congressional district, and those loans had usually gone to people of influence—bankers, businessmen, and political officials representing local government agencies. On any given day there was a line of senators and congressmen waiting outside his office, hoping for a moment to push one or more pending loan applications. Jones was always solicitous of them, always willing to listen, always prepared to turn on the Texas "good old boy" charm, and always reminding them of pending legislation affecting his baby—the RFC. And when he was not in his own office listening to congressional requests, Jones was up on Capitol Hill, "chewing the fat" in congressional offices, playing cards, talking money, having a drink, fixing a problem, repaying a political debt.[17]

[16] Jones quoted in Clifford Durr, COHR, p. 39.
[17] William Clayton, COHR, p. 100; Chester Morrill, COHR, pp. 182–83; Stanley Reed, COHR, p. 82; Jerome Frank, COHR, pp. 50–51.

He had more than just RFC money backing him. Jones understood politics, and had an uncanny knack for seeking out the powerful and forming close relationships with them. One of his closest associates was Senator Carter Glass of Virginia, "father" of the Federal Reserve system, a ranking member of the Banking and Currency Committee, and chairman of the Appropriations Committee. Jones was also close to Senator Joseph Robinson of Arkansas, head of the Judiciary Committee. Blessed with a Texas gift for the bluff, Jones was a popular poker player in Washington; he played once a week with Harry Hopkins, successively head of the Federal Emergency Relief Administration, Civil Works Administration, and Works Progress Administration, all of which depended on regular infusions of RFC money. Secretary of the Interior Harold Ickes was the third partner in the game. Jones found Ickes a silly, insecure man, but one who had the ear of the president, and Jones nurtured that relationship. When "Tommy the Cork" Corcoran's star rose in Washington during 1933, Jones managed to get him employed as an assistant general counsel in the RFC Legal Division, and he also brought Adolf Berle, the famous member of the original brain trust, into the RFC as a consultant on railroad and banking matters.[18]

Jones was also a darling of the Texas congressional delegation. During the 1920s he became a major political power in Texas, helping to put the state on the map economically as well as politically. He worked tirelessly for Democratic candidates, filling their campaign war chests with his money and the resources of the oil, real estate, and ranching industries. In 1928, at the Democratic National Convention in Houston, Jones donated $200,000 in personal funds to the party, and the Texas delegation honored him with a favorite son nomination for president. Power in the United States Congress rested above all

[18] Henry H. Adams, *Harry Hopkins* (New York, 1977), pp. 119 and 137; Beatrice Bishop Berle and Travis Beal Jacobs, eds., *Navigating the Rapids 1918–1971. From the Papers of Adolf A. Berle* (New York, 1973), p. 84; Monica Lynne Niznik, "Thomas G. Corcoran: The Public Service of Franklin Roosevelt's 'Tommy the Cork,' " Ph.D. dissertation, University of Notre Dame, 1981, pp. 57–59.

other things on seniority, and Texas voters were loath to unseat incumbents. Texas politicians stayed in office and accumulated power, so that Jones's contact with them meant a long-term influence on political events.

Although Senators Thomas Connally and Morris Shepherd had served in Congress for years and were ranking members of the Finance, Judiciary, and Public Buildings Committees, it was the Texas delegation in the House of Representatives which wielded so much influence. Jones's closest associate and friend there was "Cactus Jack" Garner, the fierce, wild-eye-browed speaker of the House from Uvalde, Texas. Jones considered Garner his most valuable ally. Not only were they personally close, but Jones needed the power Garner exercised in the House. Even after his election as vice-president, a job he deemed as worthwhile as a "bucket of warm spit," Garner knew everyone who was anyone in Congress. When he left the House, Garner was replaced as the unofficial leader of the Texas delegation by Samuel Taliafero Rayburn, the dedicated, compassionate populist from Fannin County. The child of dirt-poor East Texas farmers, Rayburn spent his life hating Wall Street, Republicans, and the great railroads. When Jones managed to secure Rayburn's support for federal bank and railroad loans, the House listened and the RFC triumphed. By virtue of his seniority and chairmanship of the House Interstate Commerce Committee, Rayburn was invaluable to Jones. Joseph Jefferson Mansfield, chairman of the Rivers and Harbors Committee and premier distributor of pork barrel public works money, was also a Texan, as was Hatton W. Sumners, chairman of the House Judiciary Committee. Another Texan, J. Marvin Jones, chaired the House Agriculture Committee, and Fritz Lanham of Texas headed the Committee on Public Buildings and Grounds. There were other bright stars in the Texas delegation, like Wright Patman, Lyndon B. Johnson, and Maury Maverick—with whom Jones kept contact, but each of them was in the orbit of Rayburn, Garner, or Marvin Jones anyway. Jones was in constant touch with the Texas delegation, always keeping them informed of pending legislation and how it would affect the RFC. He had clout in

51

Congress because Texas had clout, and the Texas delegation loved him.[19]

In choosing his associates on the RFC board, Jones at first wanted either absolute loyalty or great political influence. During 1932, he chafed under Eugene Meyer's leadership. Not only was Meyer arrogant and combative, he was a tool of Wall Street and an enemy of the emerging financial interests of the South and West, at least in Jones's mind. Looking back at those RFC board meetings during the Hoover administration, Jones recalled that "when Mr. Meyer was no longer with us we had complete harmony."[20]

William Woodin joined the RFC board when he became secretary of the treasury. A lifelong Republican, Woodin had come to know the president during their years of service with the Warm Springs Foundation raising money to fight polio. He had spent most of his life running a family business—the American Car and Foundary Company—and had independent political views. Woodin grew weary of Republican conservatism during the 1920s, and in 1928 he endorsed Al Smith for president. Joining the Democratic party after that, he supported Roosevelt's candidacy for president in 1932. Like Jones, Woodin's basic instincts were conservative, but he was convinced that only the federal government was capable of dealing with the depression.[21]

At first, Jones seemed much more concerned with the political power of the board. When he took over at the RFC in March 1933, he filled several vacancies. Since Roosevelt wanted to reassure Republican Senator Robert M. La Follette, Jr., of his status in the New Deal, he appointed former Senator John J. Blaine to replace Atlee Pomerene, who had resigned. Jones was delighted with the nomination. Blaine's liberal credentials were impeccable, and he gave Jones a better hand in

[19] For a brilliant description of the Texas congressional delegation, see Robert A. Caro, *The Years of Lyndon Johnson: The Path to Power* (New York, 1982), pp. 217–22, 306–34.

[20] Jones, *Fifty Billion Dollars*, p. 530; Niznik, "Thomas G. Corcoran," p. 44.

[21] *New York Times*, May 4, 1934.

his political poker deck. Jones knew the RFC enjoyed support among the business elite of the conservative wing of the GOP, and among conservative Democrats, but it was vulnerable among progressive Republicans who had earlier criticized its loans. The addition of John J. Blaine, whose progressive Republicanism in Wisconsin went all the way back to former Governor Robert M. La Follette, strengthened Jones. When Wilson McCarthy resigned in 1934, Jones turned to former Nevada Senator Charles B. Henderson. He had worked with Henderson during the Nevada banking crisis late in 1932, and Henderson had strong ties to western mining and railroad interests. When Harvey Couch, the prominent Arkansas Democrat, left the board in 1934, Jones brought in former Democratic Senator Hubert Stephens of Mississippi. Each of the former senators gave Jones more leverage in Congress, as if he needed any more, and none of them questioned his basic philosophical approach to the agency.[22]

By the mid-1930s, however, Jones's preoccupation with a powerful RFC board had subsided. Perhaps his power had become so great that there was little need for former congressmen on the board. Whatever insecurities he might have harbored in 1933 and 1934 were long gone by 1935 and 1936. Jones had more than established himself as a leading figure in the New Deal. When Blaine died on April 18, 1934, Jones filled the position with Charles T. Fisher, a Republican banker who had headed the RFC's Detroit loan agency. Fisher had close ties to the Detroit automobile community, particularly to his family's Fisher Body Company and to General Motors. But at the same time, Fisher had credibility with the labor movement, and American Federation of Labor (AFL) President William Green endorsed the appointment. When Stephens left the board in 1936, Jones accepted the recommendation of Speaker of the House Henry Rainey of Illinois that Emil Schram suc-

[22] Patrick J. Maney, *"Young Bob" La Follette. A Biography of Robert M. La Follette, Jr., 1895–1953* (Columbia, 1978), pp. 104, 120, and 134; *New York Times*, January 24 and August 17, 1934, and March 14, 1935; see the Henderson endorsement in FDRPL, OF 643-A, RFC Endorsements, Box 22.

ceed him. Schram had headed the RFC's Drainage, Levee, and Irrigation Division since 1933.[23]

The other spots on the RFC board during the 1930s went to friends and associates of Jesse Jones or Franklin D. Roosevelt. Shortly after taking over at the RFC, Jones had to fill three vacancies on the RFC board caused by the resignation of Republicans Charles Miller, Gardner Cowles, and Ogden Mills. All three vacancies, according to the original RFC Act, had to go to Republicans. Jones asked the president to nominate Republican Carroll B. Merriam, president of the Topeka Central Trust Company, and a director of the Santa Fe Railroad and the Kansas Power and Light Company. Jones had worked with Merriam in Washington for the American Red Cross during World War I. John J. Blaine had filled the second Republican opening, and Roosevelt called on Frederic Taber of Massachusetts, an old Harvard classmate, to fill the third vacancy. Jones had no problem with the Taber appointment.[24]

Two other people had positions on the RFC board during the New Deal, and both of them were very close to Jones. When Charles T. Fisher left in 1936 at the request of Governor Frank Murphy of Michigan to become Michigan bank commissioner, Jones filled the spot with Howard J. Klossner, a Minnesota Republican who had already spent seven years in the RFC Examining Division. When Jones became federal loan administrator in 1939 and Emil Schram took over as chairman of the RFC, Sam H. Husbands, a South Carolina Democrat and also a longtime member of the RFC Examining Division, filled the vacancy. Both Husbands and Klossner were fanatically loyal to Jones.[25]

In June 1933, the first RFC board under the New Deal con-

[23] Jones, *Fifty Billion Dollars*, pp. 521–30; C. B. Merriam to Stephen Early, April 14, 1936, FDRPL, OF 643, RFC, Box 4; Emil Schram to Franklin D. Roosevelt, January 3, 1937, FDRPL, OF 42-B, Electric Farm and Home Authority; *New York Times*, March 14, 1935; Jesse Jones to Franklin D. Roosevelt, June 5, 1936, FDRPL, OF 643-A, RFC Endorsements, Box 21.

[24] Jones, *Fifty Billion Dollars*, pp. 521–30; *New York Times*, June 10–11, 1933.

[25] Jones, *Fifty Billion Dollars*, pp. 529–31; Clifford Durr, COHR, p. 72.

sisted of Democrats Jesse Jones, Wilson McCarthy, and Harvey Couch, with William Woodin a member by virtue of his position as secretary of the treasury, and Republicans John J. Blaine, Carroll B. Merriam, and Frederic Taber. McCarthy resigned late in 1933 and was replaced by Charles Henderson. Blaine died in 1934 and Charles Fisher took his place. Hubert Stephens came on board when Couch resigned in August 1934. Emil Schram replaced Stephens in 1936. Howard Klossner succeeded Fisher in 1936, and Sam H. Husbands took over for Emil Schram in 1939 when Schram replaced Jones as RFC chairman. The later appointees to the RFC board were in one important respect no different from the earlier ones: they stood in awe of Jesse Jones, deferred consistently to his judgment, and accepted his domination of the agency as a fact of life.[26]

Only one dark cloud appeared on Jones's horizon at the RFC. Ever since January 1932, the secretary of the treasury had an ex-officio position on the RFC board. Ogden Mills had been very active under the Hoover administration, but William Woodin was a different story. His health was already failing when he took over at Treasury in March 1933, and he was only able to attend two RFC board meetings during the year. Jones liked Woodin personally and had his complete support, but Woodin could not hold up any longer. He sent his resignation to Roosevelt in October, but the president asked him to take a leave of absence instead of resigning. Woodin went to his home in Colorado to recuperate but it was no use. He resigned in December. Roosevelt had already appointed Henry Morgenthau, Jr., an old friend and governor of the Farm Credit Administration, as acting secretary of the treasury. In January 1934 Morgenthau took Woodin's place at Treasury and on the RFC board.[27] Morgenthau proved to be a thorn in Jones's side.

Morgenthau, a large, bald-pated man whose eyes squinted

---

[26] Jesse Jones to Franklin D. Roosevelt, January 13, 1936, FDRPL, OF 643, RFC, Box 4; *New York Times*, January 21, 1935, January 2, 1937, and January 25, 1938.

[27] Jones, *Fifty Billion Dollars*, p. 524.

behind pince-nez, had a dour public image. Shy and withdrawn, he appeared uncomfortable at press conferences, and journalists usually got the better of him. Roosevelt jokingly called him "Henry The Morgue." Jokes aside, Roosevelt loved Morgenthau. The son of a wealthy real estate developer, Morgenthau attended Phillips Exeter Academy and Cornell, and in 1913, with his father's help, he purchased several hundred acres of farmland in Dutchess County, about fifteen miles from the Roosevelt estate at Hyde Park. The two young Hudson River squires formed a close personal relationship. During Roosevelt's long recuperation from the polio attack in the 1920s, the two men met all the time, talking politics and playing endless games of parcheesi. When Roosevelt made his political comeback in the late 1920s, Morgenthau acted as his driver, aide, and advance man. As governor of New York, Roosevelt appointed the gentleman-farmer commissioner of conservation, and when Roosevelt entered the White House, Morgenthau ultimately found himself running Treasury.[28]

Jones's problems with Morgenthau were philosophical and personal. Although both men were fiscally conservative, Morgenthau was ideologically so, and throughout the 1930s he campaigned vigorously for balanced budgets and cuts in government spending as the only way of restoring business confidence and stimulating a permanent recovery. Morgenthau winced at the explosion of government agencies, insisted that most of them were only temporary, and worked behind the scenes with Roosevelt to cut relief spending in general and RFC programs in particular. He offended Jones's refined sense of territoriality. Jones often lifted his own eyebrows at many New Deal programs, but he was by no means a laissez-faire ideologue. On the contrary, Jones was passionately committed to the efficacy of state capitalism. The Reconstruction Finance Corporation was a conservative agency capable of helping restore balance to the money markets, business confidence, and consumer spending. The federal government was capable of

[28] For the best work on the life of Henry Morgenthau, Jr., see John Morton Blum, *From the Morgenthau Diaries*, 3 vol. (Boston, 1959, 1965, and 1967).

promoting economic growth without hamstringing business. The New Deal, in Jones's view, was state capitalism at its best and needed no apologies.

Personal differences between the two men were great. Jones found Morgenthau cold and detached, about as far from a Texas "good old boy" as anyone could be. Punctual, hardworking, and businesslike, Morgenthau had little time for social pleasantries or, in Jones's words, "chewing the fat." He also felt that Morgenthau was out of his depth at Treasury, that his presence and power in Washington was completely personal, a gift of friendship from the president. Jones knew, of course, that he had to be careful with Morgenthau because his relationship with the president was inviolate. Roosevelt could laugh heartily at the "Morgenthau jokes" circulating through Washington, but anybody with the least political sense also knew there was a limit to the president's sense of humor. He and Morgenthau went back too far. The president felt that way about only a handful of people—Harry Hopkins, Harold Ickes, Louis Howe—and Henry Morgenthau was one of the privileged few.

Throughout the 1930s the other members of the RFC board came to share Jones's view of Morgenthau as a financial lightweight wedded to anachronistic ideas. The RFC board was created in Jones's image and Morgenthau knew it. He quickly stopped attending the meetings, and Jones used Tommy Corcoran as his liaison with Treasury. Blessed with the gift of the gab and a keen understanding of human nature, Corcoran managed to penetrate even Morgenthau's personality barriers and helped keep the relationship between the two men functional. Jones had an acute political sense about him, and even when he was enraged at Morgenthau's latest attempt to reduce RFC power, he kept the anger in tow, preferring to approach the president with tempered, undeniable economic arguments. Roosevelt almost always listened.[29]

If Morgenthau was an irritant to Jones, his replacement on

[29] Jones, *Fifty Billion Dollars*, pp. 304–6; Berle and Jacobs, *Navigating the Rapids*, p. 344; Niznik, "Thomas G. Corcoran," pp. 57–59.

the RFC board proved to be an extraordinary asset. Thomas "Tommy the Cork" Corcoran had come to the RFC in 1932 during the Hoover administration after graduating from the Harvard Law School, clerking with Supreme Court Justice Oliver Wendell Holmes, Jr., and working on corporate reorganizations with the New York law firm of Colton and Franklin. At Cambridge he had quickly impressed Professor Felix Frankfurter with his wit and unparalleled analytical skills, as well as the obvious political gifts his Irish Catholic heritage had bequeathed him. In 1933 Frankfurter introduced Corcoran to newly-elected President Franklin D. Roosevelt, and the president made him a special assistant to both Secretary of the Treasury William Woodin and Attorney General Homer Cummings. In 1934, Corcoran returned to the RFC as special counsel and liaison to Henry Morgenthau, and he remained there until his return to private practice in 1941. Beginning in June 1933, as an aide to Morgenthau and before his return as special counsel, Corcoran acted as an ex-officio member of the RFC board.[30]

Corcoran played an influential role on the RFC, even though his position as special counsel gave him no automatic power. His own abilities, as well as Jones's indulgence, did. While working on the Truth-in-Securities legislation in 1933, which became the Securities Act, Corcoran met Benjamin Cohen, who had come to Washington with Harvard Law School professor James Landis to work on the bill. Together, Corcoran and Cohen wrote the more comprehensive Securities Exchange Act of 1934, and the team of Cohen and Corcoran was born. It was an extraordinary collaboration, responsible in whole or in part for a wealth of New Deal legislation, including the Federal Housing Administration, Tennessee Valley Authority, and the Public Utility Holding Company Act of 1935. They two worked behind the scenes in Washington, displaying a "passion for anonymity" which actually enhanced their influence. They shared a Georgetown town house with several

[30] Niznik, "Thomas G. Corcoran," pp. 57–59.

other New Deal lawyers and worked incessantly, with Cohen serving as legislative draftsman and Corcoran using his effervescent personality to shepherd the bills through Congress. The two men earned the title of the "Gold Dust Twins" after a popular soap advertisement which encouraged the householder to "let the Gold Dust Twins do your work." They were also called "Frankfurter's two chief little hot dogs" and "the Brains Twins."

Corcoran's center of operations was the RFC, where he established a base of power reaching throughout the New Deal by virtue of the bright young lawyers he placed in important government agencies. Stanley Reed, RFC general counsel and later an associate justice of the Supreme Court, was nominally Corcoran's boss, but he let Corcoran have complete rein because the young Irish lawyer was one of Roosevelt's favorites. Jones liked having Corcoran around because of his unfailing good humor, unmatched lobbying skills in Congress, and constant but good-tempered demands that the scope of the RFC expand beyond government banking to economic planning and management of the private businesses with which it had become involved.

Corcoran was somewhat out of place in the early New Deal. Coming out of the Harvard Law School under the tutelage of Felix Frankfurter, he was suspicious of the planning and business commonwealth rhetoric of 1933 and 1934. The National Recovery Administration (NRA) and Agricultural Adjustment Administration (AAA) left too much power in the hands of big corporate and financial interests, while real reform demanded a Brandeisian approach—restoration of a competitive economy and regulation of financial practices. Although Jesse Jones had little faith the Brandeisian antitrust campaigns, he did share with Corcoran a strong conviction that Wall Street had gotten out of hand in the 1920s, and that the federal government had the ability and the responsibility to rescue capitalism. Jones respected Corcoran's passion as well as his wit, and although he never took the RFC down the road Corcoran was trying to map out, he nevertheless listened carefully and gave Corcoran a free hand. Under the two of them the RFC became an enormous governmental entity, the major institution in American finance, dwarfing Wall Street in power and symbolizing the shift of political and economic power from New York to Washington, D.C. In its first two years under the New Deal, the Reconstruction Finance Corporation became the largest investor in the economy.

Corcoran's office in the Legal Division was a hive of activity. Felix Frankfurter would recommend good Harvard lawyers for jobs, Corcoran would bring Reed and Jones in on the recommendations, and then he would find spots for them, if not in other agencies then in the RFC, where they waited for permanent assignments elsewhere. During the mid-1930s, the RFC was home for a host of influential New Dealers, including people like Reed and Corcoran, Benjamin Cohen, Paul Freund, Adolf Berle, Clifford Durr, Stewart McDonald, Allen Throop, Richard Quay, Blackwell Smith, Edward Burling, Jr., Joseph Cotten, Jr., Frank Watson, and Jerome Frank. With its offices, clerks, equipment, wire services, secretaries, accountants, bank examiners, lawyers, comptrollers, and every other financial skill available in the world, the Reconstruction Finance Corporation became a major center of power in Washington. Insiders in Washington affectionately described Corcoran's office at the RFC as the "Felix Frankfurter-Thomas Corcoran Civil Service Program." Separated by a generation in age, Jones and Corcoran nevertheless formed a close friendship during the 1930s, one which served both them and the RFC.[31]

The last, and by far the most important, factor in the Jones empire at the Reconstruction Finance Corporation was Franklin D. Roosevelt. The two men had enormous respect for one another, but it was a respect based on power, not affection. Jones's birth as a Tennessee dirt farmer and successful struggle for the American dream had left him skeptical of human nature and basically willing to accept the current structure of the economy, except he did want to do something about the power of Wall Street. Jones saw the New Deal relief measures as nec-

[31] Ibid., pp. 52–53.

essary evils; the AAA and NRA as harebrained experiments certain to degenerate in political controversy; and such measures as the Securities Act of 1933, the Securities Exchange Act of 1934, the Banking Act of 1935, and the Public Utility Holding Company Act of 1935 as long overdue. But if Jones had doubts about many of the president's ideas, he had no doubts about the man's power. Roosevelt sat on the crest of a great political wave in the United States, and Jones wanted to go along for the ride. He was solicitous of the president, careful to keep him informed, and always seeking his opinion. In 1934, for example, Democratic Congressman Adolf Sabath of Chicago proposed amending the RFC Act to allow the agency to make massive loans to school districts for teachers' salaries. In a letter to the president, Jones asked Roosevelt what position he should take on the bill so he could inform the Texas delegation of his opinion.[32] The letter served two purposes. Jones wanted to appear deferential to the president's opinion while at the same time illustrating his continuing influence with the Texas congressional delegation.

Roosevelt had the same respect for Jones, although the feelings probably more closely resembled those of the mongoose for the cobra. He was uncomfortable with Jones's independence and not always sure of Jones's loyalty, but Jones also brought great strength to the administration. One of the New Deal's greatest political weaknesses was its lack of ties to the conservative business community, and Roosevelt viewed Jones as a real asset there. Businessmen had enormous respect for Jones, and the president often used the RFC chairman on important political fence-building assignments among them. The president also understood Jones's political support among the Texas congressional delegation, votes Roosevelt always viewed as keys to most controversial New Deal legislation. Finally, the president saw the RFC as a bureaucratic tool perfectly designed to fit his administrative style—flexible, pragmatic, powerful, and independent. Blessed with massive financial resources, unparalleled congressional support, political insula-

---

[32] Jesse Jones to Franklin D. Roosevelt, May 18, 1934, FDRPL, OF 643, RFC.

tion, and a dynamic, highly respected leader, the RFC gave the president freedom of action and power without strings attached. Roosevelt needed Jones and the RFC as badly as the RFC and Jones needed Roosevelt.[33] It was a marriage made in heaven for both of them.

[33] Schlesinger, *The Coming of the New Deal*, p. 431; Chester Morrill, COHR, p. 182; Clifford Durr, COHR, pp. 36–39; William Clayton, COHR, p. 100; Jerome Frank, COHR, pp. 50–51; Stanley Reed, COHR, p. 82, 96; Jones, *Fifty Billion Dollars*, pp. 522–35.

CHAPTER IV

Reconstruction of the Banking
System, 1933–1934

FEW PRESIDENTS had entered the White House under more inauspicious circumstances. On March 4, 1933, the economy was in a state of collapse. The banking system had closed under the weight of its own liabilities; businessmen were laying off workers in record numbers; and consumers were hoarding money as a hedge against the future. The banking holiday on March 6 brought some relief, and the Emergency Banking Act of March 9 gave the RFC the power to invest in thousands of private institutions. But few people took much comfort. Hopes were high but doubts were strong. There had just been too many economic surprises in the recent past. For over a year Jesse Jones, Wilson McCarthy, and Harvey Couch had been pushing the idea of bank reconstruction as the prerequisite for a revival of commercial credit. During 1932 they had all naively assumed that short-term RFC loans to banks and railroads would do the trick, providing temporary liquidity to break the cycle of panic and doubt. The collapse of the banking system in February 1933 was proof that the financial malaise was more serious than they had once thought, and that more drastic government reconstruction measures were necessary. But what had not changed was their belief in the need for a credit revival. Not until businessmen had access to working and equity capital could recovery be expected. Roosevelt shared their conviction, or at least was willing to give it the credence he extended to so many other recovery theories in 1933.

The purpose of the holiday had been to buy time before depositors pushed the entire banking system to ruin. Somehow the federal government had to restore public confidence and make sure all reopened banks were liquid enough to do business. Between March 4 and March 13 William Woodin, Ogden Mills, Arthur Ballantine, Francis G. Awalt, Walter Wyatt, Adolf Berle, Eugene Meyer, and Jesse Jones debated whether to reopen most of the banks and perpetuate the liquidity crisis or open only a few select banks and risk the possibility of a severe credit deflation. But with President Roosevelt wanting banking services available in small towns as well as large urban centers, they decided to reopen as many banks as possible, even those with marginal economic problems, if they were sound enough to operate profitably without restrictions. The federal government would guarantee the financial integrity of each reopened bank and restore public confidence. The fate of the money markets rested on the fragile condition of public opinion. If depositors doubted the condition of the banking system, their collective fear could destroy the economy.[1] President Roosevelt and Secretary of the Treasury Woodin announced that no member of the Federal Reserve system would reopen until it had satisfied them that it was sound.[2]

Teams of bank examiners from the RFC, Federal Reserve banks, the Treasury Department, and the comptroller of the currency fanned out across the country in a crash program to analyze the financial condition of each national bank. Time was at a premium. Any prolonged delay in reviving the banking system would create frustration and, worse yet, public skepticism about the actual condition of the banks. All national banks whose capital structures were unimpaired received licenses permitting them to reopen at the direction of the president. National banks with impaired capital but with assets valuable enough to repay all depositors remained closed until the crisis passed and they could receive RFC assistance. Banks whose capital was gone and whose assets were incapable of a full return to depositors and creditors were placed in the hands of conservators who could reorganize them with RFC assistance or liquidate them.[3]

[1] RFC, Minutes, 14 (March 11, 1933), 822–23; Notes of the Meeting of the Board of Directors of the Federal Reserve Bank of New York, March 8–11, 1933, Discussion Notes, Harrison Papers.

[2] New York Times, March 11, 1933.

[3] Cyril B. Upham and Edwin Lamke, Closed and Distressed Banks (Washington, D.C., 1934), pp. 46–47; Jones, Fifty Billion Dollars, p. 22.

The federal government had no authority to dictate reopening regulations to state-chartered banks, but Woodin asked state banking authorities to use the same licensing process.[4] They usually cooperated. In Iowa, for example, the governor directed the state superintendent of banking to take control of state-chartered banks on March 11. Each state bank had to submit a statement of condition which examiners used to determine its ability to reopen. Examinations were hasty and sometimes haphazard, but state officials completed the job. No state wanted its banks closed for examination while banks throughout the country were opening. Nor did the federal government. Nothing was more likely to trigger another liquidity crisis.[5]

With the bank examinations underway, the administration worked out a reopening schedule. All banks in the Federal Reserve system located in a Federal Reserve Bank city would reopen on March 13 if they possessed a license to do so. The RFC would also reopen for business. If all went well on the thirteenth, licensed member banks of the Federal Reserve system which operated in a city with an active clearinghouse association could reopen on March 14. If that proved equally tranquil, remaining licensed banks could open on March 15.[6] Woodin asked state banking officials to use the same schedule. The RFC directed its loan agency managers to release funds only to licensed banks.[7]

On the evening of March 12, the night before the first reopenings, Franklin D. Roosevelt went on the radio with the first of his famous "fireside chats." Written largely by Ogden Mills and Arthur Ballantine, the speech was a masterstroke.[8] In a mild, soothing voice, he explained the nature of the banking crisis, why it had occurred, and how the reopenings would

---

[4] *Federal Reserve Bulletin*, 19 (March 1933), 127–29.

[5] Muchmore, "The Banking Crisis of 1933: Some Iowa Evidence," 638.

[6] See the telegram from the Treasury Department to the governors of the Federal Reserve banks, March 12, 1933, NA, RG 234, RFC, Administrative Subject File.

[7] RFC, Minutes, 14 (March 14, 1933), 958.

[8] Ballantine, "When All the Banks Closed," p. 140; Jackson Reynolds, COHR, pp. 170–72.

proceed. He assured people that all reopened banks were sound. Roosevelt asked people to be patient and calm, to resist fear and skepticism, and to trust him that stability was returning.[9]

Few other presidents had spoken more powerful words. Complete calm reigned on March 13. By the end of business on March 15, 12,756 banks had reopened, 69 percent of the 18,390 banks operating on March 3, 1933. Of the 6,816 member banks of the Federal Reserve system, 5,038 received licenses.[10] Even more encouraging was that people began returning hoarded money. Between March 13 and March 30, more than $660 million flowed back into the money markets, and by the end of the month the total had reached nearly $1 billion. The administration had restored the banking system to its pre-1933 condition, and public confidence seemed secure. During the rest of the year, only 221 banks failed; 9 national banks, 6 state member banks of the Federal Reserve, and 206 state nonmember banks. That too reassured people that the banking system was stable.[11]

The uneventful reopening gave the RFC its first opportunity to look carefully at the basic condition of the money markets and consider major policy changes. On the original RFC board, Jones, McCarthy, and Couch had staked out a philosophical position different from that of Eugene Meyer, Ogden Mills, H. Paul Bestor, and Charles Dawes. The three Democrats, though committed to the reconstruction of the banking system, resented the influence of the eastern banking establishment. In the case of railroad loans, for example, they hated bailing out indebted lines because the money quickly found its

[9] Samuel I. Rosenman, ed., *The Public Papers and Addresses of Franklin D. Roosevelt*, vol. II. *The Year of Crisis, 1933* (New York, 1938), p. 61.

[10] "Weekly Review of Economic Conditions," March 18, 1933 and April 4, 1933, NA, RG 234, RFC, Statistical Division. Melvin Traylor, head of the First National Bank of Chicago, told J.F.T. O'Connor that depositors were more calm after the holiday than they had been in years. See J.F.T. O'Connor Diary, May 16, 1933, O'Connor Papers.

[11] "Weekly Review of Economic Conditions," April 4, 1933, NA, RG 234, RFC, Statistical Division; *Annual Report of the Comptroller of the Currency for 1933* (Washington, D.C., 1934), pp. 662–63.

way to the major Wall Street firms. Instead of just making the loans, Jones, McCarthy, and Couch wanted the RFC to help the railroads renegotiate their outstanding obligations with those Wall Street firms, securing lower interest rates and more long-range stability. Meyer, Mills, and Bestor were more interested in simply making the loans and buying the railroads more time.[12]

Bred in the rough-and-tumble, entrepreneurial spirit of southwestern and western business, the Democrats were also more flexible than the Republicans on the board, more willing to tolerate an expansion of RFC authority and to accept it as a permanent rather than temporary institution. While Hoover, Meyer, Mills, Bestor, and Dawes wanted to leave RFC interest rates high and loan terms stringent, Jones, McCarthy, and Couch wanted lower rates and greater activity. They also felt that the Republicans had ignored, or at least been rather insensitive to, the needs of western and southern banks, small businesses, and farmers. They found the Republican philosophy governing RFC operations too conservative and cautious, too stingy, and too severe in its loan terms.[13]

The new board immediately reevaluated RFC policies. Under Hoover the RFC had functioned conservatively, always worried about preempting the prerogatives of private business. The board insisted that all loans be repaid promptly and that collateral fully secure the corporation's investment. Collateral requirements were strict. They loaned only 80 percent of the market value of the highest grade securities and no more than

[12] Charles Hamlin Diary, April 2, 1932, Hamlin Papers; *New York Times*, March 19, 1932; *Wall Street Journal*, March 12, 1932; "Intelligent Rail Relief," *Magazine of Wall Street*, 50 (May 14, 1932), 72.

[13] Jones, *Fifty Billion Dollars*, pp. 84, 517–19; Eugene Meyer, COHR, p. 676; Wilson, *Harvey Couch*, pp. 145, 156–57; Atlee Pomerene to Charles Dawes, April 25, 1932, Dawes Papers; Charles Dawes to Butler Hare, May 23, 1932, and Ralph Hore to Herbert Hoover, May 25, 1932, NA, RG 234, RFC, Administrative Subject File; Eugene Meyer to Hiram Johnson, June 1, 1932, in RFC, Minutes, 5 (June 1, 1932), 3; Eugene Meyer to Charles McNary, April 1, 1932, in RFC, Minutes, 3 (April 1, 1932), 4–5; Charles Hamlin Diary, March 1 and June 7, 1932, Hamlin Papers; *Chicago Tribune*, June 7, 1932; Stanley Reed, OH, HHPL, p. 8.

50 percent of the market value of other assets. A bank accepting an RFC loan had to deposit its most liquid assets at only a fraction of their previous value as collateral. The RFC also had the right, which it frequently exercised, to demand more collateral when securities and asset values declined. All loans had to be repaid in six months. Finally, the RFC set its interest rate at 6 percent on bank and railroad loans and 7 percent on agricultural loans, both well above prevailing money market rates. Rates were high on purpose. Hoover feared the idea of state capitalism. It would be too easy for the federal government to displace private institutions from the money market. So he wanted to make sure the government alternative was expensive and inconvenient—a last resort.[14] An editorial in *Business Week* severely criticized Hoover's RFC for its cautiousness:

> What is the RFC?
>
> Is it a pawnshop, or a fire department? If it is a pawnshop in which necessitous borrowers are compelled to hock assets worth two or three times the amount of the loan, we are opposed to it. . . . We see no reason why the government should be engaged in a careful pawnbroking enterprise, niggling over security, haggling over interest, competing with other lenders.
>
> Is the RFC a fire department? If so, what is the idea in counting out the buckets of water?[15]

Jesse Jones had none of Hoover's reservations. He was committed to the idea of state capitalism, at least as far as the banking system was concerned. Although he wanted to use government funds wisely and prudently, Jones was willing to revive the banking system even if it took billions of dollars. Because

---

[14] RFC, *Loan Agency Bulletin No. 1* (Washington, D.C., 1932), p. 1; Jesse Jones to M. H. Gossett, March 17, 1932, Jones Papers; RFC, *Loan Agency Bulletin No. 8* (Washington, D.C., 1932), p. 1. For an example of RFC regulations, see Minutes of the Advisory Committee of the Atlanta Loan Agency, February 5, 1932, NA, RG 234, RFC, Secretarial Division.

[15] "R.F.C.: Pawnbroker or Fire Department," *Business Week*, March 1, 1933, p. 32.

of strict collateral requirements, high interest rates, and short-term loans, the RFC helped basically sound enterprises in need of temporary liquidity.[16] For weaker banks the strict conditions of an RFC loan offered no solutions. Most banks in serious trouble needed long-term capital, not temporary infusions of short-term funds. The Emergency Banking Act had given the RFC authority to provide investment capital, and at the same time Jesse Jones and the new RFC board relaxed collateral requirements and reduced the loan rate by 1/2 percent. It was a modest beginning, but a beginning nonetheless.[17]

With relaxed loan requirements, the RFC joined the Treasury Department and the comptroller of the currency in working on closed banks. They had to decide which banks could be reorganized and which had to be liquidated. Under Title II of the Emergency Banking Act, they appointed a conservator for each closed bank. The conservator could liquidate assets at any time to prevent further declines in value or hold them intact until reorganization plans were complete. William Woodin, Jesse Jones, and Comptroller of the Currency J.F.T. O'Connor met every day to discuss policy matters and reorganization plans for nonlicensed banks, i.e., those not permitted to reopen after the holiday.[18]

They classified closed banks into three groups. The first group included those banks which could be reopened without reorganization. Either because federal examiners had been late or because there had been some question about the value of their assets, they had not reopened by March 15. After that they had been examined and declared sound. Between March 15 and April 12, over 1,300 banks reopened without major assistance from the RFC.[19] There were still 4,215 unlicensed

---

[16] Olson, *Herbert Hoover and the Reconstruction Finance Corporation*, pp. 116–19.

[17] *New York Times*, June 12, 1933.

[18] J.F.T. O'Connor, *The Banking Crisis and Recovery under the Roosevelt Administration* (Chicago, 1935), p. 30.

[19] Upham and Lamke, *Closed and Distressed Banks*, pp. 124–25; *Annual Report of the Comptroller of the Currency for 1933*, p. 663; *Federal Reserve*

banks, of which 1,108 were national banks, 148 state member banks, and 2,959 nonmember banks. They constituted the second and third groups. One set of them had impaired assets but could reopen with large-scale RFC loans and investment capital. The other group was beyond help. They had to be liquidated.

The remaining 4,215 unlicensed banks were placed in the hands of conservators if they were national banks or state banking authorities if they were state-chartered. More than 1,100 of them were liquidated in 1933 because their assets were so badly eroded that no stronger bank would even consider buying them out. RFC funds would only have postponed the inevitable.[20] The remaining 3,100 banks had to be reorganized before reopening. Both state and federal banking authorities used the same procedures. They turned to the capital correction plan when only the capital of the bank was impaired. They wrote off bad assets by charging them against the bank's capital account. At the point the bank possessed sound assets which at least equaled its liabilities, sales of new stock to the RFC or to investors restored the capital. In some instances depositors subordinated a percentage of their claims to decrease the bank's liabilities.[21]

Another approach involved liquidating a bank after its solvency had been assured through subordination of depositors' claims and sale of its sound assets to another bank. Between the application of the capital and profits of the old bank and the depositors' claims which had been secured, bad assets were eliminated. The new bank then assumed its liabilities. The RFC supplied new capital.[22] On March 19, for example, the RFC

Bulletin, 20 (April, 1933), 251; "Weekly Review of Economic Conditions," May 6, 1933, NA, RG 234, RFC, Statistical Division.

[20] *Annual Report of the Comptroller of the Currency for 1933*, p. 663.

[21] O'Connor, *The Banking Crisis*, p. 42; James Couzens to J.F.T. O'Connor, September 14, 1934, O'Connor Papers.

[22] O'Connor, *The Banking Crisis*, pp. 43–44; Ellis Merry, "Bank Reorganization and Recapitalization in Michigan," unpublished manuscript, NA, RG 234, RFC, Administrative Subject File, Banking Emergency of 1933, Michigan Bank Moratorium.

loaned $35 million to the conservators of the Guardian National Bank of Commerce and the First National Bank of Detroit to liquefy their assets, and then bought $12.5 million in preferred stock of a newly organized bank. Reorganization depended on the ability of the new bank to raise an additional $12.5 million from sales of common stock.[23] In both plans, RFC assistance was the key to success. By October 1933 there were only 2,300 banks still closed since the holiday.

But those banks posed a special challenge to the RFC. On June 16, 1933, Congress had passed the Banking Act of 1933 establishing, among other things, a Federal Deposit Insurance Corporation to guarantee bank deposits and protect the money supply from a liquidity crisis. The idea of deposit insurance went back to the early 1930s when the number of bank failures reached catastrophic levels. The two most prominent bills came from Senator Carter Glass of Virginia and Congressman Henry Steagall of Alabama. Glass wanted establishment of a liquidation corporation, a federal agency to expedite receiverships so that depositors could get some of their money from closed banks. Steagall wanted a government corporation to do more than just expedite receiverships. He wanted the government to guarantee an individual account up to a predetermined maximum. It would be an insurance program financed by the premiums of member banks. Steagall felt such a program would protect the money supply against public panic. Assured of getting their money even if a bank closed, depositors would not be so inclined to demand their funds simultaneously and destroy the bank in a liquidity crisis. Because of the opposition of Herbert Hoover, the reluctance of Carter Glass over the guarantee provision, and the outright hatred of most bankers, the deposit guarantee bill did not triumph until after Franklin D. Roosevelt's inauguration. A Senate-House conference committee joined the Steagall bill for deposit guarantee with Carter Glass's other bill separating commercial

[23] RFC, Minutes, 14 (March 19, 1933), 1555; 14 (March 21, 1933), 1657–61.

from investment banking. Roosevelt signed the measure on June 16, 1933.[24]

But the FDIC also posed a new problem for federal banking authorities. Because FDIC directors wanted to protect the circulating medium, they wanted every bank in the country enrolled. But the Banking Act of 1933 specified that only sound banks whose assets exceeded liabilities were eligible. None of the banks still closed were eligible, and a good number of open banks were only marginally eligible. The RFC assumed the task of getting as many banks as possible—closed as well as open—in the FDIC when it opened on January 1, 1934.

Although the Emergency Banking Act changed RFC activities, its rationale remained the same. No less than Ogden Mills, Arthur Ballantine, Herbert Hoover, and Francis G. Awalt, the New Dealers wanted to expand bank credit. They believed economic recovery could not be sustained until bankers abandoned their liquidity preferences and extended more credit to businessmen. Like their predecessors, the New Dealers in the RFC assumed that significant demand for working capital existed in the economy. Under Hoover, the RFC had tried to stimulate bank credit by liquefying bank assets through short-term loans. They failed. Under Franklin Roosevelt and Jesse Jones, the RFC tried to strengthen banks through loans and capital investments, whether they were closed or open, in order to qualify them for the FDIC and create the psychological security necessary for aggressive commercial lending. Once banks started lending and businesses started borrowing, the economy would revive.

But it was not that easy. By the end of October, with only two months left before the FDIC opened, there were still 2,300 banks closed and hundreds more in marginal condition. Between June and October the RFC loaned more than $300 mil-

[24] Jones, *Fifty Billion Dollars*, p. 45; Carter Golembe, "The Deposit Insurance Legislation of 1933: An Examination of Its Antecedents and Its Purposes," *Political Science Quarterly*, 37 (February 1950), 153–54. For the best discussion of New Deal banking legislation, see Helen M. Burns, *The American Banking Community and New Deal Banking Reforms: 1933–1935* (New York, 1974).

lion, mostly to closed banks undergoing liquidation or reorganization.[25] But before reconstruction was complete, bank capital had to be replenished. The RFC's preferred stock program hit a snag when bankers resisted. Dividends on the stock had to yield at least 6 percent and voting rights had to accompany the stock. The bank also had to use its net profits regularly to retire the RFC's investment. Finally, the RFC refused more than the investment of common stockholders.[26]

The RFC made some initial investments just after the holiday. Late in March, for example, they reorganized the Union Trust Company of Cleveland with a $35 million loan and a $10 million purchase of preferred stock to be matched by a $10 million subscription by common stockholders.[27] Still, most bankers were afraid of the program. Some saw it as a government attempt to take over the banking system. Others worried that RFC purchases of preferred stock would impose a difficult dividend and redemption burden on the banks. Because the RFC insisted that preferred stock dividends and amortization had first claim on bank profits, many bankers feared their earnings would fail to satisfy the government and common stockholders. Finally, many bankers thought the public would interpret RFC capital investment as a sign of weakness. In March the corporation bought nearly $13.7 million in preferred stock, but in April the total was only $7.4 million. They bought $9.1 million in May but only $4.8 million in June. The July total was over $12 million, but after that the program basically stopped, not because of the RFC but because private bankers were not participating. Only $2.8 million was purchased in August and only $3.75 million in September.[28]

[25] *Annual Report of the Comptroller of the Currency for 1933*, p. 663; RFC, *Quarterly Report for April 1 to June 30, 1933*, Table 6.

[26] RFC, *Circular No. 6* (Washington, D.C., 1933), p. 1; W. F. Sheehan to W. T. Hastings, August 16, 1933, NA, RG 234, RFC, Preferred Stock.

[27] RFC, Minutes, 14 (March 29, 1933), 2688–91; William Woodin to RFC board of directors, June 14, 1933, FDRPL, OF 643, RFC; *New York Times*, March 30, 1933.

[28] RFC, *Quarterly Report for April 1 to June 30, 1934* (Washington, D.C., 1934), Table 6.

The presence of thousands of closed banks was both an economic and a political problem. In rural areas especially, where most bank failures had occurred, millions of depositors were becoming increasingly restless about their money. Congressmen from the South and Midwest were clamoring for government assistance, and President Roosevelt took their demands seriously. Jones was not so sure. Most of the banks still closed after the holiday were in wretched shape and governed by equally wretched management, and he was loath to throw good RFC money after bad. Jones also felt that the orderly liquidation of those banks would help the economy, eliminating inefficiency and allowing larger bank chains with more capital to establish branches in their place. Roosevelt began making strong suggestions that the RFC develop some method of assisting those closed banks, but Jones resisted.[29]

Roosevelt continued to insist until finally Jones caved in. Senator Elmer Thomas, a populist and Democrat from Oklahoma, emerged as the spokesman for the victims of closed banks. In his opinion, the Democrats had made a lot of political capital out of the RFC by accusing the Hoover administration of giving millions to large banks while turning a cold shoulder to their rural cousins. Now Jones was doing the same thing. Roosevelt saw Thomas's argument for what it was—a sincere demand with the potential for political disaster. He wanted the RFC to launch a crash program to loan funds to closed banks. Eventually Jones came around to the idea as the lesser of two evils. Thomas began sponsoring legislation to have the RFC purchase outright the assets of all closed banks, distribute the money to depositors, and then liquidate the assets itself and take the losses. For Jones's balance-sheet mind, the proposal was unthinkable; state capitalism was one thing, bad business quite another. He went along with Roosevelt.[30]

[29] Niznik, "Thomas G. Corcoran," pp. 51–52; Henry Bruere, COHR, pp. 153–54; Discussion Notes, October 16, 1933, Harrison Papers; Carroll B. Merriam to Marvin McIntyre, October 31, 1934, FDRPL, OF 643, RFC.

[30] Discussion Notes, December 18, 1933, Harrison Papers; *New York Times*, April 16 and 29, May 2 and 6, and June 20, 1934; J.F.T. O'Connor Diary, February 26 and March 27, 1934, O'Connor Papers.

To direct the closed bank loan program and remove it from the control of Jesse Jones, Roosevelt established a Deposit Liquidation Board consisting of J.F.T. O'Connor, comptroller of the currency; Dean Acheson, under secretary of the treasury; Jesse Jones; Eugene Black, chairman of the Federal Reserve Board; and Carroll B. Merriam of the RFC board as chairman. The Deposit Liquidation Board hoped to expedite loans to receivers and conservators of state and national banks, complete the reorganization process, and provide an early distribution of funds to depositors. The RFC would then hold the assets as collateral until more favorable market conditions had raised their value. Frustrated depositors would finally have their money. Jones did not like having to work with "outsiders" like O'Connor, Black, and Acheson, but he had little choice. Roosevelt had to deflect the criticism of Thomas and his supporters.[31]

On October 17 the Deposit Liquidation Board appointed advisory committees of prominent bankers for each of the twelve Federal Reserve districts. State banking authorities cooperated. Local committees in each state examined closed bank assets and recommended loans. The advisory board forwarded an application for funds to the local RFC agency, and finally to the RFC in Washington. Instead of the usual 5.5 percent interest rate on RFC loans, the Deposit Liquidation Board charged only 4 percent. The board evaluated assets not at their immediate value, as RFC examiners had done in the past, but at the value the corporation felt it could get out of them during an orderly liquidation period of three to five years in a recovering stock and bond market. The board loaned money on 80 percent of the liquidation value of those assets, much higher than the 50 to 70 percent which had been the rule in 1932.[32] Although still concerned about the RFC's profit margin and liquidity, Jesse Jones and his associates had become more willing to take risks in their bank loans. Liberated by the holiday as

[31] Speech by Jesse Jones to the American Bankers' Association, September 5, 1933, Jones Papers; *New York Times*, October 16–19, 1933.

[32] J.F.T. O'Connor Diary, May 17, 1933, O'Connor Papers; Henry Bruere, COHR, pp. 153–53; *Federal Reserve Bulletin*, 19 (November 1933), 672–73.

well as by the departure of conservatives like Ogden Mills, Eugene Meyer, and Charles Dawes, they could afford to be more generous in their operations.

They were also not preoccupied, as the Hoover administration had been, with dismantling the RFC as soon as possible. If it had to be a long-term approach to the economy, so be it, as long as it did not substantially alter the structure of American institutions. Their intentions, however, were irrelevant unless bankers cooperated and the Deposit Liquidation Board did encounter resistance. Many state banking departments fought the program because it undermined a traditional source of patronage. Bank receiverships were choice gifts politicians bestowed upon their supporters. Receivers often demanded extravagant commissions and delayed liquidation as long as possible. State banking officials worried that the liquidation of closed banks would be taken over by the Deposit Liquidation Board; that the value of commissions would be reduced; and that a definite and fixed liability to the RFC would replace the indefinite, open-ended liability to depositors. They did not want the RFC to hurry up the process.[33]

Despite resistance, the Deposit Liquidation Board made progress, though not to the extent the administration had originally hoped. By January 18, 1934, the board had authorized loans to 710 closed banks totaling over $300 million, and Merriam continued the program until April 15, 1934, loaning another $120 million before he started dismantling the local and district committees. The board continued to function until early 1936 by which time it had loaned over $800 million. As far as Jesse Jones was concerned, the board was a success. Tens of thousands of depositors had received their money earlier than would have been possible before the establishment of the Deposit Liquidation Board and the reorganization of hundreds of banks had been expedited.[34]

[33] Carroll B. Merriam to R. E. Reichert, October 31, 1933, and Carroll B. Merriam to the RFC board of directors, November 11, 1933, NA, RG 234, RFC, Records of the Deposit Liquidation Board; Jesse Jones to Franklin D. Roosevelt, October 16, 1933, FDRPL, OF 643, RFC; *Federal Reserve Bulletin*, 19 (November 1933), 670–71.

[34] W. T. Kemper to Carroll B. Merriam, October 26, 1933; J. H. McCoy to

But Roosevelt and Jones both knew that liquefying bank assets was not the real objective. What the economy really needed was more commercial credit. During the 1930s several recovery theories competed for influence, but early in the New Deal the faith in a government-business partnership reigned supreme. Resting on the legacy of the War Industries Board during World War I and the associational activities of American business during the 1920s, the National Recovery Administration dreamed of rationalizing the economy by eliminating destructive competition and coordinating research, development, production, and prices. Throughout the summer of 1933, NRA chief General Hugh Johnson scurried around the country establishing industry-wide codes of fair competition and securing corporate endorsements. The administration was also trying to avert strikes in the textile, steel, automobile, and shipping industries, any one of which could retard recovery.

The NRA crusade imposed a new sense of urgency on Jesse Jones and the RFC. Once the recovery made even a hesitant beginning, the banking community would have to be prepared to sustain it through large-scale commercial lending. Without a sound credit base, the recovery would be stillborn. Throughout the summer and fall of 1933 Jones and Roosevelt had pushed that point of view to get bankers to sell preferred stock to the RFC. With new capital, banks could give "the credit necessary for the recovery program."[35] But the volume of bank

---

Carroll B. Merriam, November 8, 1933; E. B. Schwulst to Carroll B. Merriam, December 20, 1933; Carroll B. Merriam to R. G. Clay, October 17, 1933; Carroll B. Merriam to all district chairmen of the Deposit Liquidation Board, January 18, 1934, all in NA, RG 234, RFC, Records of the Deposit Liquidation Board; *Annual Report of the Comptroller of the Currency for 1933*, p. 663; Carroll B. Merriam to Stephen Early, January 4, 1936, FDRPL, OF 643, RFC.

[35] RFC, *Quarterly Report for October 1 to December 31, 1934*, Table 6; Carroll B. Merriam to R. G. Clay, October 17, 1934, NA, RG 234, RFC, Records of the Deposit Liquidation Board. An interesting sidelight to the RFC loan policy in 1933 involved the volume of funds going to large banks, particularly since New Dealers had leveled this criticism at the RFC during the Hoover administration. During the first ten months of the New Deal, the RFC loaned $665 million to open and closed banks. Of that amount, $312 million went to only twenty-two banks. Approximately 47 percent of all RFC loans in 1933 went to only twenty-two banks, a record of support to large bankers which even exceeded Hoover's generosity for them. Also see RFC, Minutes, Index to

loans declined drastically after Roosevelt took office. Between January 10 and June 30, 1933, outstanding commercial credit dropped from $26 to only $22.3 billion. Just like Hoover, Roosevelt had been unable to overcome bankers' liquidity fears. On their part, bankers maintained that Roosevelt and Jones, just like Hoover and Meyer before them, were grossly exaggerating the demand for loans among businessmen.[36]

Faced with declining bank loans, the necessity of implementing the NRA codes, a slowing pace of bank reorganizations, and establishment of the FDIC, Roosevelt had Jones launch a campaign to get bankers to accept RFC investment. Both men believed the state of the economy rested on a foundation of public confidence, which depended directly on the health of the banking system. All banks licensed after the holiday had to be healthy enough to join the FDIC and strong enough to stay open. Many still had eroded assets and impaired capital, even though they had reopened. They needed RFC capital to write off their poor assets and decrease their liabilities. Only then could they enter the FDIC.[37] Once in the FDIC, they would probably be safe from the fickle whims of nervous depositors.

The RFC began soliciting applicants for the preferred stock program. To convince small banks that issuing preferred stock was not a sign of weakness, Jones asked several of the country's largest and most prestigious financial institutions to accept the program. He also established a special division in the RFC to process the thousands of applications for preferred stock purchases he expected. On October 23 Roosevelt expressed the hope that

> all banks will take advantage of this opportunity . . . to put themselves in an easy cash position to help in the work of

---

the Minutes, 2 (1933). All RFC loans during 1933 are listed alphabetically in the Index.

[36] Franklin D. Roosevelt to Jesse Jones, August 31, 1933, Jones Papers; P. B. Dunn to J.F.T. O'Connor, March 10, 1934, O'Connor Papers; *Federal Reserve Bulletin* 21 (December 1935), 803; 19 (October 1933), 597.

[37] Notes of the Meeting of the Board of Directors of the Federal Reserve Bank of New York, April 24, 1933, Discussion Notes, Harrison Papers.

recovery. To accept the government's offer to purchase preferred stock does not mean that a bank is weak, but that it is eager to cooperate in the recovery effort to the fullest extent and thus undertake to put additional capital to work, capital working for recovery.[38]

Closed banks undergoing reorganization could issue preferred stock for the capital necessary to reopen and join the FDIC, while strong banks could issue preferred stock, join the FDIC, and expand their commercial loans. Jones was not at all excited about committing RFC funds to rebuilding the assets of closed banks. Most of them were weak and burdened with poor management, and he feared the investment would be a losing proposition. But the pressure to do something was too strong. On October 23, 1933, Jones established the Non-Member Preferred Stock Board as a separate division of the RFC. It would direct the crash program.[39]

Harvey Couch chaired the Non-Member Preferred Stock Board, and he was joined by Eugene Black, Dean Acheson, Director of the Budget Lewis Douglas, J.F.T. O'Connor, FDIC chairman Walter J. Cummings, and Henry Bruere, a New York banker and economic adviser to Roosevelt. The board first met on November 1 and by November 11 had a nationwide organization of local advisory committees ready to evaluate applications. In mid-November Couch estimated that more than 2,500 nonmember banks would need RFC investment capital before they could qualify for FDIC membership.[40]

To make the program seem more attractive, the RFC reduced the dividend rate on preferred stock from 6 to 4 percent, deemphasized the liquidity and marketability of bank assets, and evaluated high-grade securities at their potential, not market,

[38] *New York Times*, August 2 and 3, and October 24, 1933.

[39] *New York Times*, October 24, 1933; Walter Wyatt, COHR, pp. 49–52, 93–95.

[40] *Annual Report of the Comptroller of the Currency for 1933*, p. 7; speech by Jesse Jones over NBC Radio, November 1, 1933, Jones Papers; *Federal Reserve Bulletin*, 19 (November 1933), 673; Harvey Couch to Franklin D. Roosevelt, November 11, 1933 and Carroll B. Merriam to Henry Bruere, November 30, 1933, FDRPL, OF 643, RFC.

value. The RFC gave book or cost value to the highest grade bonds, market value for bonds in default, face value for slow but sound assets, and a reasonable valuation for doubtful assets like real estate. It was a marked change from the cautiousness and banker-oriented fears which had characterized the RFC during 1932 and early 1933.[41]

In mid-October the RFC received a boost when the New York Clearing House Association endorsed the preferred stock plan. Although the bankers were still not very enthusiastic about the program, they knew they would have to have a permit to enter the FDIC on January 1, and that FDIC membership was essential for survival. The endorsement was a victory for Jones. If the soundest banks participated, small banks would surely feel that RFC investment was not a sign of weakness. During November the RFC purchased $18 million in preferred stock, the highest monthly total since the beginning of the program. More important, however, were the announcements from the First National Bank of Chicago and the Continental Illinois Bank and Trust Company that they would sell the RFC some stock.[42] The real breakthrough came in December when the National City Bank of New York sold $50 million in preferred stock to the RFC. Jones enthusiastically wrote the president that "this new capital should multiply itself many times in credit for agriculture, business and industry."[43]

Applications then began pouring in from all over the country. On December 14 Couch told Jones and Roosevelt that all resistance to the work of the Non-Member Preferred Stock Board had evaporated.[44] During December the RFC bought

[41] Jesse Jones to all member banks of the Federal Reserve system, October 11, 1933, and Franklin D. Roosevelt to Jesse Jones, September 26, 1933, NA, RG 234, RFC, Preferred Stock; Jones, *Fifty Billion Dollars*, p. 36; Alva B. Adams to J.F.T. O'Connor, November 22, 1934, O'Connor Papers.

[42] Percy H. Johnston to Jesse Jones, October 18, 1933, NA, RG 234, RFC, Preferred Stock; RFC, *Quarterly Report for April 1 to June 30, 1934*, Table 6; *New York Times*, September 10, 1933.

[43] Jesse Jones to Franklin D. Roosevelt, December 4, 1933, FDRPL, OF 643, RFC.

[44] Harvey Couch to Franklin D. Roosevelt, December 14, 1933, FDRPL, OF 643, RFC.

more than $310 million in the preferred stock or capital notes of hundreds of banks, and approved 3,208 applications for capital funds.[45] But it was impossible to process all the money before January 1, 1934. Jones estimated more than 2,000 open banks had liabilities exceeding the market value of their assets. They were not eligible for the FDIC, and Jones was concerned that depositors would withdraw their money when they learned the banks would not be protected by government insurance. On December 28 Jones explained the problem to Henry Morgenthau, acting secretary of the treasury. They worked out a plan allowing those banks to join the FDIC on January 1, 1934, with the RFC agreeing, through loans and capital investment, to make them solvent in six months. The plan worked. On January 1 Walter Cummings announced that the FDIC had accepted 13,423 banks as members and had rejected only 141.[46]

The Non-Member Preferred Stock Board continued its work throughout 1934, as did the Deposit Liquidation Board, and Jones redeemed his promise to Morgenthau. By the end of April, the RFC had purchased more than $1.1 billion in the preferred stock and capital notes of 6,500 banks. By September 1934 the RFC owned stock in half the nation's banks. Another 900 banks never licensed after the holiday completed liquidation. By the end of 1934 there were only 10 national banks still unlicensed, 6 state member banks, and 213 nonmember banks. Another 1,000 banks had joined the FDIC by the end of 1934, bringing the total to 14,400. Bond and securities values had made a substantial recovery, increasing 25 percent from their holiday lows. Finally, bank deposits in December 1934

[45] RFC, *Quarterly Report for April 1 to June 30, 1934* (Washington, D.C., 1934), Table 6; Harvey Couch to Franklin D. Roosevelt, January 2, 1934, FDRPL, OF 643, RFC.

[46] *Annual Report of the Comptroller of the Currency for 1933*, p. 5; Jones, *Fifty Billion Dollars*, pp. 29–30; Stanley Reed, COHR, pp. 90–94. To allow the RFC to keep up with the increased demand for preferred stock money, Congress appropriated an additional $850 million in January 1934 as part of the legislation to continue RFC lending authority for another year. See Franklin D. Roosevelt to Jesse Jones, January 21, 1934, FDRPL, OF 643, RFC.

stood at over $44 billion, an increase of $7 billion over the holiday totals.[47] Not until June 1935 did the RFC end the preferred stock program, when the total reached $1.3 billion in 6,800 banks. The RFC by that time owned more than one-third of all outstanding capital in the entire banking system.[48] But the real work had been accomplished in 1933 and early 1934. In 1934 only 61 licensed commercial banks failed, and only 32 failed in 1935. Stability had returned to the money markets.[49]

But stability in the money markets did not translate automatically into economic recovery. Although New Dealers had used the RFC to end the cycle of financial panic and institutional collapse, they failed, as Hoover had done, in their primary objective: raising the volume of bank credit and commercial loans. The process of liquefying frozen assets and repairing capital structures had not led to more commercial credit. By the end of 1935 the volume of bank loans had fallen to only $20.3 billion, compared to $38.1 billion in early 1931. Instead of commercial loans, banks were turning to government securities. In 1929 only 21 percent of bank funds were invested in government securities, but that had risen to 58 percent in 1934.[50] Just after the bank holiday in March 1933, Jesse Jones had envisioned the RFC buying preferred stock only in troubled banks, but the continuing erosion in commercial credit had convinced him to make the purchases in any bank

[47] *Federal Reserve Bulletin*, 21 (December 1935), 803, 878; 19 (December 1933), 751; 20 (November 1934), 733 and 763; "Review of Economic Conditions," April 5, 1933, NA, RG 234, RFC, Statistical Division.

[48] See the unpublished reports by the RFC on the progress of the preferred stock program, August 13 and 29, 1934; March 28, 1935 and June 7, 1935, NA, RG 234, RFC, Preferred Stock; RFC, *Quarterly Report for October 1 to December 31, 1938* (Washington, D.C., 1939), Table 6; American Bankers' Association, *Banking After the Crisis* (New York, 1934), p. 17.

[49] Notes of the Meeting of the Board of Directors of the Federal Reserve Bank of New York, February 4, 1934, Discussion Notes, Harrison Papers; Fischer, *The American Banking Structure*, p. 225; Theodore Andersen, *A Century of Banking in Wisconsin* (Madison, Wis., 1954), p. 56.

[50] *Federal Reserve Bulletin*, 21 (December 1935), 803; "Review of Economic Conditions," October 7, 1933 and January 17, 1934, NA, RG 234, RFC, Statistical Division; American Bankers' Association, *Changes in Bank Earning Assets*, pp. 13–14.

or trust company willing to participate. Since an increase in commercial credit was, in the administration's mind, the prerequisite for the success of the NRA, Jesse Jones in 1934 began leading a campaign for a major expansion in RFC authority. The money markets in 1933 had all been in a far more perilous condition than most people had once assumed; the need for government intervention was more compelling; and the connection between credit, interest rates, and industrial production was more confusing. Doubts about the economic future, the extent of RFC involvement in the private sector of the economy, and a continuing commitment to a revival of commercial credit all transformed the RFC into a major recovery agency during the First New Deal.

CHAPTER V

The New Deal Credit Revolution, 1933–1934

SEVERAL recovery theories competed for influence during the Great Depression. On the far right, conservatives clamored for economies in government and balanced budgets as the only way of restoring business confidence and reviving production and employment. At the other end of the spectrum, socialists like Norman Thomas wanted to create a welfare state and government ownership of major industries. And in between there was a host of inflationists, monetarists, laissez-faire ideologues, technocrats, pump primers, and monopolists. Too pragmatic and too dependent on a variety of competing interest groups to follow any ideological course, Franklin D. Roosevelt had the New Deal chart a conservative middle ground using state capitalism to rebuild the economy.

In 1933 and 1934 the advocates of a business-government commonwealth had the upper hand. The idea of cooperative planning between the federal government and the private sector rested on three major programs. One of them was the National Recovery Administration attempt to stop deflation and declining profits by eliminating destructive competition, inefficiency, and waste. Suspension of antitrust laws permitted major companies in a particular industry to work with the government in establishing production quotas, fair prices, marketing codes, and fair labor practices. Once approved by the president, the codes had the force of law, and when no code appeared for an industry the president could impose one himself. Planning advocates believed the codes would restore prosperity. The success of the War Industries Board during World War I, as well as the technocratic managerialism and private associationalism of the 1920s, had convinced a number of prominent Americans that the National Recovery Administration would work. Once deflation and declining profits had been stopped, business confidence would revive, and so would employment and production.[1]

The second part of the early New Deal recovery effort addressed the traditional problems of overproduction and depressed farm prices by establishing the Agricultural Adjustment Administration. The brainchild of such agricultural economists as John Black of the University of Minnesota, Milburn Wilson of Montana State University, and Rexford G. Tugwell of Columbia University, the AAA became law on May 12, 1933. It designated cotton, wheat, tobacco, hogs, rice, and milk as basic commodities, and called on the secretary of agriculture to negotiate marketing agreements with individual farmers to reduce production. By reducing supplies the administration hoped to raise commodity prices toward parity levels. The Agricultural Adjustment Administration became the backbone of American agricultural policy for the next two generations. Payments would be financed by taxes levied on processors and distributors, and the RFC made short-term loans to food processors hurt by the law.[2]

But the success of the NRA and AAA depended upon restoring liquidity to the money markets. Unless commercial banks were willing to make working capital loans to legitimate businesses, the NRA's hopes of reviving the economy would be stillborn. Unless mortgage money became available to finance commercial and residential construction, the economy would be unable to lift itself out of the current morass. And unless rural mortgage and marketing institutions were free of their mountains of frozen assets, the efforts of the AAA would fail because nearly half the country's farmers would lose their land in mortgage foreclosures and tax auctions. Eventually, the NRA

---

[1] See Robert Himmelberg, *The Origins of the National Recovery Administration: Business, Government, and the Trade Association Issue, 1921–1933* (New York, 1976). Also see Ellis W. Hawley, *The New Deal and the Problem of Monopoly* (New York, 1966).

[2] For the origins of the Agricultural Adjustment Administration, see Van L. Perkins, *Crisis in Agriculture: The Agricultural Adjustment Administration and the New Deal, 1933* (Berkeley, 1969).

and the AAA became embroiled in arguments over constitutionality and faced the concerted opposition of small farmers and
businessmen, organized labor, and Brandeisian liberals. The
NRA proved to be a miserable failure, while the AAA was, at
best, a mixed blessing. But the effort to provide a financial
transfusion for the money markets and end the cycle of deflation and bankruptcy was by far the most successful of the experiments in state capitalism and the most enduring legacy of
the early New Deal.

The central agency in the New Deal crusade to liquefy the
money markets was the Reconstruction Finance Corporation.
The success of the War Finance Corporation during World
War I had built the public faith in federal credit operations,
and during the 1920s the government had moved into the agricultural credit markets when the farm depression all but destroyed thousands of rural banks. Federal Land banks and
Federal Intermediate Credit banks refinanced farm debt and
provided short-term working capital loans to some farmers.
The Emergency Relief and Construction Act of 1932 created
regional agricultural credit corporations to help farmers get
marketing loans, and the RFC gave them $36 million in capital.
The Home Land Bank Act of 1932 provided federal funds to
discount the mortgages of troubled building and loan associations, and the RFC supplied $125 million in working capital.
Hoover and his RFC associates had naively assumed that government loans to banks, savings banks, building and loan associations, insurance companies, and regional agricultural
credit corporations would relieve their liquidity fears and reopen private credit channels. The banking crisis of 1933 had
demonstrated clearly that short-term government loans were
not enough, and that a major, long-term bolstering of the
money markets was necessary.[3]

Throughout 1932 and early 1933, Roosevelt's "Brain
Trust" had worried about the credit crisis. Unless some liquidity was restored to the money markets, all recovery efforts

[3] Olson, *Herbert Hoover and the Reconstruction Finance Corporation*, pp.
11–12, 92.

would be stillborn. Adolf A. Berle, Jr., one of the original members of the brain trust, along with Raymond Moley and Rexford G. Tugwell, felt strongest about the credit crisis. Son of a Congregational minister, Berle graduated from Harvard Law School at the age of twenty-one and became a corporation lawyer and later a law professor at Columbia University. In 1932, with Gardiner Means, he wrote *The Modern Corporation and Private Property*, one of the most important books of the interwar period. Berle and Means argued that the competitive economy of the nineteenth century had given way to a new economic order, where 200 of the largest corporations controlled most economic activity and where corporate power rested in the hands of a managerial elite rather than stockholders or the public.[4]

In a 1932 memorandum to Governor Franklin D. Roosevelt of New York, Berle created the analogy of a huge amount of accumulated goods and the capacity to make goods stuck on one side of a plate glass window, and an equally enormous volume of poverty and suffering on the other side, with no means of breaking the window because of the paralysis of the money markets. Hoover was confining the Reconstruction Finance Corporation to bank rescue via short-term loans, which did little to get money into the hands of people. It all meant "that if you were going to have a money economy at all it would have to be the federal credit that was involved."[5] Berle and Tugwell both agreed that some credit situations, like the utilities empires and jerry-built investment holding companies, were not worth saving because of their speculative natures, but the whole range of bank assets, high grade corporate and railroad bonds, home mortgages, and farm mortgages had to be scaled down or refinanced. Federal bankruptcy and receivership laws needed to be changed. Later in his life Berle recalled that

> the greatest single need [in 1933], it seemed to me, was to undergird the credit of the perfectly legitimate operations

---

[4] Adolf A. Berle, Jr., and Gardiner Means, *The Modern Corporation and Private Property* (New York, 1933), pp. 18–46.

[5] Adolf Berle, COHR, pp. 176–77. Also see pp. 170–71.

which were the basis of the . . . economy, when practically every one of them was facing default, sometimes because they couldn't pay their charges but more often because their debts were falling due and there was no place they could refinance them. And that was as true of the little farmer in Iowa as it was of the big railroad systems. So essentially the idea was to undergird the credit and simultaneously to get some spending power into the population. . . .[6]

The original idea of the RFC as a temporary agency giving short-term liquidity to banks and trust companies would have to be replaced by a state capitalism involving some sort of federal support of the credit structure.

In 1933 and 1934, the New Deal approached the credit crisis from three directions. In addition to the preferred stock program and massive loans for banks, the RFC became deeply involved in the rest of the money market as well. By 1935 the RFC had loaned more than $1.4 billion to 10,576 banks and trust companies; $1.2 billion in loans for distribution to the depositors of closed banks and had prepared the way for the successful implementation of the FDIC; $1.26 billion in bank preferred stock and capital notes; $143 million to nearly 1,100 building and loan associations; $103 million to 133 insurance companies; $21 million to joint stock land banks; $14 million to livestock credit corporations; and $6 million to agricultural credit corporations. Jones reduced interest rates from the 5 to 7 percent levels of the Hoover administration to 3 to 4 percent, hoping that with increased liquidity financial institutions would start funneling credit funds to businesses and consumers.[7]

The New Deal credit revolution also addressed bankruptcy laws. Mortgage debt was frozen because there was no secondary market for mortgages. Defaults by large corporations and

---

[6] Ibid., pp. 176–77. Elliott A. Rosen, *Hoover, Roosevelt, and the Brains Trust: From Depression to New Deal* (New York, 1977), pp. 325–26; Raymond Moley, *The First New Deal* (New York, 1966), p. 231.

[7] RFC, *Summary of the Activities of the Reconstruction Finance Corporation and its Condition as of December 31, 1935*, p. 5.

small borrowers were unprecedented. The corporate bond market was a disaster; Berle feared that as much as $1 billion in corporate bonds might be defaulted on in 1934. Complicated bankruptcy laws allowed even a tiny minority of stockholders to delay reorganization plans for years, leaving assets uselessly tied up in the courts. The Deposit Liquidation Board's program to disburse quickly the deposits in failed banks was one method of overcoming the delays, but other means of breaking the logjam had to be developed. Title II of the Emergency Banking Act had ended the complicated delays in reorganizing closed national banks, and corporations needed similar legislation.

Late in 1933 a drive to facilitate corporate reorganization gained support among people like Adolf Berle, Jesse Jones, Henry Morgenthau, Jr., and Secretary of Commerce Daniel Roper. Existing bankruptcy regulations allowed a minority of stockholders or creditors to block any attempts at refinancing or scaling down debts. In the spring of 1934, Senator Frederick Van Nuys of Indiana and Representative Tom D. McKeown of Oklahoma sponsored a corporate reorganization measure to prevent unnecessary delays. Roosevelt signed it on June 7, 1933. The measure permitted an insolvent corporation to apply for reorganization if 25 percent of the creditors in each class of claims and 10 percent of the whole approved. All creditors were bound to a reorganization plan sanctioned by a federal court and accepted by 67 percent of the holders of the total amount of claims.[8] With reorganization simpler, the chance of reviving the value of corporate bonds was much better, and in a recovering bond market, the capital structures of banks, savings banks, building and loan associations, insurance companies, and foundations would be much stronger.

The condition of the municipal bond market was also weak. In December 1933 Adolf Berle wrote to Jesse Jones warning him that more than $500 million in municipal securities were in danger of default. Hundreds of towns and cities were hard-pressed to meet current expenses as well as fixed costs. Indus-

[8] *New York Times*, June 8, 1934.

try groups like the Investment Bankers' Association as well as the urban political machines demanded federal intervention. An administration measure reached both houses of Congress in May 1934. Senator Carter Glass of Virginia opposed the bill because he was convinced it would destroy the municipal bond market, but Senator Patrick McCarran of Nevada offered a compromise providing cities the opportunity of scaling down their debts with federal court approval. With the consent of 51 percent of the holders of its outstanding obligations, a city could take a refinancing plan to the courts. If the court found it equitable and 75 percent of its debtors agreed, the plan would go into effect. Cities had two years to apply for debt restructuring. President Roosevelt signed the measure on May 24, 1934. Although the Municipal Bankruptcy Act was not widely used in refinancing municipal indebtedness, it enjoyed the unique support of Wall Street and the mayors of the largest American cities, and helped rebuild public confidence in the bond market.[9]

Another group of public bonds was frozen solid in the early 1930s. Ever since the outbreak of World War I, farmers and bankers in rural areas had organized drainage, irrigation, and levee districts to finance water projects. Blessed with public charters, the districts issued bonds to financial institutions and used the proceeds to build water systems. With revenues from user fees, the districts paid dividends on the bonds. But during the 1920s and early 1930s, with commodity prices down and farmers unable to pay their bills, the drainage, levee, and irrigation districts began defaulting on their bonds. Maintaining the integrity of those bonds as financial assets required government action, and in the spring of 1933 Congress authorized the RFC to make loans to those agricultural districts.[10]

The last change in federal bankruptcy laws during the early New Deal was the Frazier-Lemke Farm Bankruptcy Act of

---

[9] *New York Times*, May 24, 1934; Berle and Jacobs, *Navigating the Rapids*, pp. 91–93.

[10] Frederic Taber Diary, November 11, 1935, Taber Papers; C. H. McCotter to Carroll Bozarth, May 17, 1935, FDRPL, OF 643, RFC; RFC, *Press Release No. 1356* (Washington, D.C., 1937).

1934. William Lemke, Republican congressman from North Dakota, was militant on agricultural issues and determined to bring farmers financial relief from burdensome mortgages. At the same time, thousands of rural banks were stuck or about to be stuck with depreciated farms as collateral for defaulted loans. The Frazier-Lemke Act permitted federal courts to scale down a farmer's debts until they compared favorably with the appraised value of his property. The farmer could continue to work the same land with the same equipment and chattels. If he succeeded in retiring his debts at the scaled-down figure, the property would be his and all encumbrances removed. In its final form, the Frazier-Lemke Act allowed farmers to repurchase their property at an interest rate of 1 percent over a six-year period. If creditors opposed such a settlement, the farmer could retain possession of the land for five years without foreclosure. Although the Supreme Court held the law unconstitutional in 1935, on the grounds it deprived creditors of property without due process, the Frazier-Lemke Act nevertheless brought some economic stability to farm states and, in the long run, helped end the cycle of default, repossession, and land sales which were eroding the capital of small, rural banks.[11]

The third part of the New Deal credit revolution involved direct government loans so people could make back payments and keep hold of their property. Farmers were in real trouble. Huge mortgage debts accumulated during the boom years of World War I had become unbearable burdens in the bust years of the 1920s and 1930s. Groups like the National Farm Holiday Association, the Grange, and the National Farmers' Union protested the combination of low commodity prices and high interest payments. Roosevelt sent a message to Congress on April 3, 1933, calling for legislation to help farmers refinance their debts, and in response Congress passed the Emergency Farm Mortgage Act as an amendment to the Agricultural Adjustment Act.

The bill authorized Federal Land banks to issue up to $2 bil-

---

[11] David H. Bennett, *Demagogues in the Depression: American Radicals and the Union Party, 1932–1936* (New Brunswick, 1969), pp. 96–98.

lion in tax exempt bonds at 4 percent for new loans or refinancing existing mortgages. It also permitted the direct exchange of bonds for existing mortgages. A loan ceiling of $50,000 per farm or $25,000 per individual was established. Between 1933 and 1935 the RFC supported the Emergency Farm Mortgage Act by giving $200 million to the farm loan commissioner to assist farmers in redeeming farm property lost through foreclosure after July 1, 1931, refinancing minor debts, and working capital loans. The maximum loan could not exceed $5,000 at 5 percent. Farmers could repay the money in ten annual installments, with no principal payments due for five years. Under the Emergency Farm Mortgage Act, the RFC also extended nearly $400 million to the Federal Land banks to assist its refinancing program.[12]

To consolidate all the federal farm credit programs, President Roosevelt issued an executive order on March 27, 1933, creating the Farm Credit Administration. The FCA received its statutory authority on May 27, 1933, when Congress passed the Farm Credit Act. Written by Texas congressman Marvin Jones and Cornell economist William Myers, the Farm Credit Act established local credit institutions to ease working capital and marketing problems. A Central Bank for Cooperatives and twelve regional banks for cooperatives replaced the Federal Farm Board and made loans to national farm cooperatives. Each loan had to exceed $500,000. It also established a Production Credit Corporation with $7.5 million in each Federal Land Bank district. The corporations promoted formation of Production Credit Associations of ten or more farmers which could borrow from the Federal Intermediate Credit banks. Roosevelt named Henry Morgenthau as governor of the Farm Credit Administration. In eighteen months the FCA refinanced more than 20 percent of all farm mortgages in the United States, saving millions of farmers from foreclosures and thousands of rural banks from bankruptcy. During the 1920s a large number of joint stock land banks and livestock credit

[12] *Congressional Digest*, 12 (May 1933), 156–57; RFC, *Summary of Activities of the Reconstruction Finance Corporation*, p. 5.

corporations had enjoyed the power to issue tax-exempt bonds to refinance farm and ranch mortgages. The RFC had a fund of $100 million to liquefy their assets. The Farm Mortgage Refinancing Act in January 1934 established a Federal Farm Mortgage Corporation to issue up to $2 billion in bonds to refinance farm debts. During 1933 and 1934, the RFC supplied the Farm Credit Administration with a total of $1.16 billion to finance the Federal Land banks, Federal Intermediate Credit banks, Federal Farm Mortgage Corporation, regional agricultural credit corporations, and the Production Credit Corporations.[13] The PCC loaned money to the Product Credit Associations (PCAs), which then reloaned it to farmers.

Although the real problem was overproduction, millions of farmers also believed that low prices were an outgrowth of peculiar marketing conditions. Because crops came on the market soon after harvest, prices were artificially low on a seasonal basis. For more than a half century farm groups had demanded some scheme for the orderly marketing of commodities. On October 16, 1933, President Roosevelt issued Executive Order 6340 creating the Commodity Credit Corporation. The origins of the Commodity Credit Corporation reach back to the subtreasury plans of the populists in the 1890s, and more recently to the agricultural marketing legislation of the 1920s, the stabilization corporations of the Hoover administration, and RFC farm loans in 1932. The Commodity Credit Corporation allowed farmers to hold their crops off the market until seasonal gluts had disappeared. It also hoped to stimulate farm loans by private banks through loan guarantees. To maintain normal credit channels, the Commodity Credit Corporation promised private bankers it would purchase on demand all of the marketing loans they had extended. When banks refused to

---

[13] W. Gifford Hoag, *The Farm Credit System. A History of Financial Self-Help* (New York, 1976); W. N. Stokes, Jr., *Credit to Farmers. The Story of the Federal Intermediate Credit Banks and Production Credit Associations* (New York, 1973); RFC, *Summary of Activities of the Reconstruction Finance Corporation*, p. 5; Henry Morgenthau, Jr., *Farm Loans and Mortgage Refinancing Through the Federal Land Bank System* (Washington, D.C., 1933), pp. 3–4.

make the loans, the Commodity Credit Corporation would loan directly.[14]

The New Deal's farm credit programs had political as well as economic ramifications. The protest movements in the Midwest had been gaining momentum throughout 1932 and 1933, and during the famous "Hundred Days" John Simpson of the National Farmers' Union and Milo Reno of the National Farm Holiday Association postponed their demonstrations to see if the New Deal was really serious about farm relief. Refinancing farm debt and assisting in marketing commodities were responses to political unrest, but the real economic rationale behind the Farm Credit Administration was to strengthen the rural banking structure and prepare it to resume normal credit functions.

The New Deal was also committed to reviving the real estate markets and construction industry. After the boom years of the 1920s, the real estate bubble had burst, leaving building and loan associations, mutual savings banks, and insurance companies with billions of dollars of frozen assets. RFC loans to insurance companies and building and loan associations had helped, as had the $500 million of the Federal Home Loan bank system, but real estate markets were badly shaken and the construction industry all but moribund. The new Home Loan banks only discounted the paper of home mortgage institutions, not making direct loans to individuals or businesses. Although short-term loans had provided a small secondary market for mortgages, they had little effect on depressed mortgage markets and the construction industry. Most of the early New Dealers believed economic recovery would not appear until residential and commercial construction had revived, and they knew the federal government would have to do more than just provide a limited secondary market for mortgages.[15]

The first order of business was refinancing urban mortgages. By early 1933, more than 40 percent of the country's $20 bil-

[14] Jones, *Fifty Billion Dollars*, pp. 88–104; Jesse Jones to Franklin D. Roosevelt, October 16, 1933, FDRPL, OF 643, RFC.

[15] Thomas B. Marvell, *The Federal Home Loan Bank Board* (New York, 1969), pp. 20–21.

lion in home mortgages were in default, and most mortgage lending institutions had serious troubles. Stuck with frozen, unmarketable assets, they could not meet depositors' demands nor respond to loan requests. Loan defaults were undermining housing values and the asset portfolios of thousands of lending institutions. About 10 percent of the country's building and loan associations failed between 1929 and 1932, and more were destined to go under unless the federal government intervened. Short-term RFC loans to building and loan associations and mutual savings banks in 1932 had postponed the crisis, but a financial disaster was nevertheless looming on the horizon when Roosevelt took office in March 1933.[16]

As soon as Congress went into special session in March, Senator Joseph Robinson of Arkansas sponsored legislation to deal with the home mortgage problem, and Roosevelt signed the law creating a Home Owners' Loan Corporation on June 13, 1933. Capitalized with $200 million from the RFC, the HOLC could issue up $2 billion in bonds. That was increased to $3 billion in June 1934 and $4.75 billion in May 1935. The Home Owners' Loan Act of April 1934 guaranteed the principal and interest of HOLC bonds. Under the program, HOLC bonds would be traded for mortgages (up to a maximum of $14,000) and changed into a single first mortgage. The HOLC could issue cash advances for payment of taxes and repairs up to 50 percent of the value of the property. It could also redeem properties lost by foreclosure after January 1, 1930. Repayments were spread over fifteen years at 5 percent interest. John H. Fahey, a Boston journalist and progressive, became head of the Home Owners' Loan Corporation.[17] Like the Farm Credit Administration, the Home Owners' Loan Corporation was a political response to the plight and protest of desperate homeowners as well as an attempt to relieve building and loan as-

[16] Ibid., pp. 18–20; Walter J. Woerheide, *The Savings and Loan Industry. Current Problems and Possible Solutions* (Westport, Conn., 1984), pp. 3–24; Frederick E. Balderston, *Thrifts in Crisis. Structural Transformation of the Savings and Loan Industry* (Cambridge, Mass., 1985), pp. 1–2.

[17] *Congressional Digest*, 15 (April 1936), 107–8; *New York Times*, November 20, 1950.

sociations of the frozen assets they had accumulated since 1929.

To stimulate the construction industry, Congress passed the National Housing Act in June 1934 establishing the Federal Housing Administration. The President's Emergency Commission on Housing spent much of 1933 and early 1934 studying the problem, and Utah banker Marriner Eccles, soon to become governor of the Federal Reserve Board, wrote the legislation. Like the HOLC, the FHA received $200 million in operating capital from the RFC and had authority to insure loans made by private institutions to middle-income families who wanted to repair their homes or build new ones. The FHA could establish national mortgage associations and sell notes to buy up mortgages, and the RFC could purchase those obligations. The National Housing Act also established a Federal Savings and Loan Insurance Corporation to insure the deposits of building and loan associations and prevent runs on institutions by panic-stricken depositors.[18]

But even as the administration was busy preparing the legislation to create the new federal credit institutions, they realized that even more extensive government intervention into the money markets was necessary. By May 1933 several major insurance companies were verging on failure. The railroad industry, upon which thousands of money market institutions depended because of heavy investment in railroad bonds, was sicker than ever, with freight volume and revenue falling, and fixed debts and interest payments mounting. The erosion of commercial credit, part of a long-term trend reaching well back into the 1920s, fueled fears about a continuing depression. If legitimate businesses could not get working capital through normal credit channels, the entire program of the National Recovery Administration would fail. Although members of the Hoover administration had believed the depression was a temporary aberration feeding on public ignorance and fear, New Dealers began to realize in 1933 and 1934 that it was far more serious. The money markets seemed permanently

[18] *Monthly Labor Review*, 39 (August 1934), 369–70.

frozen in a liquidity crisis which only the federal government could break.

Railroads were the most intractable problem and had an early priority in New Deal recovery efforts. The Great Depression was an unmitigated disaster. Between 1929 and 1932, freight and revenues declined from 1,419,000 tons and $4.9 billion to 679,000,000 tons and only $2.5 billion. Passenger revenues were down from $876 million in 1929 to $306 million in 1933. Railroad employment had fallen more than 41 percent since 1929, and total employee compensation was down by more than 50 percent. The railroads had cut operating expenses in half and reduced dividends, but their income fell from a net of $977 million in 1929 to a loss of $122 million in 1932, more than offsetting any savings. The burden of fixed costs added to the misery. Heavily indebted with long-term bonds used to finance construction and expansion, the railroads were stuck with huge interest payments each year. Between 1929 and 1932, those interest payments actually increased, from $581 million in 1929 to $591 million in 1932.[19]

The Hoover administration had approached the railroad problem as a temporary aberration unique to the depression. With heavy debt structures and declining revenues, many railroads were defaulting on interest payments and undermining the railroad bond market, where hundreds of banks, insurance companies, and savings banks had invested billions of dollars. Hoover, Mills, Meyer, and Dawes had assumed that short-term RFC loans would enable troubled railroads to meet their debt service payments until the recovery arrived. In the meantime, the asset portfolios of money market institutions holding railroad bonds would hold their value. So in 1932 and early 1933 the RFC made more than $350 million in loans to sixty-one railroads. Most of the money went to fifteen companies,

---

[19] U.S. Bureau of the Census, *Historical Statistics of the United States, Colonial Times to 1957* (Washington, D.C., 1960), pp. 430–31, 434–35; U.S. Department of Commerce, *Transportation Statistics in the United States. Part I. Railroads, Their Lessors, and Propriety Companies, 1956* (Washington, D.C., 1957), Table 155.

and the bulk of it went to meet maturing funded debt, interest payments, and delinquent loans.[20]

Politically and economically they could not have been more off base in dealing with the problem. The RFC Railroad Division had ignited a storm of protest early in 1932 by making a $12.8 million loan to the Missouri-Pacific Railroad. One day before the RFC opened for business in 1932, the J. P. Morgan and Company had made the Missouri-Pacific Railroad a $1.5 million loan, payable as soon as the railroad had received an RFC loan. The larger loan was extended a few months later. Half of the loan was destined for immediate transfer to the J. P. Morgan and Company and Kuhn, Loeb and Company, two of Wall Street's most powerful investment firms. Jesse Jones had bitterly opposed the loan, but the views of Meyer and Dawes prevailed. In the hands of progressive Republicans and liberal Democrats during 1932, the loan, as well as a number of other loans, became political nightmares, proof that the Hoover administration was more interested in bailing out the wealthy than the poor. Republican Senator William Borah of Idaho insisted

> no good reason has been shown for approving a government loan to enable the applicant to make a 50 percent payment on the bank loans maturing April 1. I would have no difficulty in joining in such approval if there were any evidence that the loan is needed in the public interest. But no one has made or attempted to make such a showing.[21]

People like William Borah, Robert M. La Follette, Jr., of Wisconsin, Bronson Cutting of New Mexico, and George Norris of Nebraska saw the RFC as a tool of Wall Street, allowing the firms to get their money and avoid nasty reorganizations. During 1932 the RFC loaned the Missouri Pacific a total of more than $23 million, and to top it off the railroad declared bankruptcy on March 31, 1933.[22]

[20] *Commercial & Financial Chronicle*, January 28, 1933; Jones, *Fifty Billion Dollars*, pp. 120–22.

[21] *Congressional Record*, 75 (March 28, 1932), 6906–7.

[22] Jones, *Fifty Billion Dollars*, pp. 122–27; *Congressional Record*, 75 (March 29, 1932), 6989; (March 30, 1932), 7102–5.

But assisting the banking houses was exactly what the Hoover administration intended to do. The RFC railroad loan program was not an end in itself; it existed to stabilize railroad bonds and underwrite commercial bank and money market assets. If the Missouri-Pacific Railroad defaulted, the value of its bonds would fall and hurt every bank holding them. Some RFC money would naturally flow to the institutions which had extended capital and credit to the major railroads. It was unavoidable.[23] After levying such intense criticism of the "trickle-down" theory during the presidential campaign of 1932, New Dealers had no intention of letting their RFC fall into a similar trap. Jones was adamant. The last thing he wanted was RFC money bailing out conservative Wall Street bankers who had helped get the railroads and the economy in its current fix.

Hoover's railroad program, however, was not just a political nightmare; it was also economically bankrupt. In assuming the problem was temporary he ignored the long-term structural problems in American transportation. Railroads were not just suffering from depression-induced revenue declines. Passenger revenues had started dropping after World War I, from $1.3 billion in 1920 to $876 million in 1929. Railroad cars in service peaked in 1924 and then began a long decline. Truck registrations increased from 100,000 in 1914 to 1.1 million in 1920, 3.5 million in 1929, and 5.2 million in 1941. Automobile registrations went from 1.2 million in 1913 to 23.1 million in 1929. Air passenger service was up from 100,000 in 1929 to 3.5 million in 1941.[24] The railroad crisis transcended the Great Depression; the railroads were in a long-term decline from which they would never recover. Most RFC loans to railroads in 1932 had six-month maturities, guaranteeing the companies would be back at the RFC doorstep again for more money.

The major railroad creditors, of course, knew that the industry was in trouble. Despite more than $250 million in RFC

[23] *Wall Street Journal*, April 1–2, 1932; *Washington Post*, April 1, 1932; "Railroad Loans," unpublished manuscript, HHPL, PP, SF, RFC; *Commercial & Financial Chronicle*, April 9, 1932; James Couzens to Atlee Pomerene, August 13, 1932, in RFC, Minutes, 7 (August 18, 1932), 856–57.

[24] U.S. Bureau of the Census, *Historical Statistics*, pp. 430–31, 462.

railroad loans in 1932, the railroad bond market was still in desperate straits. New York Central bonds, for example, had sold at a high of 256 in 1929, but had sagged to a low of only 9 in 1932. The Missouri Pacific had dropped from 101 to 1, the Pennsylvania from 110 to 6, and the Southern Pacific from 157 to 6. During 1932 a total of 122 Class I railroads had been unable to meet their fixed expenses. Of the more than $10 billion in outstanding railroad debt, nearly 70 percent was held by insurance companies, savings banks, and major private endowments. Those institutions were facing a financial catastrophe. In October 1932, at the request of major insurance companies and such universities as Harvard, Yale, Columbia, and Chicago, whose endowments were heavily invested in railroad securities, a National Transportation Committee headed by former president Calvin Coolidge began studying the railroad industry. Two prominent Democrats, Alfred E. Smith and Bernard Baruch, were on the committee. In February 1933 the committee issued its report—*The American Transportation Problem*. In their opinion, the railroad industry was facing stiff, permanent competition from the airlines, automobiles, and trucks, and only massive consolidation could ever make it competitive again. Waste, duplication, and overexpansion characterized the railroad industry.[25] As long as the major railways were trapped in a revenue-debt squeeze, railroad bonds would remain depressed, and the investment position of banks, insurance companies, savings banks, and endowed universities would remain compromised.

Joseph B. Eastman, a prominent Democrat and member of the Interstate Commerce Commission, wholeheartedly accepted the Coolidge committee report and began a major campaign for railroad legislation. On June 16, 1933, Congress passed the Emergency Railroad Transportation Act. To eliminate the political problems created by RFC railroad loans in 1932, the law prohibited the extension of RFC credit to any railroads the ICC determined were headed for reorganiza-

---

[25] Earl Latham, *The Politics of Railroad Coordination, 1933–1936* (Cambridge, Mass., 1959), pp. 11–13; Jones, *Fifty Billion Dollars*, p. 616.

tion.[26] The measure also frankly acknowledged that the industry was in for a long-term struggle by allowing the RFC to make up to ten-year term loans, as long as the railroad was amortizing them throughout the period. To bring economic order to the railroad industry, the bill created a federal coordinator of transportation with the authority to divide railroads into eastern, southern, and western groups. Each group would select a coordinating committee of railroad managers to eliminate duplication and promote joint use of tracks and terminals; encourage financial reorganization to cut fixed costs; and study ways of improving transportation. Although the general philosophy of the law was for the committees to coordinate voluntary action to eliminate waste, the federal transportation coordinator could order uncooperative carriers to participate. Before taking any formal action, the coordinator had to consult with labor leaders, and neither railroad employment nor salaries could be reduced below their May 1933 levels, except for a modest 5 percent reduction to handle resignations, retirements, and deaths. All decisions of the federal coordinator could be appealed to the ICC or to the federal courts. Finally, the act exempted carriers from antitrust laws. The objective was simple: to make the railroads competitive with new technologies emerging in the transportation sector of the economy.[27]

With railroad bonds a chronic problem, the financial difficulties of life insurance companies were not likely to go away soon. By 1920 railroad bonds constituted nearly 90 percent of the corporate bond holdings of life insurance companies, and approximately 27 percent of total assets. Ever since 1910 railroad bonds had been losing value and causing concern to life insurance executives. The *Savings Bank Journal* index of railroad bond values had declined from 112.7 in 1909 to 69.2 in 1919, and by 1929 life insurance companies had reduced their railway bonds to only 16 percent of total assets. By January

[26] "The Reconstruction Finance Corporation Act and Other Laws Relating Thereto, 1932-1950," unpublished manuscript, NA, RG 234, RFC, Secretary's Office, RFC Legislation File, Box 1.

[27] Latham, *The Politics of Railroad Coordination*, pp. 56–83.

1932 the railroad bond index was down to 37. The RFC loaned more than $67 million to insurance companies in 1932, but by the end of the year the index had fallen to only 26. RFC loans had provided only short-term relief. With desperate policy-holders exercising their options for low-interest cash loans on their policies, life insurance companies faced liquidity problems similar to, if not as severe as, those of thousands of commercial banks.[28]

Jesse Jones and the RFC proposed a preferred stock purchase plan to provide long-term liquidity to life insurance companies, similar to the bank reconstruction program of the Emergency Banking Act of 1933. Senator Duncan Fletcher, a Democrat from Florida and chairman of the Banking and Currency Committee, sponsored legislation giving the RFC authority to purchase the preferred stock of life insurance companies or to make long-term loans secured by preferred stock. Blessed with the active support of Jesse Jones, Senator Carter Glass, and Congressman Sam Rayburn, the bill sailed through Congress and President Roosevelt signed it on June 10, 1933.[29]

During the 1930s New Deal credit agencies saved the private money market. The Federal Deposit Insurance Corporation and Federal Savings and Loan Insurance Corporation solved the problem of bank panics and forced liquidation of assets. Federal deposit guarantees eliminated the need for frenzied withdrawals and protected the money supply. The Farm Credit Administration loaned $6.87 billion by 1940, established more than 600 Production Credit Associations, and refinanced nearly one-third of all farm mortgages in the United States. By June 1940 the Commodity Credit Corporation had

[28] Commission on Money and Credit, *Life Insurance Companies as Financial Institutions* (Englewood Cliffs, N.J., 1962), p. 48; Weldon Welfling, *Mutual Savings Banks. The Evolution of a Financial Intermediary* (Cleveland, 1968), p. 74; *Federal Reserve Bulletin*, 18 (December 1932), 759.

[29] Karen Orren, *Corporate Power and Social Change. The Politics of the Life Insurance Industry* (Baltimore, 1974), pp. 30–31; "The Reconstruction Finance Corporation Act and Other Laws," pp. 1–4; U.S. Congress, Senate, Committee on Banking and Currency, *Hearings on S. 1094, Purchase of Preferred Stock of Insurance Companies by R.F.C.*, 73d Cong., 1st Sess., 1934; "Transcripts of Board Notes," August 21, 1933, NA, RG 234, RFC.

loaned $889 million on 16.7 million bales of cotton; $470 million on 897 million bushels of corn; $166 million on 253 million bushels of wheat; and $46 million on 253 million pounds of tobacco. By 1939 the RFC had made loans of $142 million to 632 drainage, levee, and irrigation districts. Between June 1934 and December 1940, the Federal Housing Administration made $4.1 billion in insured loans, reducing the need for second and third mortgages on homes and making home ownership more affordable to larger numbers of people. By June 1936, when it stopped making new loans, the Home Owners' Loan Corporation had refinanced more than 20 percent of mortgaged homes in the United States and one-sixth of the total urban mortgage debt. It had made nearly one million loans totaling more than $3 billion.

The development of the federal credit structure had once been viewed as a temporary, short-term program to restore liquidity to the money markets until bankers and financiers had regained the confidence and security to begin making working capital loans again. But if the New Deal credit agencies were anything, they were not temporary. The most important of them in the 1930s, the Reconstruction Finance Corporation, played a central role in the New Deal recovery program. By late 1933 the National Recovery Administration seemed caught in a real dilemma. Under General Hugh Johnson's frenzy of establishing industry-wide codes of fair competition, the NRA plan to consolidate American industry into a cooperative commonwealth seemed on track, as was the RFC program to reconstruct the banking system. But despite those early successes, bank credit remained the great intangible. Congressmen from all over the country were receiving complaints from businessmen unable to secure working capital. Demands for government action to supply that credit, as well as the faith in state capitalism of influential New Dealers like Rexford Tugwell and Adolf Berle, put the Reconstruction Finance Corporation at the center of the recovery debate during 1934 and 1935.

The Emergence of a Financial Power, 1933–1935

THE NEW DEAL coalition was one of the most enduring in American history, and keeping its diverse constituencies together was a juggling act Roosevelt performed with consummate skill. Jesse Jones often found himself on center stage walking a tightrope between a variety of competing interests. Devaluation of the dollar, abandonment of the gold standard, and purchases of gold in 1933 and 1934 were bizarre episodes, and Jesse Jones was right in the middle of events because Roosevelt used the RFC to buy gold.

Pressure to inflate commodity prices came from several different directions. Democrats in the South and Midwest, particularly congressmen with rural constituencies, still had a populist faith in currency expansion. Led by Senator Elmer Thomas of Oklahoma, inflation rallies spread throughout rural America in 1933 and enjoyed support from the National Farmers' Union and the National Farm Holiday Association. They demanded an increase in paper currency, believing that commodity prices would rise as paper currency deflated. With higher crop prices farmers would be free of the economic burdens they had carried since World War I. Democrats like Senators Hugo Black of Alabama and Pat Harrison of Mississippi supported the idea, as did congressmen like Sam Rayburn of Texas and John Rankin of Tennessee. If Roosevelt had any hope of controlling Congress and getting recovery and relief measures, he had to respond to inflationist demands.[1]

While farmers were calling for more paper money, western mining interests wanted to remonetize silver, another populist dream. Some of them, like Senators Burton K. Wheeler of

---

[1] William E. Leuchtenburg, *Franklin D. Roosevelt and the New Deal, 1932–1940* (New York, 1963), pp. 37–38, 50–51.

Montana or William King of Utah, genuinely believed that restoration of the silver standard would expand the money supply and raise commodity prices. Others, like Senator Key Pittman of Nevada, supported silver remonetization out of political expediency. Government silver purchases would revive the moribund silver industry. The silver bloc in Congress, like its inflationist counterpart in the South and Midwest, could not be ignored.[2]

Finally, a small but vocal group of economists, led by Professors Irving Fisher of Yale and George Warren and Frank Pearson of Cornell, believed commodity prices were linked to the price of gold and its relation to paper currency. They called the theory the "commodity dollar." If the federal government purchased gold in large volumes and raised its price gradually, the value of the dollar would fall and commodity prices rise. If commodity prices went up, deflation would stop, normal credit markets revive, and employment and production increase. Henry Morgenthau had studied under Warren at Cornell and was fascinated with the theory. Morgenthau brought Warren to Washington as a consultant in the Department of Commerce. Roosevelt viewed the "commodity dollar" with academic skepticism but political fascination. It offered one way of satisfying inflationists, and there was at least a chance it would work. For Roosevelt, it was worth a try.[3]

He had already moved in that direction. The collapse of the banking system in February and March of 1933 forced abandonment of the gold standard. The Emergency Banking Act gave Roosevelt control over the money supply, and with several executive orders in the spring he outlawed gold hoarding, gold exports, and the gold payment clause in all contracts. Currency was no longer maintained in terms of gold, and the federal government had unprecedented control over the money supply.[4] Senator Elmer Thomas also gave Roosevelt broad authority to manipulate the money supply in Title III of

---

[2] Schlesinger, *The Coming of the New Deal*, pp. 248–52.

[3] Joseph Reeve, *Monetary Reform Movements* (Washington, D.C., 1943), pp. 162–84; Schlesinger, *The Coming of the New Deal*, pp. 236–38.

[4] Leuchtenburg, *Franklin D. Roosevelt and the New Deal*, pp. 43, 50–51.

the Agricultural Adjustment Act, which gave Roosevelt the discretionary power to issue up to $3 billion in new paper currency, reduce the gold content of the dollar, and freely coin silver. It enjoyed the strong support of commodity dollar advocates, the silver bloc, and southern and midwestern inflationists.[5]

In mid-August 1933 Roosevelt told Morgenthau he wanted to devalue the dollar with gold purchases. The decision ignited a bitter debate and demonstrated the president's independence of conservative ideologies. Under Secretary of the Treasury Dean Acheson firmly opposed him. Born to a prosperous New England family and a graduate of Yale and the Harvard Law School, Acheson was a blue blood who came to Washington after serving as private secretary to Supreme Court Justice Louis Brandeis and working with the law firm of Covington and Burling. When William Woodin became ill in 1933, Treasury duties fell to Acheson, although the president frequently consulted with Morgenthau about Treasury business. Acheson resented Morgenthau's influence, but his opposition to gold buying had little to do with politics. Acheson thought the commodity dollar was ludicrous. He had no intention of implementing it, and his opposition was outspoken and moralistic. Tired of Acheson's obstructionism, Roosevelt fired him in November. By that time Roosevelt had named Morgenthau acting secretary of the treasury.[6]

Acheson was not alone in his opposition. Lewis Douglas, director of the Bureau of the Budget, was almost apoplectic in his opposition. When the president abandoned the gold standard back in the spring, Douglas had predicted "the end of western civilization." Gold buying was just as bad. A well-known fiscal conservative, Douglas resigned his congressional seat in 1933 to take over at the budget office, where he advocated drastic spending cuts as the only way of restoring business confidence, reviving investment, and ending the depression. Douglas be-

[5] James S. Olson, ed., *Historical Dictionary of the New Deal. From Inauguration to Preparation for War* (Westport, Conn., 1985), pp. 7–8, 494–95.

[6] William Woodin to Dean Acheson, October 24, 1933, FDRPL, OF 643, RFC.

came disaffected in 1933 over budget-busting relief bills, and Roosevelt began to see him as hopelessly doctrinaire. Douglas represented the hard money conservatism of Wall Street, hated the economic theories of George Warren, and resisted remonetization of silver.[7] Opposition to gold buying was the beginning of the end of his influence in the administration.

Oliver M. Sprague joined the cacophony. A professor of economics at Harvard since 1913, Sprague knew Roosevelt during the president's undergraduate years in Cambridge. In June 1933 Morgenthau hired him as an adviser and executive assistant. Although Sprague was sympathetic to much of the early New Deal, he took exception to gold buying. Roosevelt tired of Sprague, and saw him as a tool of large, eastern financial interests. He forced Sprague's resignation just three weeks into the gold buying campaign.[8]

More opposition came from the Federal Reserve Board. In May 1933 Roosevelt replaced Eugene Meyer as governor of the Federal Reserve Board with Eugene M. Black, a conservative banker and attorney serving as head of the Federal Reserve Bank of Atlanta. Throughout the late 1920s and early 1930s Black had predicted a national banking crisis, and he gained widespread recognition when those apparitions came true. Black had close ties with the American Bankers' Association and other financial trade groups, and he looked on the gold buying scheme as pure foolishness. Black was not as adamant about it as Sprague, Douglas, and Acheson, and his independence at "the Fed" insulated him from Roosevelt's wrath, but he nevertheless strongly opposed the program. George Harrison of the Federal Reserve Bank of New York, along with the entire Wall Street investment community, thought gold buying would destroy the money markets.[9]

James Warburg, the renegade Wall Street financier and ad-

---

[7] James E. Sargent, "FDR and Lewis Douglas: Budget Balancing and the Early New Deal," *Prologue* 6 (Spring 1974), 33–44.

[8] *New York Times*, May 25, 1953.

[9] *New York Times*, December 20, 1934; Discussion Notes, October 26, 1933, Harrison Papers; Niznik, "Thomas G. Corcoran," pp. 60–64; Walter Wyatt, COHR, pp. 88–90.

viser to President Roosevelt, also thought gold buying was a prescription for economic catastrophe. When Elmer Thomas had managed to get it placed in the Agricultural Adjustment Act, Warburg never expected Roosevelt to implement it. Although a financier and president of the International Manhattan Company, Warburg was a loyal Democrat, a brilliant, flexible pragmatist who saw in the federal government one means of stabilizing the economy. Suspicious of Roosevelt's monetary views in 1932, Warburg had turned down an appointment as under secretary of the treasury, but he nevertheless became a close adviser to the president until gold buying. The idea scared Warburg. He thought it would destroy business confidence and asked Roosevelt to abandon it, but the president tired of the debate and decided that Warburg, despite his Democratic credentials, was too tradition-bound and Wall Street-oriented. Warburg left the administration publicly attacking New Deal monetary policies.[10]

Despite the opposition of so many people, Roosevelt was not alone in his commitment to gold buying. Secretary of Agriculture Henry A. Wallace wanted to give it a try to satisfy people in the farm belt who were convinced it would work. Secretary of the Interior Harold Ickes was loyal only because of Roosevelt's preoccupation with it. Special adviser Raymond Moley also backed the idea. Stanley Reed, the RFC general counsel, suggested using the RFC to buy gold, and Attorney General Homer Cummings upheld its constitutionality. Morgenthau was interested in making a profit for the government off the rising price of gold and in creating a gold fund so that the government would not always need Wall Street to underwrite bond issues. The Wall Street financial community always made government issues more difficult because they wanted to limit deficit spending.[11]

[10] New York Times, June 4, 1969; Blum, From the Morgenthau Diaries, vol. I. Years of Crisis, 1928–1938, pp. 66–67; James Warburg, COHR, pp. 1449–58.

[11] Homer Cummings to Franklin D. Roosevelt, October 26, 1933, FDRPL, OF 643, RFC; John Morton Blum, From the Morgenthau Diaries, vol. I, pp. 66–67; Walter Wyatt, COHR, pp. 88–90.

Jesse Jones had no faith in the "commodity dollar," but he was also circumspect about his views. Support for inflation was strong in the Texas congressional delegation, and Jones knew how much Roosevelt wanted to give it a try; so he went along much as Ickes did. Jones suspected that opposition to gold buying would end his influence in the New Deal, like it was doing to Acheson, Douglas, Sprague, and Warburg. And there was one part of gold buying that Jones loved. Anything that raised so much ire on Wall Street couldn't be all bad. Jones was delighted about the protests and posturings of J. P. Morgan, Charles Mitchell of the National City Bank, Winthrop Aldrich of the Chase National Bank, and George Harrison of the Federal Reserve Board of New York. He swallowed his misgivings and made the best of it. The RFC board issued $50 million and later $100 million more in short-term obligations to make the purchases.[12]

Late in October 1933, Jesse Jones, George Warren, and Henry Morgenthau met each morning at the president's bed to set a gold price. The daily price was irrelevant as long as the trend was up. To keep speculators off balance they fluctuated the daily price, but the general trend was up, from $29.01 an ounce on October 23, 1933, to $34.06 on January 17, 1934. By the end of October the price of gold in the United States was higher than London or Paris quotes because the RFC was confining its purchases to the domestic market. Much to George Harrison's chagrin, Jones used the Federal Reserve Bank of New York to purchase gold abroad on behalf of the RFC. Harrison hated it and Jones loved to watch him squirm. At the morning meetings, amidst laughter and coin flips and silly compromises, the four men reached a daily price. Jones and Morgenthau occasionally winced at how unscientific their methods were, but they did raise the price of gold and reduce

---

[12] Niznik, "Thomas G. Corcoran," pp. 60–64; Henry Morgenthau to Jesse Jones, December 7, 19, 1933, and January 2, 1934, NA, RG 234, RFC, Records of the Gold Reserve Act of 1934, Box 1; Harvey Couch to Franklin D. Roosevelt, October 20, 1933, and Jesse Jones to Franklin D. Roosevelt, October 28, 1933, FDRPL, OF 643, RFC.

the gold content of the dollar. Eventually the RFC bought a total of more than four million ounces of gold for $134 million.[13]

The gold buying program ended abruptly in January 1934. It was not working, at least not in the automatic way Warren, Fisher, and Pearson had predicted. Commodity prices dropped even more in the last quarter of 1933, despite the rising price of gold, and international monetary exchanges were destabilized by the artificial manipulation of the dollar. In the long run the devaluation probably helped American trade by making exports more competitive on world markets, but the "commodity dollar" was not bringing recovery. Still, the program had worked some magic. Roosevelt could at least hold his head high among inflationists. He had made an honest effort. As far as Jones was concerned, the program had done little damage and had brought a profit on gold buying of nearly $143 million to the RFC. His instincts for the bottom line were handsomely rewarded. The RFC stopped buying gold in mid-January, and on January 30, 1934, Roosevelt signed the Gold Reserve Act giving him the power to fix the price of gold. The next day he set the price at $35 an ounce, an amount fixing the dollar at 59 percent of its pre-1933 level. The legislation gave the federal government more power over credit, money, and exchange rates than ever before. Roosevelt then gave western "silverites" their reward with the Silver Purchase Act of 1934 declaring the proportion of silver to gold in the monetary system should be increased until the monetary stock was 25 percent silver and 75 percent gold or until the market price of silver reached $1.29 an ounce and that the Treasury Department issue silver certificates to equal the amount paid for the silver.[14]

[13] Discussion Notes, October 26 and November 2, 1933, Harrison Papers; Jesse Jones to Franklin D. Roosevelt, December 7, 1933, NA, RG 234, RFC, White House Correspondence, Box 20; Blum, *From the Morgenthau Diaries*, vol. I, pp. 69–71; Franklin D. Roosevelt to Jesse Jones, November 1, 1933; Jesse Jones to George Harrison, October 31, 1933; Jesse Jones to Franklin D. Roosevelt, December 7, 1933, all in FDRPL, OF 643, RFC; Jones, *Fifty Billion Dollars*, pp. 245–54.

[14] Jones, *Fifty Billion Dollars*, pp. 253–54. For a discussion of the entire New Deal silver program, see John A. Brennan, *Silver and the First New Deal* (Reno, Nev., 1969).

The controversy over gold buying was just part of a larger debate between 1933 and 1935 over the nature of the RFC and the New Deal. From the brain trust came the vision of the RFC as the primary focus of New Deal reconstruction efforts. Three people in particular—Rexford G. Tugwell, Adolf Berle, and Raymond Moley—saw the RFC as the primary institution in the development of state capitalism. An expert in agricultural economics at Columbia University, Tugwell was a major figure in the development of early New Deal programs. He saw the Great Depression as an enormous human tragedy but also as an opportunity to implement fundamental economic changes. Eschewing the Brandeisian emphasis on competition and antitrust, Tugwell accepted centralization and technology as modern facts of life, and thought the government should, through long-range planning and technical expertise, directly manage the economy. The federal government was not just a bureaucratic regulator; it was the only institution capable of defining national economic goals, allocating resources, and establishing prices, wages, and production objectives. He believed in the socialization of corporate management, not of corporate assets, and hoped to leave consumer power, entrepreneurial instincts, and private property intact. Tugwell found mass spending ideas as repugnant as progressivism because they would do nothing to restructure the economic relationship between the haves and the have-nots. Functioning as a great capital bank, the RFC would sit at the center of a new economic order.[15]

Berle and Tugwell had few differences over the structure of the economy, but Berle was more optimistic about human nature and the capacity of corporations to accept a new relationship with the government. While Tugwell wanted to impose his ideas immediately, Berle was willing to let the planning institutions develop more deliberately. Like Tugwell, he saw the RFC as the central institution in rebuilding the economy. By

[15] Paul Conkin, *The New Deal* (New York, 1967), pp. 37–39; Rosen, *Hoover, Roosevelt, and the Brains Trust*, pp. 151–94, 357–59, 374–75. Also see Bernard Sternsher, *Rexford Tugwell and the New Deal* (New York, 1964).

late 1933 and early 1934, the federal government in general and the RFC in particular had an unprecedented opportunity. Its creditor relationship with thousands of banks, savings banks, building and loan associations, and railroads allowed the RFC to make industrial policy—control the flow of capital, determine dividend rates, hire and fire management, and limit corporate salaries. The fact that it owned preferred stock in thousands of banks only made that power more certain, as did its potential to make similar investments in major insurance companies. Berle was also convinced that the railroad situation was hopeless. Government intervention was inevitable and the RFC should act as a huge holding company forcing liquidation, reorganization, and consolidation. Berle also advocated the establishment of some type of government credit bank to make the same loans and investments in manufacturing and service companies that the RFC was making in financial institutions. Although his formal position on the RFC ended in late 1933, Berle had a close relationship with Jesse Jones, worked as a consultant on railroad matters throughout the 1930s, and tried to shape Jones's thinking on recovery.[16]

Thomas Corcoran looked at the potential of the RFC from another perspective—the antitrust, progressive tradition of Felix Frankfurter and Louis Brandeis. From his position in the RFC Legal Division, Corcoran wanted an RFC assault on Wall Street and the major credit institutions of the country, not to break them up or take them over but to force low-interest rates and scaled-down debt refinancing. For Corcoran, the major Wall Street investment firms were making huge profits by charging interest rates far in excess of market levels, and the money markets would not be healthy again until railroad securities, mortgages, and corporate bonds were refinanced at lower levels with longer maturities. Along with Harold Rosenwald, a Harvard law graduate and RFC attorney, Corcoran drafted a memorandum in January 1933 proposing major

[16] Schlesinger, *The Coming of the New Deal*, pp. 432–33; Adolf Berle, COHR, pp. 170–71; Rosen, *Hoover, Roosevelt, and the Brains Trust*, pp. 325–26; Adolf Berle to Jesse Jones, December 28, 1933, FDRPL, Berle Papers, Box 19; Berle and Jacobs, *Navigating the Rapids*, pp. 35–38, 107–8.

changes in the RFC, including a new board composed exclu-
sively of Democrats; conversion of the RFC into a planning
agency to coordinate recovery programs; and using RFC
money to "force reorganization" of banking, urban real estate,
irrigation projects, and railroads. As for the future of the RFC,
Corcoran called for the agency to

> organize centralized cooperative organizations and plans,
> for which this Corporation will provide capital and direc-
> tion, to use its strength in the most concentrated economical
> way by meeting difficulties at wholesale and not at retail and
> giving private capital the nerve to venture by government
> partnership.[17]

Although Corcoran's attitude toward the business community
was more hostile than Berle's, their ideas for the RFC dove-
tailed nicely in 1933.

Another demand for increased RFC authority came from
Secretary of Commerce Daniel Roper. A South Carolina attorney who had held several government posts during his career,
Roper was the voice of the business community in the New
Deal, generating support for such measures as the Securities
Act of 1933, the Securities Exchange Act of 1934, the National
Industrial Recovery Act of 1933, and the Agricultural Adjustment Act of 1933. Convinced that several major insurance
companies had made terrible economic decisions during the
1920s, Roper began calling for the RFC to supervise strictly
their investment activities. Although he was advocating government regulation rather than economic planning and control, he nevertheless wanted the RFC to play a far more active
role in the life of the insurance industry.[18]

But while Tugwell, Berle, Corcoran, and Roper were calling
for a tremendous expansion in RFC authority, others wanted it
confined to the role Hoover had envisioned for it. In the federal
banking bureaucracy there was a growing resentment about

---

[17] Niznik, "Thomas G. Corcoran," pp. 41–42, 47–50.
[18] Daniel Roper to Franklin D. Roosevelt, October 6, 1933, FDRPL, OF 643,
RFC.

the RFC, primarily because Jones's aggressiveness and the corporation's increasing power were eclipsing the power of "the Fed." Before his sudden death in 1934, Governor Eugene Black frequently protested Jones's omnipresence in Washington financial circles and how the RFC, not the Federal Reserve Board, was the dominant force in the money markets. In New York, the governors of the Federal Reserve Bank, particularly George Harrison and Owen Young, expressed similar sentiments. During the bank reconstruction process in the spring and summer of 1933, Harrison repeatedly called for an end to RFC loans. Instead, he wanted the Federal Reserve banks to make the loans with the RFC guaranteeing them. Jones disagreed and prevailed with the president. While Berle, Corcoran, and Tugwell wanted the RFC to become a permanent agency controlling the flow of capital throughout the entire economy, conservatives wanted it to remain purely a temporary, emergency institution.[19]

Others in the federal banking structure were jealous of the RFC. Leo Crowley, head of the FDIC, frequently clashed with Jones over RFC loan policies, arguing they were unnecessarily harsh on the banking community. He accused the RFC in June 1934 of exacerbating banking difficulties by ruthlessly writing down assets and insisting on liquid collateral. Jones denied the claim and insisted that confidence in the banking system required such an approach. Late in 1935, Crowley again accused the RFC of playing too direct a role in banking affairs and urging bankers to retire their preferred stock. Jones disagreed and wrote an open letter to every bank in the country urging them to keep the preferred stock for a while longer until the stability of the money markets had been assured.[20]

J.F.T. O'Connor, comptroller of the currency, also wanted the RFC scaled down because it had become too powerful a fixture in American banking. In December 1935, just as the Christmas shopping season moved into full swing, he urged

[19] Walter Wyatt, COHR, pp. 88–90; Discussion Notes, April 27, 1933, and February 5, 1934, Harrison Papers; Stanley Reed, COHR, pp. 122–23.
[20] *New York Times*, June 20, 1934, November 13 and December 6, 1935.

the receivers of closed banks to refuse all RFC loans because the 4 percent interest rate was too high. Jones argued that 4 percent was necessary to cover costs and produce enough revenue to make up for any losses. Jones also urged receivers to hurry up and distribute RFC money to depositors so they would be able to spend it for Christmas.[21]

More opposition came from the budget balancers who thought the RFC was acquiring too much power. Henry Morgenthau was, according to Adolf Berle, "insanely jealous" of Jesse Jones and worked continuously to rein in the RFC and cut its budget. Morgenthau did not like the power, independence, and access Jones had to Roosevelt. Roosevelt too would have preferred to phase out the RFC and limit Jones's political power, and occasionally he tried, only to find new economic problems requiring RFC attention. Budget Director Lewis Douglas also expressed concern in 1933 and 1934 about the power the RFC was accumulating and the money it had at its disposal. If business confidence was ever to return, the RFC had to be curbed and the federal budget balanced. Continuing deficits, whether for bank reconstruction or unemployment relief, would prolong the depression.[22]

Finally, Wall Street wanted the RFC cut down to size, but their demands had little effect on the president. While they were opposing the gold buying scheme, Wall Street insiders were hoping to reduce RFC power. James Warburg wanted to consolidate the RFC, Federal Reserve system, and the new federal credit agencies under the control of Budget Director Lewis Douglas. He doubted whether Jones would be able to get all the closed banks ready for membership in the FDIC and feared the gold buying program would cause a panic and stampede capital to foreign markets. Warning of a new banking crisis, Warburg wanted Douglas to become the New Deal financier, get rid of Jones, and reduce the budget. Roosevelt disagreed.

[21] Jesse Jones to Franklin D. Roosevelt, December 5, 1935, FDRPL, OF 643, RFC; *Baltimore Sun*, November 28, 1935; Henry Morgenthau Diaries, December 3, 1935, Morgenthau Papers.

[22] Berle and Jacobs, *Navigating the Rapids*, p. 142; Stanley Reed, COHR, pp. 122–23.

He was already tired of the doomsaying about buying gold and saw the plan to cut down the RFC as another self-serving Wall Street scheme to maintain their control over the money markets.[23]

Wall Street and the commercial banking community were also quite critical of the RFC insistence that local stockholders match RFC investment. Jesse Jones felt that stockholders were responsible for their own institutions and were obligated to participate in the program. Bankers, however, wanted government investment without risking any of their own funds. George Harrison and Owen Young called on the RFC to abandon its requirement of matching private investment funds and bail out the troubled banks. Jones conferred with the president, however, and they both decided to keep the pressure on stockholders to commit their own funds to the reconstruction effort. The investment community resented Jones's power but could do little to thwart it.[24]

Jones and the RFC occupied that broad political ground between the planning and regulation schemes of Berle, Tugwell, and Corcoran on the one hand and the budget-balancing, limited government of Warburg, Douglas, Morgenthau, and Harrison on the other. By opposing the gold buying scheme so vocally, conservatives lost credibility in the administration, and Warburg and Douglas even lost their jobs. Roosevelt also doubted the political feasibility of national economic planning. He had enormous faith in Berle, Tugwell, and Corcoran, but he knew the country was not ready for any drastic alteration in the structure of the economy. Roosevelt made economic decisions in a political context, and although Jesse Jones and the RFC acquired the power in 1933 and 1934 to alter the relationship between the federal government and the private sector, they did not take full advantage of it. Instead of reorganizing the flow of capital, setting wages and production goals, and making personnel decisions, the RFC and federal

[23] James Warburg, COHR, pp. 1449–62, 1469, 1553, 1564.

[24] Discussion Notes, February 4–5, 1934, Harrison Papers; Jesse Jones to Franklin D. Roosevelt, September 3, 1934, FDRPL, OF 643, RFC; James Warburg, COHR, p. 1469.

credit agencies confined their activities to liquefying the money markets rather than changing their nature. State capitalism as it evolved during the New Deal was aimed at liberating the economy from its chains, not reallocating the existing flow of resources.

There were plenty of opportunities to do more. The railroad problem was especially difficult, and the RFC found itself deeply involved in the intricacies of railroad finance. In 1934 no less than thirty-two of the largest forty-six American railroads operated at a loss, and in 1935, despite a modest upturn in the economy, that number was still twenty-eight. The RFC estimated that thirty-two roads were in serious danger of bankruptcy. RFC loans, even at the reduced interest rates levied in 1933, had failed to stem the tide of defaults and securities declines. The assets of insurance companies and mutual savings banks remained severely compromised.[25]

By 1935, despite authorized RFC loans totaling $458 million, the problem was just as bad. Low-interest, long-term government loans only postponed the inevitable, especially since freight revenues continued to decline. The Chicago and Northwestern Railroad was one example. To pay interest charges and repair capital equipment, the RFC loaned it $21 million in 1932, nearly $4 million in 1933, and $7 million in 1934, and extended all those loans at the end of the year. But at the same time the Chicago and Northwestern had operating losses of $7.9 million in 1933, $8.2 million in 1934, and $11.1 million in 1935. It was a lost cause. The railroad declared bankruptcy on June 28, 1935. Despite more than $10 million in RFC loans, the St. Louis-San Francisco Railway went under in February 1933 after declaring a $10.1 million operating loss in 1932.[26] Dozens of other roads, and the financial institutions holding their paper, were in similar trouble.

Nothing was happening to address the real problems: heavy debt structures, overbuilding, competition from long-haul

[25] See the railroad earnings report filed with J. W. Barriger III to Adolf Berle, June 14, 1939, Berle Papers, Box 66, FDRPL, OF 643, RFC.

[26] Herbert Spero, *Reconstruction Finance Corporation Loans to Railroads*, pp. 42–59.

trucks, and declining freight revenues. The Emergency Railroad Transportation Act of 1933 had created the office of federal coordinator of transportation to consolidate the roads, but Joseph B. Eastman had little assistance. When he tried to force consolidation, he encountered bitter opposition from railroad management afraid of losing corporate independence; railroad workers afraid of losing their jobs; various communities afraid of losing railroad service; and large shippers afraid of losing cheap, competitive rates. The reduction in fixed costs so desperately needed by the railroads did not occur, and Congress allowed the federal coordinator's office to cease operating in June 1936.[27]

That left Eastman even more convinced that government ownership of the railroads was the only answer. Born in Katonah, New York, Eastman had attended Amherst College and after graduating spent a year in law school at Boston University. He took a position with the Public Franchise League in Boston in 1905 and began working with Louis Brandeis investigating the Boston Elevated Railway Company and the New York, New Haven & Hartford Railroad. Eastman became an expert in public transportation, and in 1919 President Woodrow Wilson appointed him to the Interstate Commerce Commission, a position he held for the rest of his life. By the 1930s he was known as the most liberal mind in the public utility field as well as a legal expert in transportation. Years of experience before the 1930s, as well as his term as the federal coordinator of transportation, convinced him that only a government takeover of the industry would overcome the power of vested interests resisting consolidation. Others in the administration, such as Adolf Berle and New York banker and presidential adviser Henry Bruere, were calling for a drastic, forced consolidation, but not a government takeover.[28]

[27] Latham, *The Politics of Railroad Coordination*, pp. 3, 35, 90–96, 119, 191, 196–201.

[28] *New York Times*, March 16, 1944; Latham, *The Politics of Railroad Coordination*, pp. 17–19, 24–25, 86–101; Berle and Jacobs, *Navigating the Rapids*, pp. 75–90; Henry Morgenthau Diaries, March 31, 1938, Morgenthau Papers.

The RFC loan program was still politically touchy, just as it had been in 1932. Two weeks into the New Deal, RFC loans to the Chicago and Northwestern Railroad became controversial because the City of Chicago wanted a loan to pay teachers' salaries. The protest convinced Roosevelt that the school district loan was imperative if the government had any hope of continuing RFC railroad financing.[29] In 1934 Senator Huey Long of Louisiana accused the RFC of making a $52 million loan to the Baltimore and Ohio Railroad. Actually, the RFC had a $25 million repayment due from the B & O on August 1, 1934, and to meet the note and purchase necessary equipment, the road offered a $50 million, five-year secured bond issue. The RFC evaluated the collateral at $90 million and offered to take up any of the unsold bonds. Investors eventually bought $36 million of the bonds and the B & O paid its RFC note with $12 million in cash and $13 million in bonds.[30]

As usual, Jesse Jones steered clear of both extremes. Regardless of how astute Berle and Eastman were about the transportation problem, government ownership or forced consolidation was just not in the cards, any more than nationalization of the banks had been a serious alternative back in March 1933. Even the precedent of the Plumb plan during World War I, with its takeover of the railroads, was not enough. The public was not ready for socialism in transportation, and there was no support for it in Congress or the administration. But Jones also looked askance at the progressive critics of RFC railroad loans. Herbert Hoover had been right. RFC money had flowed into railroads not to line the pockets of executives or their Wall Street bankers but to prevent defaults on the railroad bonds held by so many banks, savings banks, and insurance companies. Stability in the money markets and the access of depositors and policyholders to their funds rested to a large extent on the railroad bond market. In Jones's opinion, progressive critics did not understand the connection.

[29] John Fitzpatrick to Franklin D. Roosevelt, March 22, 1933, FDRPL, OF 643, RFC.
[30] Jesse Jones to Franklin D. Roosevelt, March 7, 1935, FDRPL, OF 643, RFC.

Clearly the RFC had to do more than offer low-interest loans, and between 1933 and 1935 it gradually became more deeply involved in railroad finance, though not as deeply as Berle and Eastman would have preferred. The RFC Act had required ICC approval before the Corporation could make a loan to a railroad, and the ICC did not like government money going to companies verging on bankruptcy. It was hard enough to get railroad leaders to consolidate, and the ICC believed bankruptcies and reorganizations would facilitate that process and speed the recovery of the industry. Jones and Berle, however, were more concerned about the immediate condition of the money markets and the impact of railroad defaults. They wanted the ICC to relax its stipulation of RFC loans only to solvent lines. By 1934 it had become an absolute necessity or the RFC would be hamstrung, large numbers of railroads would go under, and hundreds of financial institutions would fail. By late 1934 the ICC was relenting and giving the RFC more latitude, regardless of the road's financial condition, because Joseph Eastman had realized that his dream of bringing about massive railroad consolidation was unlikely at best.[31]

But relaxation of ICC standards was hardly enough. More than 80 percent of RFC railroad loans were used to meet interest payments, maturing bonds and equipment trusts, back taxes, and bank loans. By the end of 1935 the RFC had loaned just over $500 million to various railroads, of which $146 million were in default and $248 million still outstanding.[32] Instead of offering short-term loans, the RFC began to assist railroads in refinancing their indebtedness. Otherwise RFC loans would only bail out the Wall Street investment firms holding maturing bonds. The goal was to reduce the fixed interest-bearing securities to the point that the railroads, even under

[31] Adolf Berle to Franklin D. Roosevelt, December 16, 1932, quoted in Berle and Jacobs, *Navigating the Rapids*, pp. 82–83; Adolf Berle to Franklin D. Roosevelt, November 3, 1934, FDRPL, PPF 1306, Adolf Berle.

[32] RFC, "Earnings Statements," April 30, 1936, NA, RG 234, RFC, Railroad Division; speech by Charles Henderson to the National Association of Life Underwriters, August 27, 1937, NA, RG 234, RFC, Speeches of Key Personnel.

difficult economic circumstances, could service the debt and maintain bond values.[33]

Reducing fixed charges required more than cajoling, and the RFC entered the railroad securities market whenever Jones decided Wall Street bankers were charging too much. Late in 1935, for example, he decided to assist the Great Northern Railway. The Great Northern had been paying 7 percent on a $115 million bond issue for the last fifteen years, and the bonds were due to mature in July. Bankers agreed to finance a new issue at 5 percent and charged a $1 million underwriting fee. Jones thought the rate usurious and tried to get the bankers to finance the bond issue at 4 percent. When they refused he offered to have the RFC buy up any unsold 4 percent bonds the road would issue with no underwriting charge. When the bankers protested such bald government intervention, Jones argued that the RFC had "no desire to supplement you bankers, but would like to cooperate with you and the railroads to the end that railroad financing can be done at much less cost to the railroads." The bankers caved in and the Great Northern sold all $115 million of the issue to the public.[34]

Another problem was deteriorating railroad equipment. Unlike so many other businesses, the roads had to continue operating, even at a loss, because local economies depended on freight service. With so many roads unable to meet fixed expenses, purchases of new equipment and repair of old equipment were postponed and efficiency suffered. If the roads were to be competitive, they needed state-of-the-art technology, and

[33] *New York Times*, February 22, 1935.

[34] *New York Times*, January 12, 1936; RFC, *Press Release No. 1195* (Washington, D.C., December 18, 1935), NA, RG 234, RFC, Secretarial Division; Jones, *Fifty Billion Dollars*, pp. 113–15; speech by Jesse Jones to the American Bankers' Association, November 12, 1935, NA, RG 234, RFC, Speeches of Key Personnel. For another example, the Boston and Maine Railroad, with $26 million from an RFC purchase of new 4 percent first mortgage bonds, readjusted its bonded indebtedness. The plan gave consenting bondholders 50 percent of their holdings in new twenty-year 4 percent fixed-interest bonds and 50 percent in new 4.5 percent thirty-year income bonds in lieu of present holdings. See Federal Loan Agency Press Release Number 29, June 7, 1940, FDRPL, OF 643, RFC.

in 1934 the RFC began making loans with railroad equipment trust certificates as collateral. In 1936, for example, the RFC handled the sale of equipment trust certificates for the Pennsylvania Railroad. With the RFC offering to purchase them if necessary, the road had no difficulty selling $18.7 million at 4 percent to the Wall Street investment firm of Saloman Brothers.[35]

Legislative authority to buy railroad securities and equipment trust certificates came with the RFC Extension Act of January 1935. Stanley Reed had first forwarded an amendment allowing the RFC to write down a railroad loan or buy its securities in February 1934, and Senator Duncan Fletcher of Florida had moved it through committee. The bill became part of the RFC extension legislation and passed Congress on January 31, 1935, authorizing the RFC to buy railroad obligations, including equipment trust certificates, or lend money to receivers or trustees. At any one time the RFC could not have more than $350 million outstanding in such investments.[36]

The most complicated, and perhaps most revealing, of the RFC railroad loans went to the Baltimore and Ohio. For thirteen years the RFC managed the B & O's finances and kept it afloat. The B & O was burdened with annual fixed charges of more than $32 million, and it had operated at a loss of $6.3 million in 1932, a profit of $205,000 in 1933, and a loss of $3.8 million in 1934. By that time the RFC had loaned the road $72 million. Including its RFC loans, the road would have a total of $185 million in maturities coming due in the next four years. Roosevelt wanted to see if those debts could be scaled down, and in 1934 the RFC underwrote a new $50 million bond issue at 4.5 percent.[37] As part of that arrangement the RFC bought more than $13 million in B & O bonds. By 1938 the loans totaled more than $82 million, but that year the B & O lost more than $13 million. It began capital reorganization on September 3, 1938. Adolf Berle wanted the RFC to buy the

[35] RFC, *Press Release No. 1238* (Washington, D.C., April 23, 1936).

[36] *New York Times*, January 20 and 23, and February 1, 1935.

[37] Franklin D. Roosevelt to Jesse Jones, July 1, 1934, FDRPL, OF 643, RFC; J. W. Barriger to Adolf Berle, June 14, 1939, Berle Papers, Box 66.

road and operate it by exchanging its own securities for B & O bonds, but Jones and Roosevelt refused. Instead, the RFC extended due dates on B & O loans well into the 1940s to keep it operating.[38] RFC loans to the Baltimore and Ohio periodically raised the ire of some progressive congressmen, as they had with Senator Huey Long in 1934, but Jones remained convinced that the health of the money markets made those loans absolutely necessary.

Occasionally the RFC similarly intervened in the municipal bond market to keep rates low and help cities refinance debts. In 1934, for example, New York City tried to float a $75 million bond issue, but only Chase National Bank bid, and their offer was 6 percent for the first year and 4 percent until maturity. Mayor Fiorello La Guardia was outraged and asked Jones if the RFC would buy the bonds. Jones allowed La Guardia to use the threat of an RFC purchase. Winthrop Aldrich of Chase protested the RFC offer, but he relented and agreed to take the bonds at 3.75 percent. The untangling of the New York City bond crisis had a direct impact on the municipal bond market in 1934 and 1935. In 1939 the RFC purchased $20 million of a 3.5 percent bond issue from the City of Philadelphia. The bonds were secured by revenues from the Philadelphia Gas Works.[39]

Economic conditions in the 1930s gave the government an unprecedented opportunity to seize control of the money markets and capital financing, but the RFC stopped short of that kind of power. Under Jesse Jones the RFC had become the most powerful institution in the money markets, but it functioned neither as a huge, private bank nor as an all-powerful government agency making fundamental economic decisions about prices, employment, investment, production, and wages. President Roosevelt and Jesse Jones resisted demands to transform the RFC into the central agency of a planned economy because they both wanted to preserve the basic structure of American

[38] Jones, *Fifty Billion Dollars*, pp. 138–40; Berle and Jacobs, *Navigating the Rapids*, p. 178.
[39] Jones, *Fifty Billion Dollars*, pp. 178–79; Berle and Jacobs, *Navigating the Rapids*, p. 96.

capitalism. Nor was the RFC a government bank operating for a profit. Time and again Jones instructed RFC loan agency managers to be patient with borrowers; the government's main objective was not repayment but preservation of money market assets. Forced liquidation, except when absolutely necessary, was not the road to recovery, and he repeatedly had the RFC postpone repayments, accept partial payments, and refinance indebtedness.[40]

With its investment in preferred stock, capital notes, railroad bonds, municipal bonds and trust certificates, and collateral of enormous variety, the RFC had acquired in 1933 and 1934 powerful voting rights in thousands of American corporations. The RFC was the single largest investor in the country. Businessmen were always worried about the potential of government assistance becoming government control. Usually the RFC purchased as much preferred stock as there was common stock outstanding, doubling bank capital and giving it a controlling interest, but RFC policy was quite clear: leave competent bankers, insurance company executives, building and loan officers, and railroad managers in charge of their own institutions, with the RFC offering advice and capital. Neither Roosevelt nor Jones, despite the counsel of Rexford Tugwell and Adolf Berle, pushed beyond that role.[41]

There were many times when the RFC exercised its voting rights in making management decisions. In a letter to Vice President John Nance Garner on November 6, 1934, Jones said:

> I am making it clear to the roads that need to come to the Government for help that we must have some look-in on the management. Probably a fair criticism of railroad executives would be that they are always reluctant to allow any sort of governmental interference. That is perfectly all right so long

[40] Jesse Jones to RFC Loan Agency Managers, October 15, 1934, FDRPL, OF 643, RFC.

[41] Stanley Reed, COHR, pp. 74, 79, 105–6; Leuchtenburg, *Franklin D. Roosevelt and the New Deal*, pp. 71–72; William Appleman Williams, *The Contours of American History* (New York, 1961), pp. 438, 441–42.

as they do not have to come to the Government for money, but if the Government must be the banker, it should exact intelligent and efficient management.[42]

But Jones had no intention of planning the country's economic future. He just wanted to protect the RFC investment. He "had no desire to control or manage the banks."[43] Occasionally Jesse Jones would suggest a management change, or at least an addition to a board of directors. The Prudence Company of New York, for example, had taken more than $20 million from the RFC, and the RFC insisted on the resignation of its president, Arthur H. Waterman, as a condition of the loan. In place Jones put William H. Wheelock, an outstanding mortgage banker, and assigned RFC mortgage specialist Jerome Thralls to monitor corporate decisions. In April 1934 the RFC bought controlling interest in the Maryland Casualty Company, and sent Silliman Evans and Edward G. Lowry of the RFC to take over its presidency and vice presidency. Most of the time RFC management decisions were quite private and gave the companies involved the opportunity to get rid of the very people who had made the corporate decisions leading to insolvency. Jones felt that prudence with government money dictated some personnel changes.[44]

Now and then management disputes became public issues when companies charged the RFC with promoting socialism. The most celebrated example was the Continental Illinois Bank and Trust Company. Founded by George and Arthur Reynolds, the bank had lost a fortune in the collapse of the Samuel Insull utilities empire. Its deposits had declined from more than $1 billion in 1939 to less than $450 million in 1933, and it had lost $110 million in 1933 and 1934. A large correspondent bank in the Midwest, the Continental Illinois would have taken hundreds of smaller banks with it if bankruptcy became necessary. In October 1933 the RFC purchased $50 mil-

---

[42] Jesse Jones to John Nance Garner, November 6, 1934, FDRPL, OF 643, RFC.

[43] *New York Times,* June 17, 1934.

[44] Jones, *Fifty Billion Dollars,* pp. 156–58.

lion in preferred stock and required that outstanding stock be reduced from $75 million to $25 million, giving the RFC control of the bank. At the January 1934 meeting of the Continental Illinois board of directors, the RFC named Walter J. Cummings, first head of the FDIC, as chairman of the board. Bank officers protested but Jones was not moved, and Cummings took over one week later. But even in the midst of the controversy, Jones felt compelled to explain that the RFC's activities with the Continental Illinois were exceptions rather than the rule. Except where previous management had been wholly inadequate, the RFC would not interfere.[45]

For political reasons, Jesse Jones often toyed with the salaries of corporate management, especially if they were, in his mind, "over-paid" Wall Streeters. Jones and Roosevelt knew that RFC loans always had the potential of political trouble—stirring up liberal Democrats and progressive Republicans who were blaming businessmen for getting the country into such an economic mess. Salary reductions were one way of showing that the RFC, even while it was pouring billions into private business, was not enriching corporate management. Amendments to the RFC Act in 1933 required Jones to certify the appropriateness of the salaries paid by every corporation accepting loans and investment money. Jones devised a declining scale of salary reductions. Corporate management receiving annual salaries of $150,000 or more would be cut to $60,000, $100,000 or more to $50,000, and other reductions accordingly. Critics of RFC loans at least got some satisfaction about the billions of government money going to the business community.[46]

The Reconstruction Finance Corporation was a faithful reflection New Deal conservatism, a compromise between those who wanted to inject the government directly into the economy and those still faithful to balanced budgets and laissez-faire. Although people like Adolf Berle, Rexford Tugwell, and

[45] Ibid., pp. 47–49; *New York Times*, January 5, 9, 10, 12, and 23, 1934.
[46] Jesse Jones to Franklin D. Roosevelt, August 26, 1933, FDRPL, OF 31, Railroads.

Thomas Corcoran wanted dramatic extensions of government control over the private sector, what they got was several years of government cooperation with the business community in a desperate attempt to save capitalism and stimulate recovery. By the end of 1935 the RFC had loaned a total of $10.6 billion to thousands of businesses and government agencies, and much of that money was investment capital. However, except for occasional management changes, salary reductions, and business advice, Jesse Jones did not use the RFC to make macroeconomic decisions. Nor did he give an ear to the counsel of people like Henry Morgenthau, Jr., Lewis Douglas, or James Warburg, who continually wanted to reduce the RFC and cut government spending. Jones was too much of a realist. The money markets were frozen and only government intervention could restore liquidity. Only restored liquidity could revive commercial credit. And only dramatic increases in commercial credit could lift the country out of the depression.

The RFC and the National Recovery Administration, 1933–1935

ALTHOUGH the new federal credit agencies had prevented the collapse of the money markets, the Roosevelt administration worried continually about working capital, business loans, and long-term financing. RFC purchases of preferred stock in thousands of banks, securities and equipment loans to dozens of railroads, and long-term loans to hundreds of savings banks, insurance companies, and building and loan associations had stabilized the money markets but had not stimulated commercial credit or long-term capital flotations. Between 1929 and 1934, new equities for long-term financing had declined from $306 million to less than $25 million, and bank loans for real estate, securities, and working capital had dropped from $23.2 billion to $10.5 billion.[1] Most economists were convinced that a permanent recovery would not materialize until the credit available to business was restored to pre-1929 levels. The revival of commercial credit was the RFC's major objective.

Classical economic theory commanded the loyalties of most economists in the early 1930s, even though the depression was challenging them at every turn. They assumed an automatic connection between bank credit, production, and employment. Bank lending released cash for an expansion of consumer income and spending. Retailers and wholesalers saw inventories diminish and placed new orders for finished products. Manufacturers hired workers to produce more, and the cycle of expansion accelerated. By reducing interest rates and reserve requirements, and purchasing bonds on the open market, Federal Reserve banks channeled new resources to

[1] RFC, "Review of Economic Conditions," October 7, 1933, NA, RG 234, RFC, Statistical Division; *Federal Reserve Bulletin*, 23 (September 1937), 923.

banks, which quickly converted them into loans and investments. Just as high interest rates slowed down an economy, low interest rates inevitably stimulated it.[2]

What they could not account for was excess reserves—deposits banks refused to loan or invest. Federal Reserve banks reduced interest rates and reserve requirements after 1929 and purchased government securities on the open market in 1932. Theoretically those monies should have quickly found their way into the economy. Instead, banks accumulated excess reserves. Federal Reserve officials, as well as influential New Dealers, also predicted that large-scale bank investment in government securities would reduce yields to the point that money market rates in general would drop, stimulating an increase in capital issues for long-term business financing.[3] When neither an increase in equity issues nor a rise in bank credit materialized, they assumed that banker fear over the panic of 1933 and the Banking and Securities Acts of 1933 was responsible.[4]

The federal credit agencies created between 1932 and 1934 were supposed to remove the fear, so that private financial institutions would start lending again. The need to liquefy banks and convince them to expand credit was a passion permeating the thinking of RFC officials between 1932 and 1935. Federal Reserve bank had reduced discount rates and made large purchases of government securities early in 1932, and by July its portfolio of government bonds had grown by more than $1 billion.[5] But excess reserves continued to mount.

To supplement RFC loans and Federal Reserve open market

[2] E. A. Goldenweisar, *Federal Reserve System in Operation* (New York, 1925), pp. 85–86; Ralph G. Hawtrey, *The Art of Central Banking* (London, 1932), pp. 167–68; John Maynard Keynes, *A Treatise on Money* (London, 1930), p. 53; Jacob Oser, *The Evolution of Economic Thought* (New York, 1963), p. 287.

[3] Discussion Notes, March 7 and 14, 1935, Harrison Papers.

[4] Discussion Notes, April 30, 1934, Harrison Papers; *New York Times*, May 14, 1933.

[5] Clay J. Anderson, *A Half-Century of Federal Reserve Policymaking, 1914–1964* (Philadelphia, 1965), pp. 68–72; American Bankers' Association, *Banking After the Crisis*, pp. 16–18.

operations, Hoover called a conference of the Banking and Industrial Committees in each Federal Reserve district. They gathered in Washington, D.C., in August 1932 to discuss ways of stimulating private credit. The Federal Reserve Bank of New York had first formed a banking and industrial committee in the spring of 1931, and by May 1932 President Hoover was encouraging similar committees in each Federal Reserve district. The August conference tried to get bankers and industrialists in the mood for financing legitimate enterprise, and although little came of the conference, the emphasis on credit revival eventually became a major recovery theme for the RFC. As credit evaporated in 1932 and excess reserves increased, the Hoover administration became more and more frustrated. The president was convinced that recovery rested on the fickle intentions of the banking community. In November, RFC Chairman Atlee Pomerene charged that any bank refusing to lend was a "parasite in the community and deserves the condemnation of every thinking man and woman."[6] Following that same tradition, Jesse Jones and Franklin D. Roosevelt campaigned throughout 1933 and 1934 for an expansion of bank credit while the RFC was trying to reconstruct the financial system. Excess reserves should be soaked up by heavier commercial lending, but by 1935 those reserves, bolstered by heavy gold imports, had risen to more than $5 billion.[7]

The "trickle-down" theory was alive and well. In both the Hoover and Roosevelt administrations, influential policymakers demanded large-scale increases in bank lending. Both administrations believed credit stringencies prolonged the depression and that recovery would lag behind a loan revival. Baffled by increasing volumes of excess reserves, both admin-

[6] Speech by Atlee Pomerene to the New England Council, November 17, 1932, NA, RG 234, RFC, Speeches of Key Personnel; Atlee Pomerene to Walter Dean, January 28, 1933, Pomerene Papers; "Minutes of the Meeting of the Chairman of the Business and Industrial Committees and Members of the Administration," August 25, 1932, NA, RG 56, Department of the Treasury.

[7] RFC, "Review of Economic Conditions," January 17, 1934, NA, RG 234, RFC, Statistical Division; Henry Morgenthau Diaries, October 28, 1935, Morgenthau Papers.

istrations had tried to increase bank credit via loans, stock purchases, and public cajoling, but bank credit continued to decline. Just as the Home Owners' Loan Corporation had been forced to go beyond the discounting provisions of the Federal Home Loan banks, so the RFC or other government agencies would have to go beyond liquefying bank assets and make direct business loans until bank lending recovered.[8]

IT WAS HARDLY a new idea. Congress had created the War Finance Corporation in 1918 to strengthen capital markets and make industrial loans. In a capital-short economy the WFC provided the funds necessary to bridge the gap between productive capacity and wartime demand. While stabilizing the money markets, the WFC also sustained the government bond market by purchasing federal bonds. During World War I the WFC loaned funds to public utilities, electric power plants, mining and chemical concerns, railroads, and banks.[9] The logic of the WFC seemed suited to the depression as well, since so many congressmen thought businesses were having trouble getting working capital. During World War I the federal government had filled the gap with WFC money; perhaps the same approach would work in 1932 as well. To provide relief and public works money to ease unemployment, President Hoover, after resisting for several months, worked with Congress in passing the Emergency Relief and Construction Act in July 1932. The legislation, in addition to providing $300 million in RFC relief loans and $1.5 billion in public works construction, allowed the Federal Reserve banks to make working capital loans to businesses unable to secure credit from commercial banks. The paper had to be short-term and eligible for dis-

[8] Eugene Meyer, COHR, pp. 617–18; Arthur E. Burns and Donald S. Watson, *Government Spending and Economic Expansion* (Washington, D.C., 1940), p. 110; Homer Cummings to Franklin D. Roosevelt, August 23, 1933, FDRPL, OF 644-B, Home Owners' Loan Corporation.

[9] Louis B. Wehle, *Hidden Threads of History* (New York, 1953), pp. 71–73; Secretary of the Treasury, *Annual Report, 1919* (Washington, D.C., 1920), pp. 105–6.

count by Federal Reserve banks, and the loan had to be adequately secured.[10]

The Federal Reserve banks were never comfortable with their new authority, and found few businesses eligible for loans, at least inside the legislative mandate of the Emergency Relief and Construction Act. The Federal Reserve Bank of New York received 1,286 loan applications, but only 250 were worthy of serious consideration. Fourteen finally got loans. Poor credit histories and lack of adequate collateral disqualified most applicants. Nor did people like George Harrison or Owen Young of the board of governors of the Federal Reserve Bank of New York have much enthusiasm for the Act. They viewed themselves as a discounting institution, not a bank offering commercial credit. As far as they were concerned, legitimate demand for bank credit was not nearly as high as many people assumed.[11]

Most bankers agreed. They argued that government officials were seriously overestimating the demand for credit. Most businesses lacked confidence in the economic future and were unwilling to burden themselves with heavy debts. Rapid declines in bank interest rates were proof, bankers claimed, that little demand existed for commercial credit. Just as important, those businesses applying for credit were usually short of working capital, earning power, or collateral, and so ineligible for loans. Commercial banks were meeting most legitimate demands for assistance. They had all undergone a liquidity crisis in 1932 and 1933, but by 1934 they were far more willing to make commercial loans. The New Deal was unfair in its judgment of the financial community and inconsistent in its approach to the credit problem. While the RFC was insisting that banks make more business loans, bank examiners with the comptroller of the currency, RFC, and FDIC were busy classifying all term loans as "slow," making bankers even more reluctant to make them.[12]

[10] *Washington Post*, June 6, 1932. Also see the unpublished minutes of the Rapidan Conference, June 5–6, 1932, HHPL, PP, SF, RFC.

[11] *New York Times*, March 17, 1934; "Direct Loans of Reserve Banks to Industry," unpublished manuscript, Harrison Papers, 1940, Binder 74.

[12] Francis M. Law to Franklin Roosevelt, October 9, 1933, FDRPL, PPF 756,

Bankers also felt the RFC was unaware of fundamental changes in the economy which had altered bank investment policies. The volume of commercial loans reached in the 1920s, which RFC officials seemed to accept as a benchmark of a healthy economy, was a temporary aberration which would never return. Commercial loans were abnormally large during the 1920s because businesses were short of working capital. World War I price increases had left thousands of businesses short of expansion capital, and they had turned to commercial banks to fill the void. Commercial credit expanded rapidly until the mid-1920s. By then many businesses had accumulated internal funds to finance expansion without bank credit. The decline in commercial loans by banks had begun long before the depression, and the volume of commercial loans would never recover to pre-depression levels.[13]

Bankers also claimed that business demand for short-term credit had fallen sharply. Many businesses were more interested in reducing indebtedness and strengthening cash balances than in expansion, especially given the extent of unemployment and falling prices. Businesses needing credit were not interested in short-term loans, since money subject to early maturities would not provide enough time to restore their badly depleted working capital. Just as short-term loans had failed to provide banks with liquidity, short-term working capital would leave businesses in a vulnerable financial position. Traditional banking theory had always restricted the business loan activities of commercial banks to short-term credit, but in the United States banks had become accustomed to making their sound, short-term loans renewable, providing borrowers with a form of equity or long-term financing. More interested in liquidity than profits, many banks between 1930

American Bankers' Association; Newton Busenback to Virginia Jencks, September 11, 1933, and Samuel Barker to Franklin Roosevelt, October 6, 1933, FDRPL, OF 706, Credit; *New York Times*, June 20, 1934; RFC, *Press Release No. 987* (Washington, D.C., 1934), p. 1; *Commercial & Financial Chronicle*, October 30, 1937; P. B. Dunn to J.F.T. O'Connor, March 10, 1934, O'Connor Papers.

[13] L. P. Ayres, "Prospects for Profits in the Banking Business," *Commercial & Financial Chronicle*, ABA Section, October 30, 1937, p. 28.

and 1934 refused to renew and demanded payment in full, forcing unprecedented liquidation which reduced the ratio of commercial loans to bank assets from 71 to 48 percent. Unwilling to go through such a liquidation again, businessmen now wanted long-term credit. But for bankers, these were the very loans bank examiners discouraged. It was a vicious cycle. Some bankers, like Samuel Barker of the Gerard Trust Company of Philadelphia, began calling for long-term RFC business loans.[14]

Despite banker misgivings and the failure of the Federal Reserve loan program, the Roosevelt administration decided to push ahead with the idea of direct business loans, and it became part of the National Recovery Administration program. The impetus for the National Industrial Recovery Act came from a variety of sources in 1933. Senator Hugo Black of Alabama was busy pushing legislation to impose a thirty-hour workweek to spread jobs and provide a minimum wage for workers. The American Federation of Labor endorsed the proposal. The business community had its own recovery proposal. Financier and industrialist Bernard Baruch, Henry Harriman of the U.S. Chamber of Commerce, and Gerard Swope of General Electric believed the depression was the result of overproduction and too much competition, and wanted the federal government to establish a mechanism for industrial self-regulation through trade associations. By relying on fair trade laws and trade associations, the federal government could eliminate destructive competition, encourage national economic planning, and improve business confidence. Corporate leaders from the oil, coal, textile, and retail trade industries were also calling on the New Deal to suspend antitrust laws and establish industrial codes regulating prices and production. Senator

[14] American Bankers' Association, *The Earning Power of Banks*, p. 13; American Bankers' Association, *Changes in Bank Earning Assets*, p. 8; Neil Jacoby and Raymond Saulnier, *Term Lending to Business* (Washington, D.C., 1942), p. 16; Neil Jacoby and Raymond Saulnier, *Business Finance and Banking* (New York, 1947), p. 5; Frederic Taber Diary, March 1, 1934, Taber Papers; Francis M. Law to Franklin D. Roosevelt, October 9, 1933, FDRPL, PPF 756, American Bankers' Association; Samuel H. Barker to Franklin D. Roosevelt, October 6, 1933, FDRPL, OF 706, Credit.

Robert Wagner of New York sponsored the self-regulation proposal and tied to it his own proposal for a massive public works construction program. A variety of social workers wanted a vigorous program of fair labor standards legislation. Another group, led by brain truster Raymond Moley and Budget Director Lewis Douglas, wanted federal licensing and code making to achieve the goals of industrial self-regulation.[15]

Inside the Wagner group, several proposals for federal loans to industry surfaced, although none was as comprehensive as Adolf Berle's call for a large government corporation directing the capital markets. Former New York congressman Meyer Jacobstein, an adviser to Robert Wagner, drafted legislation to provide federal funds to guarantee industrial investment in payroll and inventory expansion. Harold G. Moulton, president of the Brookings Institution and another adviser to Wagner, concurred. Fred I. Kent, vice president of the Bankers' Trust Company, wanted some federal guarantee of business profits, while David L. Podell, an antitrust attorney and trade association specialist, called for suspension of the antitrust laws. Moulton then came up with his own proposal for working capital loans to industry. Former AT&T executive Malcolm C. Rorty, representing the U.S. Chamber of Commerce, developed a plan for the government to subsidize business expenditures for capital goods purchases.[16] In the last negotiations to produce a final version of the National Industrial Recovery Act, the provisions for direct federal loans to business were dropped, primarily because most government officials involved hoped that the RFC bank reconstruction program would give the private sector enough liquidity to resume lending again.[17]

Advocates of direct government loans were skeptical, and

---

[15] For the diverse origins of the National Industrial Recovery Act, see Himmelberg, *The Origins of the National Recovery Administration.* Also see Ellis W. Hawley, *The New Deal and the Problem of Monopoly* (Princeton, 1966), pp. 19–52; *Wall Street Journal*, November 18, 1932.

[16] Charles F. Roos, *NRA Economic Planning* (New York, 1937), pp. 38–40.

[17] Hawley, *The New Deal and the Problem of Monopoly*, p. 25; Hugh Johnson to Franklin D. Roosevelt, January 14, 1934, FDRPL, OF 706, Credit.

their doubts were confirmed in 1933 and 1934 when commercial lending remained flat. Between June 1933 and December 1934, business loans of Federal Reserve members dropped from $4.8 to $4.7 billion, despite the billion-dollar investment the RFC had made in bank capital.[18] Belief in the need for a large-scale credit expansion intensified, as did Jesse Jones's pursuit of the preferred stock campaign. Along with people like Harold Moulton, Meyer Jacobstein, Adolf Berle, and Hugh Johnson, Jones and Roosevelt worried that the NRA would falter unless banks supplied businesses with the working capital necessary to expand production and payrolls.[19] Belief in the need for government business loans, continuing liquidation of commercial credit, early reluctance of banks to accept the preferred stock program, and frequent complaints from congressmen that business constituents were unable to get loans forced the administration to resort to direct lending.[20]

By the summer of 1933 the credit question was becoming acutely important, at least in the minds of most administration officials. Angered by the refusal of major industries to cooperate with the NRA, Hugh Johnson had initiated a crusade to sign up businesses in support of its wages and hours guidelines. The "Blue Eagle" symbol which he designed became the national symbol of the NRA, and its legend "We Do Our Part" indicated a company's willingness to cooperate in the recovery program. Throughout the summer of 1933 Johnson traveled across the country in an army plane trying to convince major industries to adopt the Blue Eagle and join the NRA. The cotton textile industry was the first major manufacturing sector to join, and during the summer Johnson managed to secure the

[18] *Federal Reserve Bulletin*, 23 (September 1937), 923.

[19] *New York Times*, April 2, and August 2 and 28, 1933; Jesse Jones to Franklin Roosevelt, September 23, 1933, FDRPL, OF 643, RFC; Franklin Roosevelt to American Bankers' Association, August 30, 1933, FDRPL, PPF 756, American Bankers' Association.

[20] C. P. Gentry to Franklin D. Roosevelt, January 10, 1934, FDRPL, OF 172, Business Policies. The whole business file in OF 172, Boxes 1 through 10, is full of complaints about the unavailability of credit.

cooperation of the shipbuilding, electrical, wool textile, garment, oil, steel, and lumber industries as well. Late in August the automobile industry, with the notable exception of the Ford Motor Company, also pledged its support. By September 1933 Hugh S. Johnson reached the peak of his popularity, and so did the country's expectations for the NRA.[21]

Johnson's success pleased and frightened Roosevelt and Jones. They were worried the NRA program would be ready to go but that the working capital necessary for an economic expansion would be unavailable. President Roosevelt and Jesse Jones, expecting some resistance from the banking community, began a public relations campaign suggesting the likelihood of direct RFC loans. On August 1, 1933, Jones made a nationwide radio address and explained the program, telling bankers to stop complaining about economic conditions, cease building up excess reserves, and release new credit in the form of commercial loans.[22] Later in the month Roosevelt rejected an offer to speak to the American Bankers' Association, but he sent Jones in his stead, instructing the RFC chairman to urge bankers to join the program as a prerequisite to furnishing "the credit necessary for the recovery program."[23]

The ABA convention was in Chicago and Francis H. Sisson of the Guaranty Trust Company, president of the association, accused the administration of unjustified attacks on the banking community. Jones was in no mood for conciliation. He spoke to them on September 5, accused half the assembled guests of running insolvent institutions, and warned them that they had better cooperate with the preferred stock campaign or face economic ruin. Jones castigated the bankers for resisting the RFC, told them to "be smart, for once," and said that the National Recovery Administration would fail unless banks provided the credit to finance the new industrial production.

[21] Bernard Bellush, *The Failure of the NRA* (New York, 1975), pp. 36–54.

[22] Franklin D. Roosevelt to American Bankers' Association, August 30, 1933, FDRPL, PPF 756, American Bankers' Association; Jesse Jones to Franklin D. Roosevelt, August 31 and September 23, 1933, FDRPL, OF 643, RFC.

[23] Franklin D. Roosevelt to Jesse Jones, August 21, 1933, Jones Papers.

He closed his address by explaining that the FDIC would relieve bankers of their "excessive liquidity fears."[24]

Still the program lagged, and late in September Jones asked Roosevelt to consider letting the RFC make direct business loans. He viewed it more as a threat than a responsibility he wanted the RFC to exercise. Such an approach, Jones thought, would go "a long way toward heartening the country, and possibly spur the banks to greater effort toward lending."[25] Although Roosevelt did not make a public statement to that effect, RFC officials dropped quiet hints and threats to their banking friends. Despite their threats, the RFC bought only $5.9 million in preferred stock during October. Commercial credit continued to dry up.[26] The administration began considering more drastic action.

By then Jones felt under seige. Compared to the success Hugh Johnson was having in getting support for the NRA from corporate leaders, the RFC's delays in securing banker cooperation were frustrating. Jones began talking about using the RFC to make direct loans to business if bankers shirked their responsibilities. The president concurred. In a letter to Secretary of the Treasury William Woodin in October, Roosevelt criticized

> members of the banking community who do not want to make loans to industry. They are in a sullen frame of mind, hoping by remaining sullen to compel foreign exchange stabilization and force our hands. If you and I force these funds on them they will have to act in accordance with our desires.[27]

[24] Speech by Jesse Jones to the American Bankers' Association, September 5, 1933, Jones Papers; Franklin D. Roosevelt to F. N. Shepherd, June 8, 1933, FDRPL, OF 643, RFC; Jesse Jones to Duncan Fletcher, May 3, 1933, NA, RG 234, RFC, Preferred Stock.

[25] Jesse Jones to Franklin D. Roosevelt, September 23, 1933, FDRPL, OF 643, RFC.

[26] RFC, *Quarterly Report for April 1 to June 30, 1934* (Washington, D.C., 1934), Table 6.

[27] Schlesinger, *The Coming of the New Deal*, p. 429.

Roosevelt remarked several days later that the RFC might just have to go into the business of banking itself.[28]

Late in August Jones had met with Eugene Black of the Federal Reserve Board and Comptroller of the Currency J.F.T. O'Connor about expanding bank credit, and after the meeting Jones wrote to the president suggesting an RFC program to loan money to new mortgage companies for reloaning to businesses. At the time Hugh Johnson endorsed the RFC preferred stock program, urging all banks to become "double-eagle and government-partnered banks." Jones had a special RFC logo designed—a blue eagle atop a field of blue and white stripes—to symbolize the NRA connection. Roosevelt talked about the possibility of reviving the National Credit Corporation to make small business loans with RFC funds. Early in September 1933, while discussing ways of getting more banks to accept RFC preferred stock investment, administration officials held a series of conferences about the credit problem. NRA officials throughout the country were being flooded with requests from manufacturers to assist them in securing working capital since banks were being uncooperative.[29]

On September 14, Secretary of Commerce Daniel Roper held a meeting at his house with Hugh Johnson, Jesse Jones, and Stanley Reed. One week later they met again with representatives of the Treasury Department and the NRA, and they decided to have the RFC advance working capital indirectly through banks and mortgage loan companies. They decided to aggressively expand the money supply. Federal Reserve open market purchases had already augmented the volume of excess reserves, and the RFC was ready to loan funds at 3 percent for six months or less to banks, trust companies, and mortgage loan companies, provided they reloaned it on a short-term basis at not more than 5 percent to businesses cooperating with the NRA. The RFC also hoped that businesses needing credit

[28] Ibid.

[29] *New York Times*, August 31 and September 16, 23, and 26, 1933; Clarence Cannon to Franklin D. Roosevelt, August 23, 1933; Richard Lloyd-Jones to Franklin D. Roosevelt, September 8, 1933; Jesse Jones to Franklin D. Roosevelt, August 31, 1933, all in FDRPL, OF 706, Credit.

would join together and form new mortgage loan companies to accept RFC funds and reloan them to the companies involved. Loan proceeds could only be used for working capital, not for debt reduction or refinancing. As part of the campaign, the RFC reduced its interest rate on long-term loans to banks from 4.5 to 4 percent. Hugh Johnson and Jesse Jones both believed the new program would meet credit needs and encourage banks to participate.[30]

The program was an immediate failure. The participating credit arrangement did not give bankers enough security, at least in terms of what they expected. They paid 3 percent for RFC money and reloaned it at not more than 5 percent. While assuming all of the risk, their return at most amounted to 2 percent, an unacceptable rate. Prevailing money market rates were not 5 percent anyway, so the interest rate was too high. Also, the process of organizing new mortgage loan companies was too cumbersome for businessmen worried about keeping their heads above water. By December 1933 the RFC had loaned just over $2 million, and the administration, more frustrated than ever about the liquidity mania, continued its verbal assault on bankers. Bankers just as vociferously denied there was really any problem. The RFC had no choice, given the thinking of the time, but to establish a program of direct assistance to business.[31]

Two RFC credit agencies—the Electric Home and Farm Authority and the Commodity Credit Corporation—reinforced the conviction that significant demand for loans really existed. Congress created the Tennessee Valley Authority in June 1933

[30] Edward A. Filene to Franklin D. Roosevelt, September 18, 1933, FDRPL, OF 706, Credit; Jesse Jones to Franklin D. Roosevelt, August 31, 1933, FDRPL, OF 643, RFC; RFC, *Circular No. 11* (Washington, D.C., 1933), pp. 1–5; RFC, *Loan Agency Bulletin No. 322* (Washington, D.C., 1933), p. 1; *New York Times*, August 28 and 31, September 3, 14, and 15, and October 1, 1933.

[31] *New York Times*, December 18, 1933, and March 7, 1934; Frederic Taber Diary, September 25, October 11, November 3 and 8, and December 6, 1933, Taber Papers; Franklin D. Roosevelt to Paul V. Betters, December 18, 1933, and Hugh Johnson to Franklin D. Roosevelt, January 15, 1934, FDRPL, OF 706, Credit; C. P. Gentry to Franklin D. Roosevelt, January 10, 1934, FDRPL, OF 172, Business Policies.

to develop flood control, hydroelectric power, and irrigation systems for the Tennessee River Valley. A major obstacle to hydroelectric development was the lack of consumer demand among poor farmers. Because of an unfamiliarity with electrical appliances, high utility rates, lack of transmission lines into rural areas, and appliance costs, hundreds of thousands of farm families were unable to consume electric energy even if they had the opportunity.

During the 1920s and early 1930s, appliance manufacturers and utilities executives had discussed the problem, but they never reached any agreement. Manufacturers felt that if the utilities reduced their rates, farmers could afford the appliances, and the increased sales would permit volume-based price reductions. Utilities executives argued that if manufacturers reduced appliance prices, farmers would buy them, consume more electricity, and permit volume-based price reductions per kilowatt hour. An impasse existed which the private sector was incapable of breaking. In the cooperative, planning-based atmosphere of the early New Deal, the federal government was willing to negotiate a compromise between consumers, utilities, and manufacturers.[32]

Late in 1933, TVA chairman Arthur Morgan proposed the creation of an Electric Appliance Agency to assist farmers in acquiring consumer goods. Roosevelt met with Jesse Jones, Lewis Douglas, Eugene Black, Attorney General Homer Cummings, Henry Morgenthau, and Stanley Reed on December 13 to discuss the proposal. Douglas opposed it, preferring to leave the problem to the private sector, but the rest were enthusiastic. On December 19, 1933, Roosevelt signed an executive order creating the Electric Home and Farm Authority under the TVA. A little while later the EHFA was transferred to the RFC. The EHFA designed was to promote the sale of electrical appliances by assuming the credit obligations of purchasers. The EHFA sold the paper to local banks, which then paid manufacturers, and the banks at any time could sell the paper to the

---

[32] "Purposes and Program with Recommendations for Expansion," March 15, 1935, FDRPL, OF 42-B, EHFA.

RFC. The RFC made $10 million available for the program. The EHFA was to increase domestic consumption of electricity in TVA-served areas by assisting manufacturers of heavy-use appliances in providing standard equipment at lower than normal prices and securing from private utilities rates which would make the use of such appliances economical for most farmers.[33]

Directed first by TVA board member David Lilienthal, then Morris Cooke of the Rural Electrification Administration (REA), and finally by Emil Schram of the RFC, the EHFA was an instant success. In 1934 the EHFA financed the sale of 70,000 refrigerators in Tennessee, Georgia, and Alabama, and then worked to convince poor farmers to expand their purchases of electric ranges and ovens, farm motors, water heaters, water pumps, milk coolers, cream separators, electric irons, milking machines, attic fans, radios, space heaters, and heavy load-bearing machinery. By the end of 1934 the EHFA had secured the cooperation of 41 electric utilities in 10 states, 70 appliance manufacturers, and 409 retail stores. The EHFA contracted with utilities willing to keep electric rates below 3 cents per kilowatt hour in urban areas and 4 cents in rural areas. The more energy consumed, the lower the rate. Manufacturers wanting to participate in the program had to produce standard-issue, low-price appliances inspected by an independent consumer group. Once a particular model had been approved by the EHFA, retailers advertised it with an EHFA seal. Consumers selected an appliance and signed an installment contract with a 5 percent down payment and a 5 percent interest rate. The EHFA either paid the dealer 90 percent of the price of the appliance or guaranteed a loan from a finance company. If the appliance worked efficiently after installation, the EHFA paid the remaining 10 percent. The participating utility collected the payment, usually no more than two to three dollars a month, with its monthly electric bill.[34]

[33] W. A. Sutherland to Marvin McIntyre, December 18, 1933; Jesse Jones to Franklin D. Roosevelt, December 16, 1933; Stanley Reed to Angus MacLean, December 16, 1933; Homer Cummings to Franklin D. Roosevelt, December 18, 1933, all in FDRPL, OF 42-B, EHFA.
[34] *Annual Report of the Electric Home and Farm Authority for 1934*

Throughout the rest of the 1930s, the Electric Home and Farm Authority expanded rapidly, increasing employment, business profits, and consumer comfort. With loans averaging about $150, the EHFA expanded from ten states in 1935 to thirty-seven states in 1941. The number of participating utilities went from only 41 in 1935 to 657 in 1941; appliance manufacturers from 70 to 428; and retail dealers from 409 to 3,824. Between 1935 and 1941, the EHFA purchased more than 255,000 installment contracts from finance companies, with a face value of more than $51 million. When it was discontinued in 1942 because of wartime electricity shortages, the EHFA had helped in the manufacture and sale of more than a million electric appliances. Few other New Deal programs worked as well.[35]

The other RFC success story in direct lending was the Commodity Credit Corporation. Rural banks, faced with collapsing commodity prices and defaulting farm and equipment loans, had been liquidating farm loans just as urban banks had been reducing industrial loans. Farmers unable to secure loans to finance production, refinance mortgages, or store commodities had to sell their crops after harvest in glutted markets at depressed prices. When RFC loans to rural bankers failed to inspire an expansion in farm credit, Hoover inserted into the Emergency Relief and Construction Act of July 1932 authority for the RFC to make loans for the "orderly marketing of farm products." The RFC could loan money to banks, agricultural credit corporations, and livestock loan companies, which would then reloan the money to individual farmers. As security for the loans, farmers pledged a lien on their warehoused crops. Farmers could then hold their crops off the market until

---

(Washington, D.C., 1935), pp. 1–10; David Lilienthal to Franklin D. Roosevelt, July 26, 1935, and Morris Cooke to Franklin D. Roosevelt, July 31, 1935, FDRPL, OF 42-B, EHFA; Electric Home and Farm Authority, *Annual Report for 1935* (Washington, D.C., 1936), pp. 1–9.

[35] See the unpublished annual reports of the Electric Home and Farm Authority, FDRPL, OF 42-B, EHFA; Jesse Jones to Franklin D. Roosevelt, September 16, 1941, and Harold Smith to Franklin D. Roosevelt, October 3, 1942, FDRPL, OF 42-B, EHFA; "Liquidation and Final Transfer of the Electric Home and Farm Authority to the Reconstruction Finance Corporation," October 31, 1942, NA, RG 234, RFC, EHFA, Box 183.

prices had risen above seasonal lows. For the first time the RFC was willing to allow commodities to serve as collateral.[36]

The program was stillborn. Rural banks refused to participate. RFC interest rates on agricultural loans were as high as 7 percent, exorbitant for the 1930s. Bankers feared that the crops they accepted as collateral would not maintain their value, and since the RFC did not guarantee the loans under the program, they refused to carry the entire burden of risk. Hoover was so frustrated he began hinting at direct government loans. With or without the cooperation of private banks, farmers had to be able to carry their crops through seasonally low prices. But under Hoover the RFC loaned only $1.5 million on commodities. More had to be done.[37]

In the fall of 1933, when the Roosevelt administration was seriously considering direct lending by the RFC, farm marketing loans became a primary consideration. The cotton crop in 1933 was enormous, and Secretary of Agriculture Henry Wallace's order that farmers "plow under every third row" as a means of reducing the surplus was having little effect. Senator Oscar Johnson of Mississippi got Roosevelt to agree to have the federal government loan 10 cents a pound on cotton, even though the prevailing market price was only 9 cents. Corn was selling in the Midwest at between 15 and 25 cents a bushel, not enough to meet production costs, and farmers were not even bothering to harvest the crop. George Peek, head of the Agricultural Adjustment Administration, wanted the government to loan on corn at 45 cents a bushel. Roosevelt agreed, and on October 16, 1933, he signed Executive Order 6340 creating the Commodity Credit Corporation as an RFC subsidiary.

It replaced the private institutions the RFC had worked with in 1932 and 1933. The RFC loaned money to the Commodity Credit Corporation, which then reloaned it to bankers, businessmen, and farmers. The new corporation assumed fiscal re-

[36] Olson, *Herbert Hoover and the Reconstruction Finance Corporation*, p. 90.

[37] RFC, *Quarterly Report for April 1 to June 30, 1933*, pp. 4–5; RFC, *Quarterly Report for October 1 to December 31, 1933* (Washington, D.C., 1934), pp. 6–8.

sponsibility for the $1.5 million the RFC had loaned under the old program, and the Agricultural Credit Division of the RFC was in charge of funding the Commodity Credit Corporation. Anxious to keep the Commodity Credit Corporation under his control, Jesse Jones nominated Lynn Talley to become general manager of the CCC. A Dallas and Houston banker, Talley had known Jesse Jones since 1910, served as governor of the Federal Reserve Bank of Dallas, and at Jones's suggestion became chairman of the Bank of America during its financial crisis in 1932. He came to Washington with Jones in 1932 to serve as special counsel to the RFC, and his loyalty to Jones was unwavering. John Goodloe, a Kentucky attorney and member of the RFC Legal Division, became vice president of the Commodity Credit Corporation. The board consisted of Talley, Henry Wallace, Henry Morgenthau, and Herman Oliphant of the Farm Credit Administration, George Peek, Stanley Reed, and three RFC directors. With $3 million in operating funds from the Department of Agriculture and a credit line of up to $250 million with the RFC, the Commodity Credit Corporation was under way late in October.[38]

It was deluged with requests for money. To maintain normal credit channels, Talley promised private bankers he would purchase all their paper on demand. When banks refused to make loans, the Commodity Credit Corporation would loan directly. Its program was simple. Farmers would borrow money using their crop as collateral. If prices rose higher than the value of the collateral, they could sell the crop and repay the loan. If prices sagged, the Commodity Credit Corporation stored the crop until more favorable prices had appeared. Jesse

[38] RFC, *Quarterly Report for January 1 to March 31, 1933*, pp. 5–10; U.S. Congress, House, *Document No. 449. Summary of the Activities of the Commodity Credit Corporation through June 30, 1939*, 76th Cong., 1st Sess., 1939, pp. 1–2; Jesse Jones to Franklin D. Roosevelt, October 16, 1933, FDRPL, OF 643, RFC; Jerome Frank, COHR, pp. 40–42, 129, and 155; Rexford Tugwell, COHR, pp. 50–51; Executive Order No. 6340, "Authorizing the Formation of a Corporation to be Known as the Commodity Credit Corporation," FDRPL, OF 736, Commodity Credit Corporation; Franklin D. Roosevelt to Jesse Jones, November 7, 1933, FDRPL, OF 643, RFC.

Jones was convinced the program would cost the government little, if any, money in the long run because banks would find the loans profitable and would sell very few of them to the government.[39]

Jones was right and wrong. The Commodity Credit Corporation eventually sustained only $26 million in losses, but bankers sold their loans rather than carrying them on their own. At first, Roosevelt and Jones saw cotton farmers as the major borrowers from the CCC, and between 1933 and 1935 the Corporation made more than $310 million in cotton loans. It paid 10 cents a pound in 1933, and up to 11 cents a pound in 1934 and 1935 for a high-grade crop. But the need for credit existed throughout the farm belt, and more than $125 million went to corn farmers. Eventually, the CCC made loans on wheat, turpentine, rosin, figs, peanuts, raisins, butter, dates, wool, tobacco, prunes, cowhides, calfskins, sheep pelts, and mohair. Early in 1936 it had made nearly $600 million in loans.[40] Because of the demand, CCC capital was increased from $3 million to $100 million in 1936, with the RFC making the subscription. Its borrowing power eventually reached $900 million by 1939. The Commodity Credit Corporation charged 4 percent for its loans until 1939 when the rate was reduced to 3 percent.[41]

Demands on the Commodity Credit Corporation were not

[39] Jesse Jones to Franklin D. Roosevelt, October 16, 1933, FDRPL, OF 643, RFC; John D. Goodloe to Henry Steagall, March 13, 1935, NA, RG 234, RFC, White House Correspondence; RFC, *Press Release No. 880*, October 6, 1933, NA, RG 234, RFC, Secretarial Division.

[40] Henry A. Wallace to Rudolph Forster, October 17, 1933; Henry A. Wallace and George Peek to Franklin D. Roosevelt, October 19 and October 24, 1933; Henry A. Wallace to Chester Davis, June 30, 1934; Henry Wallace to Franklin D. Roosevelt, July 28, 1934; Daniel W. Bell to Franklin D. Roosevelt, April 4, 1938; Jesse Jones to Franklin D. Roosevelt, August 21, 1934, and August 7, 1935, all in FDRPL, OF 736, Commodity Credit Corporation.

[41] Jesse Jones to Franklin D. Roosevelt, January 25, 1936, and September 8, 1937, NA, RG 234, RFC, White House Correspondence; U.S. Congress, Senate, *Hearings on S. 1084. A Bill to Continue the Functions of the Commodity Credit Corporation and Export-Import Bank of Washington*, 76th Cong., 1st Sess., 1939, p. 22; *Report of the President of the Commodity Credit Corporation, 1940* (Washington, D.C., 1940), p. 3.

constant. On the 1935 cotton crop, for example, the agency loaned 10 cents a pound, but the next winter cotton was selling at 12 cents a pound, and farmers sold the crop and liquidated their loans. The CCC loaned 55 cents a bushel on 1934 corn and 45 cents on 1935 corn, and the disastrous drought of 1936 severely reduced the surplus and bailed the government out. The Commodity Credit Corporation, however, was unable to dispose of its entire crop each year, and its holdings of corn and especially cotton grew rapidly and threatened to become permanent. Jones and Talley hoped each year that a rising price would allow the government to get rid of its collateral, but when the 1937 crop came in at a whopping 19 million bales, all hopes were dashed. The CCC was here to stay. With the passage of the Agricultural Adjustment Act of 1938, the Commodity Credit Corporation became the major vehicle of Secretary of Agriculture Henry Wallace's "ever-normal granary." Government purchases of surplus crops in bumper years helped maintain price levels, and sales of stored crops in lean years kept farmers liquid and consumers happy.[42] When it was transferred as a permanent agency to the Department of Agriculture in 1939, the CCC had loaned more than $1.5 billion to more than four million farmers, on 16,674,000 bales of cotton, 897,776,000 bushels of corn, 253,391,000 bushels of wheat, and 253,249,000 pounds of tobacco, filling a void in the money markets which had existed for more than a half century.[43]

The success of the Electric Home and Farm Authority and the Commodity Credit Corporation encouraged Jesse Jones and Hugh Johnson in their conviction that demand for business credit was widespread. They were convinced even though the RFC's industrial loans through new mortgage loan companies had failed. Government loan guarantees had permitted

[42] Jones, *Fifty Billion Dollars*, pp. 89–104.

[43] Henry Morgenthau Diaries, June 22, 1939, Morgenthau Papers; U.S. Congress, House, *Document No. 449. Summary of the Activities of the Commodity Credit Corporation through June 30, 1939*, 76th Cong., 1st Sess., 1939, pp. 1–2; Jesse Jones to Franklin D. Roosevelt, July 1, 1939, FDRPL, OF 736, Commodity Credit Corporation.

thousands of banks and finance companies to participate in appliance and crop marketing loans, helping the Tennessee Valley Authority and the Agricultural Adjustment Administration achieve their objectives. The NRA needed the same assistance. Early in 1934 the administration began a campaign to boost industrial credit. The results were the Export-Import Bank of Washington and the RFC direct loan legislation of June 1934.

The collapse of foreign trade was important to New Dealers like Secretary of State Cordell Hull, who believed the end of the depression and the revival of international commerce went hand in hand. Convinced that restrictive trade policies, symbolized by the Hawley-Smoot Tariff of 1930, had precipitated a decline in exports and quickened the collapse of the economy, Hull launched a crusade in 1933 to reform tariff policy. Between 1929 and 1932 American exports had fallen by nearly a third, and Hull's bill called for bilateral trade agreements based on the reciprocal reduction of tariff rates. The act passed the House in March 1934 and the Senate in June. The Reciprocal Trade Agreements Act authorized the president to make mutual trade agreements with other nations without specific congressional approval and to raise or lower tariff rates in these agreements by up to 50 percent of the levels of the Hawley-Smoot Tariff.[44]

But for New Dealers like Jesse Jones, Hugh Johnson, Adolf Berle, Rexford Tugwell, and Cordell Hull, the chances of success for the Reciprocal Trade Agreements Act rested just as tenuously as those of the NRA on the fickle problem of industrial credit—whether or not American firms could acquire working capital to finance sales abroad. Since banks were unwilling to make loans for domestic production and commerce, the chances of them behaving otherwise for international business seemed slim indeed. The Electric Home and Farm Authority and Commodity Credit Corporation had helped hundreds of thousands of consumers and farmers, and the

[44] See James C. Pearson, *The Reciprocal Trade Agreements Program. The Policy of the United States and Its Effectiveness* (New York, 1942).

administration assumed that a new government corporation could do the same for international trade. That assumption became the Export-Import Bank of Washington.

Although protective tariff policies in the 1920s had damaged foreign trade, there had also been dramatic shifts in financing international commerce, and the Great Depression had caused more trouble. Before World War I a dozen New York firms had handled the bulk of American consumer exports. American manufacturers sold their goods to exporting firms which then retailed them abroad. Manufacturers had a difficult time acquiring reliable credit information about prospective buyers and preferred to let the export firms take the risk. But after World War I, when American goods flooded world markets, exporting firms declined in significance and banks took over, establishing offices in foreign countries and supplying manufacturers with sound credit information. Manufacturers began dealing directly with foreign buyers, using working capital supplied by American banks. Banks effectively took over for the old exporting firms. Credit risks declined because reliable information existed, and payments were facilitated by bank exchange and discount facilities.[45]

But by early in the 1930s commercial credit for manufacturers selling in foreign markets dried up, just as it had for domestic businesses. American traders began calling for long-term government credit to businesses dealing in foreign markets, particularly since so many foreign governments spared little effort subsidizing their own companies doing business with the United States. The gross unwillingness of American banks, they argued, to make export loans or underwrite equity issues put American manufacturers at a serious disadvantage. Some form of government insurance or direct lending was absolutely necessary.[46]

[45] William S. Shaterian, *Export-Import Banking* (New York, 1956), pp. 3–7.

[46] Stella Margold, *Export Credit Insurance in Europe Today* (Washington, D.C., 1934), pp. 47–49. Also see the speech by Charles E. Stuart to the Export Managers Club of New York, August 21, 1934, FDRPL, OF 971, Export-Import Bank.

The Hoover administration had gingerly approached the problem in 1932 when the Emergency Relief and Construction Act authorized the RFC to make loans to finance farm exports. Work began on an RFC loan to the North Pacific Grain Growers Association to finance a $50 million wheat sale to China and another one to the Soviet Union for cotton sales. Although the loans were not consummated before Hoover left office, the RFC had at least made a tentative beginning, picking up where the War Finance Corporation had left off. During the spring of 1933 Jesse Jones tried to complete the Soviet loan, with the Anderson Clayton & Company borrowing money from the RFC using notes from the Amtorg Trading Company, a Soviet government bank, as collateral. The RFC also loaned $4.5 million in 1933 to other commodities exporters. By that time, however, faith in solving the agricultural problem through marketing schemes had given way to the surplus reduction programs of the AAA. The idea of stimulating employment through increases in foreign trade, however, was alive and well.[47]

The Export-Import Bank originated in Roosevelt's conviction that the nonrecognition policy toward the Soviet Union was useless. The Soviets were potential allies against the Germans and Japanese as well as a lucrative market for surplus American goods. He extended diplomatic recognition to the Soviet Union in November 1933, making increased trade between the two countries much simpler. On February 2, 1934, Roosevelt issued Executive Order No. 6581 establishing the Export-Import Bank of Washington to finance trade with the Soviet Union. Soviet defaults on her World War I loans from the United States complicated trade negotiations, as did religious difficulties. Secretary of State Cordell Hull worried about religious persecution in the Soviet Union and how diplomatic recognition and increased trade would go down in the Bible Belt, but he was also interested in the success of his pend-

[47] RFC, *Quarterly Report for July 1 to September, 1933*, pp. 1–6; Jesse Jones to Franklin D. Roosevelt, June 24, 1933, FDRPL, OF 220-A, Russia. See the RFC's December 8, 1932, press release, HHPL, PP, SF, RFC, Box 232.

ing Reciprocal Trade Agreements Act, and he went along with the president.[48]

The RFC also continued to work on the Chinese loan. Henry Morgenthau, then head of the Farm Credit Administration, was siding with George Peek in opposing the AAA commitment to crop reduction, and he decided to push the Chinese loan as a means of raising cotton prices. Morgenthau believed the loan would bring an extra $100 million to cotton farmers. The State Department opposed the loan because it might offend Japan and because the Chinese were already using custom receipts to pay current expenses and had little likelihood of being able to repay it. Anxious to stimulate foreign trade, however, the president approved the loan. The RFC extended $50 million to the Chinese government to buy the cotton, but they ended up using only a tiny part of the money.[49]

Early in March 1934 Cuba requested help in purchasing and minting silver coin, a demand silver inflationists in the South and Midwest found particularly appealing, and Roosevelt established the Second Export-Import Bank of Washington to supervise the transaction.[50] As more inquiries about the extension of government export credits came into Congress and the White House, Roosevelt considered establishing a variety of banks specializing in particular countries, but eventually he had the Second Export-Import Bank expand its activities and finance trade with any nation, including Cuba. The first bank was then confined to Soviet trade. Eventually negotiations with the Soviets foundered over the debt question. Convinced World War I was a capitalist war, the Soviet Union refused to

[48] Blum, *From the Morgenthau Diaries*, vol. I, pp. 54–57; RFC, "Transcripts of Board Notes," February 24, 1933, NA, RG 234, RFC, Secretarial Division; "RFC Aids Foreign Trade," *Business Week*, February 10, 1934, pp. 6–7; *New York Times*, June 14, 1933.

[49] Blum, *From the Morgenthau Diaries*, vol. I, pp. 51–56; *New York Times*, June 5 and 25, September 7, 20, and 21, and December 20, 1933.

[50] RFC, "Transcripts of Board Notes," February 24, 1933, NA, RG 234, RFC, Secretarial Division; Hawthorne Arey, *History of the Export-Import Bank of Washington* (Washington, D.C., 1953), p. 4; RFC, *Press Release No. 979* (Washington, D.C., 1934), p. 1; RFC, Minutes, 18 (July 10, 1933), 473; Homer Cummings to Franklin D. Roosevelt, March 6, 1934, FDRPL, OF 643, RFC.

honor its debts, and the whole issue became politically too touchy for Roosevelt. Although the Soviet debt to the United States exceeded $200 million, they were willing to pay only $50 million in a settlement. The negotiations then broke down permanently. In 1935 the administration liquidated the Second Bank and transferred its obligations and responsibilities to the Export-Import Bank of Washington. In March 1934, Congress gave the executive orders creating the Export-Import Bank legislative authority.[51]

The bank's board of directors consisted of Secretary of State Cordell Hull, Secretary of Commerce Daniel Roper, and Jesse Jones. George Peek, already tired of his tenure at the AAA and still convinced that exporting surpluses was the solution to the farm crisis, took over the presidency of the EIB. The National Recovery Administration gave it $1 million in initial capital, and the RFC subscribed to $10 million in its preferred stock. Although its main objective was to increase domestic employment through supplying credit to exporters, the bank also wanted to assist banks in increasing their export loans. Having no intention of competing with commercial banks, the Export-Import Bank at first would not consider making short-term credit to borrowers. Peek and Jones believed private lenders would meet that need and the bank would be called upon to furnish only intermediate and long-term credit.[52]

To maintain normal credit channels and help banks make more loans, the EIB established cooperative arrangements with private institutions, as the RFC had done with the Electric

[51] Franklin Roosevelt to Jesse Jones, March 4, 1934, NA, RG 234, RFC, White House Correspondence; *New York Times*, May 8, 1934; RFC, *Press Release No. 1269* (Washington, D.C., 1936), p. 1; U.S. Congress, Senate, Committee on Banking and Currency, *Report No. 529. Financing of Exports and Imports by the R.F.C.*, 73d Cong., 2d Sess., 1934, p. 1; Louis Howe to Cordell Hull, July 31, 1934, and Marvin McIntyre to Franklin D. Roosevelt, July 20, 1934, FDRPL, OF 971, Export-Import Bank.

[52] See the unpublished memorandum on the Export-Import Bank board of directors, February 2, 1934, and Jesse Jones to Franklin D. Roosevelt, February 18, 1934, FDRPL, OF 643, RFC; "General Policy Statement of the Second Export-Import Bank of Washington," July 2, 1934, FDRPL, OF 971, Second Export-Import Bank of Washington.

Home and Farm Authority, the Commodity Credit Corporation, and the mortgage company loan program. Exporters applied directly to the government bank or to any commercial bank. Interest rates averaged 5 percent. An advisory committee of the American Bankers' Association counseled banks on how to work with the EIB. George Peek believed the most critical issue was to help banks resume export loans, a concern Hugh Johnson and Jesse Jones had about banks and the NRA.[53] Finally, the EIB was prepared to join commercial banks in making loans, selling its loans to them, or purchasing participations with them. Banks had to be convinced that export loans could be made with safety and reliability. The EIB could then retire from business.[54]

Peek's stay at the Export-Import Bank was shortlived. He hated the AAA acreage reduction program, could not stand Henry Wallace's domination of New Deal farm policy, and resented the president's unwillingness to do more about exporting farm surpluses. He left the administration in 1936 and endorsed Republican Alf Landon for president. By that time Jesse Jones had replaced Peek at the Export-Import Bank with Warren Lee Pierson, a California lawyer, former special counsel with the RFC, and current general counsel of the EIB. With that appointment, Jones had effective control over the bank. The RFC was firmly in charge.[55]

The administration then turned its attention to direct RFC business loans. Disillusionment with the mortgage loan program was serious at the end of 1933. Roosevelt thought banks were "bursting with money" but refusing to employ it, preferring instead to accumulate excess reserves.[56] Since businesses

[53] See the speech of George Peek to the National Foreign Trade Convention, November 2, 1934, FDRPL, OF 971, Export-Import Bank.

[54] George Peek to Franklin D. Roosevelt, December 31, 1934, FDRPL, OF 971, Export-Import Bank; James B. Alley to Henry Steagall, January 14, 1937, NA, RG 234, RFC, Records of the RFC Mortgage Company.

[55] Jones, *Fifty Billion Dollars*, pp. 214–16; George Peek to Franklin D. Roosevelt, December 31, 1934, FDRPL, OF 971, Export-Import Bank.

[56] Franklin D. Roosevelt to Paul V. Betters, December 18, 1933, FDRPL, OF 706, Credit; *New York Times*, December 18, 1933.

desperately needed credit, the only solution was government intervention, a proposal which New Deal planners like Adolf Berle, Hugh Johnson, Daniel Roper, and Rexford Tugwell had been advocating all along. Jones did not share their faith in a government credit agency directing the flow of capital throughout the economy, but he was ready to provide government loans to any legitimate business unable to secure it from private sources. In a speech to the New York Bankers' Association on February 5, 1934, he made the administration position quite clear:

> Insofar as the RFC is concerned, and President Roosevelt, the government has, and has had, only two objects in view of its preferred stock program. One to strengthen the banks in the interests of depositors, and the other to place banks in such a strong capital position as to enable them to assist in the recovery program by providing legitimate credit for agriculture, business, and industry.
>
> There is no thought of dictating management or of coercion as to bank policies or bank investments. I would be less than frank, however, if I did not say that the President would be greatly disappointed if the banks do not assume their full share in the recovery program. . . .
>
> The common cry everywhere is that the banks are not lending. We get it on every side. Your representatives in Congress continually get it, and there is a persistent demand on them to authorize the RFC to make direct loans. Unless deserving borrowers can get credit at the banks, we need not be surprised if Congress yields to this pressure. . . . if the banker fails to grasp his opportunity and to meet his responsibility, there can be but one alternative—government lending.[57]

The speech was vintage Jesse Jones, an attempt to walk the tightrope between the private business community and the grandiose dreams of the New Deal planners.

[57] Jesse Jones speech to the New York State Bankers' Association, February 5, 1934, FDRPL, OF 643, RFC.

During the winter and spring of 1934, several bills providing direct government loans surfaced in Congress. Adolf Berle had been advocating creation of federal "capital credit" banks to loan venture capital to new businesses with good earnings potential. In the economic atmosphere of the early 1930s, those firms were the most strapped for working capital. Banks were paranoid about loan expansion, and the thought of channeling money to experimental or growth industries was unthinkable. Although New Deal planners saw the proposal as an important step toward government control of the capital markets, the idea had little support in Congress or in the rest of the administration. Along with Governor Eugene Black of the Federal Reserve Board, Berle also proposed a system of twelve Intermediate Credit Banks to discount commercial paper and make direct loans of up to five years to industry. Berle also wanted the ICBs to underwrite securities issues, a move designed to shore up the defunct capital markets. Berle and Black initially envisioned a capital stock of $140 million for the banks. The Federal Reserve Board would supervise the banks.[58]

In the National Recovery Administration Hugh Johnson and W. E. Dunn, RFC-NRA liaison officer, were pushing a more ambitious proposal. Both felt the long-term capital markets were dead and government credit had to fill the gap. They wanted an intermediate government credit corporation—supervised by staff members from the RFC, Treasury, and Federal Reserve Board—to purchase marketable securities. With $50 million in capital from the RFC, the new corporation would issue up to $1 billion in preferred stock. Berle estimated that more than $1.2 billion in first-class corporate securities and $500 million in municipal securities would come due in the next year and fail to be refunded, destroying what was left of the bond market. RFC efforts to redeem municipal and railroad

---

[58] Hawley, *The New Deal and the Problem of Monopoly*, pp. 321-22; Adolf A. Berle, "A Banking System for Capital and Capital Credit," Report to the Temporary National Economic Committee, NA, RG 234, RFC, Legislative File; Schlesinger, *The Coming of the New Deal*, pp. 432–33; Discussion Notes, February 21, 1934, Harrison Papers.

bonds were only the tip of the iceberg. More dramatic government intervention was necessary.[59]

Jesse Jones was skeptical of both proposals. He wanted the RFC to fill in temporarily for banks when legitimate businesses could not get working capital, but the idea of risking RFC money on venture enterprises was beyond anything he had envisioned. Jones had no philosophical problems with state capitalism as long as it wasn't bad capitalism. He also harbored serious doubts about having a huge government corporation take over the capital markets, and it would be even worse if that agency was not the RFC. Jones realized that the RFC's mortgage loan program had been a cumbersome failure. By the end of February 1934 the RFC had made only $7.2 million in loans under the program. He remained willing to continue loaning under that program, but he also began to advocate a more extensive RFC program. By February 1934 he was calling for legislation to permit the RFC to make loans with up to ten-year maturities. Jones was willing to cooperate with the Federal Reserve in making the loans, if necessary.[60] Senator Carter Glass wanted nothing to do with any of the proposals. The collapse of the banking system in 1933 and rise of the RFC and the FDIC had displaced, in his mind, the prestige of the Federal Reserve system, and Glass was determined to make sure that new federal credit programs did not bypass the FRS. Both the Emergency Relief and Construction Act of 1932 and the Industrial Advances Act of 1934 permitted banks to discount business loans with Federal Reserve banks, but little had come of the effort, primarily because only fully secured commercial paper with ninety-day maturities or less was eligible. Glass proposed a bill which permitted Federal Reserve banks to loan up to $278 million to established commercial businesses, either directly or through bank participations. He preferred having

---

[59] W. E. Dunn, "Plan to Expand Credit for Trade and Recovery," unpublished manuscript, FDRPL, Henderson Papers, Credit, Box 4; R. H. Lansburgh to Leon Henderson, March 9, 1934, Henderson Papers.

[60] Jesse Jones to Franklin D. Roosevelt, March 18, 1934, FDRPL, OF 643, RFC; Discussion Notes, February 1, 1934, Harrison Papers; *New York Times*, March 7, 17, and 23, 1934.

Federal Reserve banks make the loans because he felt the administrative machinery was already in place, preventing duplication and preserving FRS prerogatives in the banking field.[61]

Only the RFC and Glass bills survived in Congress. The Dunn and Johnson proposal for a large-scale government agency to buy maturing corporate and municipal securities did not make it to committee. By the spring of 1934 the NRA was turning into a bureaucratic nightmare and Hugh Johnson into a political liability. Both were being assailed from all sides: southern Democrats hated the bureaucratic power it represented; progressive Republicans viewed it as a monopolistic opportunity for big business to exploit small businesses; labor leaders resented its inability to enforce Section 7(a); many economists thought its production controls were retarding recovery by suppressing employment; and small businessmen across the country claimed they could not compete against code-protected industries. In that political atmosphere plans for providing credit to the business community raised more than a little skepticism. Johnson's days were numbered. Although his resignation did not come until September 1934, his influence in the New Deal was over.[62]

The Dunn and Johnson proposal for a massive industrial credit agency to buy corporate and municipal securities did not have a prayer. Criticism of the NRA had become so intense that Roosevelt issued Executive Order No. 6632 on March 7, 1934, establishing a National Recovery Review Board to investigate charges of monopolistic domination of the NRA codes and discrimination against small business. Clarence Darrow, the outspoken attorney from Chicago, headed the board and reported directly to Roosevelt. Its hearings began on March 15 and lasted throughout the spring. Although the hearings were highly selective and the board's report statistically weak, the press widely disseminated its conclusion that NRA codes reinforced monopoly and squeezed out small business. Darrow

---

[61] W. E. Dunn to Leon Henderson, April 7, 1934, FDRPL, Henderson Papers, Credit, Box 4; *New York Times*, March 7 and April 29, 1934.

[62] Bellush, *The Failure of the NRA*, pp. 136–58.

even wrote a minority opinion that the only real answer to the depression was a planned economy with government owner-ship of the major economic units. Any plans for a government bailout of corporate securities died with the report of the National Recovery Review Board.[63]

The other industrial credit bills enjoyed the open approval of President Roosevelt. He assured Eugene Black he wanted the twelve Intermediate Credit banks; supported Senator Glass's Federal Reserve bill; and backed Jesse Jones's plan for RFC loans.[64] The Black bill for the Intermediate Credit banks did not survive Glass's knife on the Senate Banking and Currency Committee. He found the idea questionable at best, not only because it duplicated existing proposals for the RFC and Federal Reserve banks but because he feared such a bill might permanently dry up the capital markets. Roosevelt saw the writing on the wall and realized his political commitment to Glass and Jones was more compelling than his need to support a proposal of Eugene Black and Adolf Berle. By April 1934 the Banking and Currency Committee had killed the proposal.[65]

Only the Glass bill for the Federal Reserve and the RFC measure survived, and both had enemies in and out of the administration. The Wall Street banking crowd, already upset about the Securities Act of 1933 and mounting federal deficits, argued that the bill permitting the RFC to make long-term loans would be disastrous for the capital markets, postponing for years any revival of private funding of new securities issues. People like Eugene Meyer, George Harrison, and James Warburg argued that in the hands of Jesse Jones such authority would only further strip Wall Street of its former powers. Budget Director Lewis Douglas was convinced that Jones would use direct lending to socialize American industry. Even

[63] Hawley, *The New Deal and the Problem of Monopoly*, pp. 95–97.

[64] *New York Times*, March 23 and April 15, 1934; Jesse Jones to Duncan Fletcher, March 21, 1934, NA, RG 234, RFC, White House Correspondence; Frederic Taber Diary, March 19, 1934, Taber Papers; Jesse Jones to Duncan Fletcher, May 7, 1934, FDRPL, OF 64, RFC.

[65] *New York Times*, April 29, 1934; Frederic Taber Diary, March 1, 1934, Taber Papers.

if that did not come about, the very presence of such powers in the RFC would demoralize business confidence and abort any economic recovery.[66]

Marriner Eccles criticized direct RFC and Federal Reserve business loans on different grounds. He had no fears of socialism or the destruction of the private capital markets. Eccles was simply convinced the loans would do no good at all. A Utah banker who had built a family business into a financial empire which survived the liquidity crisis of the 1920s and early 1930s, Eccles testified before the Senate Finance Committee in February 1933, arguing that the depression stemmed from underconsumption and lagging private investment. He strongly advocated increases in consumer purchasing power led by federal spending as a way to stimulate more private investment. When Henry Morgenthau became acting secretary of the treasury in late 1933, he persuaded Eccles to come to Washington as his special assistant on monetary and credit matters. During the deliberations over the RFC direct loan bill, Eccles argued that the administration was misinterpreting the real problem in the economy. He agreed with bankers that credit shortages were not crippling the economy. Banks were accumulating excess reserves at the Federal Reserve and corporations were building huge cash deposits because there was so little consumer purchasing power in the economy. Even hundreds of millions of dollars in RFC and Federal Reserve credit would not address the real problem. No monetary or credit manipulations would. Although he had little influence at the time, Eccles's point of view would become more and more compelling in years to come, especially after his appointment as head of the Federal Reserve Board in 1935.[67]

Opponents had little power. Roosevelt and Jones delighted in Wall Street opposition to RFC power, and Douglas's days in

---

[66] Discussion Notes, February 1, 1934, Harrison Papers; Frederic Taber Diary, March 2, 1934, Taber Papers.

[67] Frederic Taber Diary, March 2, 1934, Taber Papers; Marriner S. Eccles, *Beckoning Frontiers* (New York, 1951), pp. 71, 118–19, 160, 260; U.S. Congress, House, Committee on Banking and Currency, *Hearings on H.R. 5357. Banking Act of 1935*, 74th Cong., 1st Sess., 1935, p. 377.

the administration were numbered. Roosevelt found him ideologically rock-ribbed and inflexible. As for Eccles, his star in
the New Deal had not risen yet. The idea of direct government
loans was still central to the work of the NRA, and some form
of government credit was inevitable. The only question was
whether the Federal Reserve banks or the RFC would run the
program. Late in April Glass managed to have the RFC measure defeated by a seven to five vote in the Banking and Currency Committee, but Jesse Jones launched a personal campaign for the measure. He claimed the Glass bill would come
nowhere near filling the demand and that the Federal Reserve
banks, at least given their recent track record, would not be
very enthusiastic about making working capital loans anyway.
In March the RFC had surveyed nearly 5,000 banks and more
than 1,000 chambers of commerce across the country and decided that full funding of the NRA potential would require
more than $700 million in direct loans. The Glass bill limited
the Federal Reserve banks to $278 million. Jones had Thomas
Corcoran working the halls of the Senate and the House intensely during late April, and Senator Alben Barkley agreed to
sponsor the measure. He got the bill restored to the Senate cal-
endar, and early in May the RFC bill gained momentum in Congress with a provision for $250 million in direct loan money.
Because of the political atmosphere created by the report of the
National Recovery Review Board, the RFC bill was scaled
down from its original authority to make ten-year loans of up
to $1 million to a maximum of five-year loans for no more
than $500,000. During the second week of May, the Glass and
Barkley bills were combined into a single measure providing
for $580 million, $280 million for the Federal Reserve banks
and $300 million for the RFC, in direct loans for working cap-
ital—not for equity, fixed capital, or previous indebtedness.
The new authority superceded the original mortgage loan
company. Congress passed the bill and Roosevelt signed it on
June 21, 1934.[68]

[68] *New York Times*, April 29, May 1, 3, 5, 8, and 15, 1934; Franklin D.
Roosevelt to Duncan Fletcher, March 19, 1934, NA, RG 234, RFC, White

The RFC bill was a perfect symbol of the state of the New Deal in the spring of 1934. The conservative financial community—represented by consistent opposition to relief spending, deficits, gold buying, and direct business loans by people like George Harrison, Lewis Douglas, and James Warburg—had little influence in the administration, but the comprehensive dreams of economic planners like Adolf Berle, Rexford Tugwell, and Hugh Johnson were also coming on hard times. Disillusionment with the NRA was mounting, as were the demands of antitrusters out to rescue small business from disaster. The spending schemes of Marriner Eccles, John Maynard Keynes, Alvin Hansen, and Lauchlin Currie were still on the horizon, political expedients to provide unemployment relief rather than economic policies designed to stimulate a recovery. The RFC was charting a conservative, albeit middle course, hoping that its long-held dream of reviving commercial credit through state capitalism would bring the elusive recovery.

House Correspondence; Jesse Jones to Franklin D. Roosevelt, March 18, 1934, and Jesse Jones to Duncan Fletcher, April 30, 1934, FDRPL, OF 643, RFC.

Decline

BY THE SUMMER of 1934 the New Deal credit establishment was firmly in place. The Electric Home and Farm Authority and Commodity Credit Corporation were making
large volumes of loans to farmers, consumers, and financial institutions. Using their success as a model, the RFC appeared
ready to stimulate and if necessary provide the working capital
business needed to assist the National Recovery Administration. The preferred stock program was investing more than $1
billion into banks and trust companies so they could begin
making loans again. The Export-Import Bank was ready to
help finance the foreign sales of American manufactured products. Finally, a series of federal bankruptcy laws had made
debt reorganization substantially easier.

Jesse Jones, however, was no Adolf Berle or Rexford Tugwell; his vision of state capitalism was much more limited. Although he was comfortable with massive volumes of RFC
loans, Jones had no intention of giving the government control
over the flow of investment and working capital. Instead, he
firmly believed that the RFC and Export-Import Bank would
revive commercial lending through cooperative arrangements
with private banks, and that RFC business loans would be
shortlived once banks saw how easy and safe they were. The
RFC established cooperative arrangements with banks in the
direct lending program, agreed to purchase participations with
banks up to 80 percent of the loan or up to 90 percent for immediate participations, and sell its own loans to banks. To undertake a direct loan program without including private banks
was more in line with what Berle and Tugwell envisioned.
Jones took a far narrower approach. Instead of converting the
RFC into a huge commercial bank, Jones wanted to encourage
an expansion of private loans as a prerequisite for NRA success.
For a few weeks after the legislation authorizing direct RFC or

Federal Reserve Bank loans, the administration contemplated having the RFC pick up only those loans which Federal Reserve banks had rejected, but Jones would have none of it. He was convinced the RFC would get stuck with bad commercial paper.[1]

To prevent being swamped with applications, Jones established strict requirements for RFC loans. Participating businesses had to be "Blue Eagle" members of an approved NRA code industry, financially solvent, and able to supply adequate security. They also had to prove failure in securing credit from a commercial bank. Loans could not be used to pay existing indebtedness, finance foreign sales or construction, or buy foreign acceptances. The RFC had the right to set corporate salaries and cancel distribution of dividends. Loans could not exceed $500,000; maturities could not exceed five years; and interest rates would not be less than prevailing rates in the private sector. With such restrictions, Jones was confident the RFC could handle the applications for business loans.[2]

He was in for a big surprise. Since 1932 officials in the Hoover and Roosevelt administrations, including both presidents, had complained about the inability of sound businesses to secure working capital loans. Exercising the blind faith of classical economists in monetary policy, they had assumed the existence of large-scale business demand for money and expected low interest rates and excess reserves to lead quickly to increased borrowing, investment, spending, and employment. But in the summer of 1934 the RFC Business Loan Division, under the direction of Frederic Taber, discovered that both the demand for loans and the soundness of prospective borrowers was not what they had expected. By September the RFC had received less than 1,200 applications and had approved only 100 of them for $8 million. Less than $400,000 had actually been disbursed. On the grounds of inadequate security, excessive indebtedness, or lack of potential earnings, the RFC rejected most

[1] *New York Times*, June 9, 1934; J.F.T. O'Connor Diary, June 26, 1934, O'Connor Papers.
[2] RFC, *Circular No. 13* (Washington, D.C., 1934), pp. 1–6.

applications. Jones was surprised at how few applications the RFC received.[3]

The experience of the Export-Import Bank was no different. To prevent being inundated with applications, the Export-Import Bank adopted strict loan guidelines. It would not offer short-term credit with maturities of less than 180 days. EIB interest rates ranged from 4.5 percent for intermediate credit to 5 percent for loans with one- to five-year maturities. Rather than directly finance foreign transactions, the bank preferred working through banks on loan participations and discounting operations. Consumer goods would be financed on six-month to one-year maturities and capital goods from one to five years.[4] In a speech to the National Foreign Trade Convention on November 2, 1934, Peek explained that the main purpose of the Export-Import Bank, beyond assisting the recovery effort, was to "find a method by which banks will resume handling this business . . . there is truth in what a good many . . . exporters say, that banks have become skittish of foreign trade." Apart from its sphere of operations, its program was no different from the RFC direct loan campaign.[5]

The number of export loan applications was less than expected, as was the credit worthiness of prospective borrowers. Commercial banks were reluctant to finance even short-term agricultural credit transactions, and most early EIB loans were short-term credit on tobacco and cotton. Commercial banks handled the loans but invariably sold them back. The Export-Import Bank also granted intermediate credit to capital goods exporters, primarily railway and heavy equipment, and advanced long-term credit to exporters and banks against obligations issued by foreign governments in settlement of claims arising out of blocked exchanges. But demand for loans did not live up to expectations, and the Export-Import Bank re-

---

[3] Transcripts of Board Notes, September 12, 1934, NA, RG 234, RFC; *New York Times*, August 31 and September 7, 8, and 23, 1934.

[4] Export-Import Bank of Washington, "General Policy Statement," unpublished manuscript, May 1935, FDRPL, OF 971, EIB.

[5] See the speech by George Peek to the National Foreign Trade Convention, November 2, 1934, FDRPL, OF 971, EIB.

jected most of the applications it received because of poor earnings potential, inadequate security, and excessive indebtedness. By the end of 1934 the Export-Import Bank had made less than $7 million in loans, and bank participations were almost nonexistent. Like the RFC, the Export-Import Bank approached loans conservatively, as much concerned about the safety of its own funds as the need to stimulate business expansion.[6]

The inauspicious beginning of the Export-Import Bank and RFC business loan program intensified the debate over the relationship between credit and recovery. The American Bankers' Association, its members no doubt smiling, felt confirmed in its belief that the administration was overestimating the extent of legitimate demand. The RFC and EIB rejection of most applications was proof. Ironically, a small group of future Keynesians like Marriner Eccles agreed. Business demand for credit would follow, not inspire, a rise in consumer spending. New Deal planners, led by Adolf Berle, continued lobbying for a system of federal industrial banks or some large-scale government corporation to make working capital and equity loans, but their influence was ebbing, a victim of the mounting criticism of the National Recovery Administration.[7]

Because of the extremes of the debate—the conviction of some that extensive business demand existed and the equally passionate doubts of others—a series of credit surveys appeared in late 1934 and early 1935 to determine the real situation. The Census Bureau sent out 16,000 questionnaires to manufacturers and received 7,669 responses. They concluded that nearly half of all businesses were having trouble getting

[6] Export-Import Bank of Washington, *Annual Report for 1934* (Washington, D.C., 1935), pp. 1–5; Daniel W. Bell to Franklin D. Roosevelt, December 19, 1935, FDRPL, OF 971, EIB.

[7] John Maynard Keynes to Marvin McIntyre, June 5, 1934, FDRPL, PPF 5235, John M. Keynes; Upham and Lamke, *Closed and Distressed Banks*, p. 226; Hawley, *The New Deal and the Problem of Monopoly*, pp. 319–322; U.S. Congress, House, Committee on Banking and Currency, *Hearings on H.R. 5357*, p. 377; Daniel W. Bell to Franklin D. Roosevelt, December 19, 1935, FDRPL, OF 971, EIB.

working capital, although there was a strong correlation between problems and net worth to debt ratios. Only one in four businesses with assets three times larger than debts reported difficulties, while more than two out of three with assets equal to or slightly larger than debts were having trouble. The report criticized "the mania of banks for liquidity" and the policy of federal bank examiners to classify many business loans as "slow."[8] A National Industrial Conference Board study at the same time reached similar conclusions: small businesses with legitimate credit needs were not getting the credit they needed to help in the recovery effort. The Department of Commerce conducted its own study late in 1934. Directed by Theodore Beckman, chief economist for the Small Industries Committee of the Business and Advisory Council, it concluded that more than $2 billion was needed, not so much in the form of working capital loans but as long-term equity financing. Small businesses were especially vulnerable. Although the working capital of American manufacturers had declined from $22.6 billion in 1929 to less than $11 billion in 1933, most of the losses hit smaller businesses. For the 413 largest corporations in the country, working capital dropped from $9.5 billion to $7.6 billion, but for the rest the decline was $12.7 billion to less than $4.5 billion. Another study by the Federal Reserve Committee on Branch, Group, and Chain Banking reached similar conclusions. A credit survey by the National Conference of Business Paper Editors concluded that businesses were reluctant to apply for federal loans because of a fear of red tape, concern about the lack of consumer demand, and a suspicion that federal loans would be followed by federal interference.[9]

The most important of the credit surveys, however, came out of the Treasury Department, and triggered a battle over

[8] Roos, *NRA Economic Planning*, pp. 388–90.

[9] *New York Times*, November 11, 1934, and September 28, 1935; Department of Commerce, "Digest of Small Industries Report," April 15, 1934, unpublished manuscript, NA, RG 234, RFC, Lending Authority of the RFC; Roos, *NRA Economic Planning*, p. 375; Upham and Lamke, *Closed and Distressed Banks*, p. 157.

federal spending and the future of the RFC which lasted more than two years. Ever since taking over Treasury from William Woodin at the end of 1933, Henry Morgenthau had campaigned for a balanced budget, increased taxes, and cuts in federal spending. While the rest of the administration had been looking on excess reserves as a potential windfall for the economy if bankers would only loan it out, Morgenthau worried that the money was fuel for an inflationary spiral once recovery was underway. Instead of deficit spending, low interest rates, and excess reserves, Morgenthau wanted just the opposite. As long as Hugh Johnson and the NRA were in the New Deal driver seat, Morgenthau's demands fell on deaf ears, even though he was as close to Roosevelt as anyone. But by late 1934, with Hugh Johnson out and the NRA embroiled in unrelenting controversy, Morgenthau's group at Treasury—which included Jacob Viner, Herman Oliphant, and George Haas—gained credibility. By late 1934, the RFC was an appealing target for budget balancers. With the banking system recovering, the need for RFC loans would soon be declining, and more than $2 billion in loans and preferred stock could be repaid. If the RFC and the New Deal credit establishment were whittled down in size, chances for a balanced budget were much much better.[10]

Whether or not those funds would be available depended on business need for credit. Late in August 1934, Morgenthau asked C. O. Hardy and Jacob Viner to conduct a thorough survey of business credit needs in the Chicago Federal Reserve District. Governor Eugene Black had first suggested the idea in 1932 but it had not seemed really necessary until the RFC's difficulties in extending commercial credit in the summer of 1934. Morgenthau wanted to know if there really were large numbers of legitimate businesses unable to obtain credit; whether most businesses had become poor credit risks because of the depression; whether banks were too liquidity conscious; and whether banks had so much money invested in government securities that funds were not available for working cap-

[10] Hawley, *The New Deal and the Problem of Monopoly*, pp. 350–52.

ital loans. Budget balancers at Treasury hoped that demand was not extensive so they could call for a reduction in the budgets of federal credit agencies.[11]

By November the Hardy-Viner report was circulating among prominent New Deal officials. It contradicted the prevailing wisdom. Declines in commercial lending were occurring throughout the country, not so much because banks were unwilling to make any business loans but because major corporations had been accumulating unused balances of liquid funds to finance an economic expansion. Also, demand for credit was down because of the depression. According to Viner, "the total amount of . . . unsatisfied demand for credit is considerably smaller than is popularly believed." But at the same time, Viner was convinced from his survey that unsatisfied demand for credit was "large enough to be a significant factor in retarding business recovery," especially after an economic expansion was already under way and surplus corporate funds had already been used. In a drive for liquidity, bankers were calling in working capital loans, even for solvent borrowers, and reluctant to make new ones. Hardy and Viner also identified a real need for long-term credit. Finally, the report criticized Jesse Jones and Leo Crowley of the FDIC. As far as Hardy and Viner were concerned, RFC business loans had been totally ineffective in 1934, and the FDIC tendency to classify all real estate and unsecured working capital loans as "slow" made bankers even more reluctant to expand commercial lending.[12]

Their criticism of the RFC was pointed, just as Morgenthau wanted it. Treasury auditors had closely examined 113 loans the RFC had rejected. Jones's refusal to make loans to pay off existing indebtedness was based on his conviction that such loans would not increase employment, but Viner and Hardy disagreed. Loans to pay off existing debts might allow going concerns to survive now and expand in the near future, rather

[11] *New York Times*, August 31, 1934.
[12] C. O. Hardy and Jacob Viner, *Report on the Availability of Bank Credit in the Seventh Federal Reserve District* (Washington, D.C., 1935), p. vi.

than go bankrupt. The RFC also required that all holders of mortgages against a company's property agree to subordinate their interests to an RFC first lien before the company could get a loan, but many creditors refused and the loans were not made. If current earnings were not sufficient to repay the debt, the RFC would not make the loan, even if the collateral would cover all losses. Finally, the RFC would not accept unsecured promissory notes as collateral, no matter how good the applicant's financial position and credit reputation. For all intents and purposes, RFC loan policies were not different from those of most commercial banks, and its loan record no more impressive. It had been part of the problem rather than the solution. In order for the RFC to have any effect at all on recovery, it would have to change its loan policies for business borrowers.[13]

Hardy and Viner encouraged bankers to make more commercial loans, advocated a relaxation of federal examination standards, primarily to allow indefinite renewal of working capital loans as long as borrowers were paying interest out of current earnings and had a sound net worth to debts ratio, and called for an end to all business loans by the Federal Reserve banks, arguing that the program should be concentrated in one federal agency, preferably the RFC or some new government credit agency. At the same time, they wanted Federal Reserve banks to discount paper with longer than six-month maturities. As for RFC loans, they wanted the corporation to loan up to ten years, just as Jesse Jones had originally wanted, and to loan for clearing existing indebtedness and fixed capital as well as working capital loans. Stringent RFC audits of prospective borrowers and collateral requirements should be relaxed.[14]

The Hardy-Viner report had a direct impact on the RFC. The decline of the NRA and the growing power of Morgenthau's Treasury group, as well as Felix Frankfurter's antitrust group, made the RFC vulnerable, since it had been so closely associ-

[13] Ibid., pp. 106–9; Henry Morgenthau Diaries, December 17, 1934, Morgenthau Papers.

[14] Hardy and Viner, *Report*, pp. 6–10; *New York Times*, December 18, 1934; Henry Morgenthau Diaries, December 17, 1934, Morgenthau Papers.

ated philosophically with the NRA. The Hardy-Viner report had not helped. In mid-November, Roosevelt established an Interdepartmental Loan Committee composed of the heads of the Public Works Administration, Farm Credit Administration, RFC, Federal Home Loan Bank Board, Federal Housing Administration, Home Owners' Loan Corporation, Export-Import Bank, Commodity Credit Corporation, Agricultural Adjustment Administration, Federal Reserve Board, and the FDIC. Henry Morgenthau chaired the committee, a fact which Jones resented but over which he had little control. From that position Morgenthau made his assault on federal spending.[15]

Jones responded to the criticism of the RFC by reevaluating more than 2,000 business loan applications. He believed such loans were the responsibility of commercial banks, not the federal government, and he made sure the prerogatives of the private sector were not destroyed. He had RFC loan agency managers reduce the red tape, allowed them to consider making loans for payment of existing indebtedness, eased restrictions on collateral eligibility, and allowed local agencies to make loans for plant renovation and construction. Jones was surprised that the RFC received only 756 applications between June and October 1934. He tried to pick up the pace of loans, and by mid-December loan authorizations had reached $35 million, although actual disbursements were less than $8 million.[16] When the Interdepartmental Loan Committee debated the Hardy-Viner report in December 1934, Leo Crowley defended the bankers, arguing that there really was not much demand for credit, and that federal examiners had changed some of their classification methods even before the report was com-

[15] Franklin D. Roosevelt to Harold Ickes, November 12, 1934, FDRPL, OF 3720, Federal Loan Agency.

[16] See the speech by Jesse Jones to the West Virginia Bankers' Association, June 8, 1934, NA, RG 234, RFC, Speeches of Key Personnel; RFC, *Press Release No. 1076* (Washington, D.C., 1934), p. 1; RFC, Minutes, 31 (August 11, 1934), 1494; Minutes, 34 (November 12, 17, and 23, 1934), 1504, 2253, and 3219; RFC, "Data on NRA Loans," November 6, 1934, NA, RG 234, RFC, Statistical Division; Frederic Taber Diary, December 6, 1934, Taber Papers; RFC, Minutes, 34 (November 23, 1934), 3219; "Transcripts of Board Notes," September 10, 1934, NA, RG 234, RFC, Secretarial Division.

plete. Jones indicated the RFC was taking another look at its policies and had already made certain adjustments.[17]

He was not about to pander to public opinion or Treasury criticism. Jones felt responsible for the RFC and public money, and he had no intention of loaning it unwisely. At a conference of RFC loan agency managers in September, he said that the

> country seems disappointed in the amount we have been able to do, and they are finding that equally true with regard to the Federal Reserve Banks. However, we must not be driven to doing unsound things by clamor and criticism and public opinion. We have to still stick to our guns under the law in making sound loans.[18]

He took seriously the requirement to make sound, secured loans, and Jones was too much of a businessman to do otherwise. Under his direction, the RFC would not embark on a large-scale commercial lending or equity financing program. That was the business of the private sector. He would not push state capitalism to the point of replacing the private money market.

Jones tried to turn the situation to the RFC's advantage. On January 31, 1935, RFC statutory authority would end without new legislation. Jones felt strongly that the RFC's preferred stock purchase plan needed more time; thousands of banks needed the security of government investment if they were to resume commercial lending at pre-depression levels. The railroad situation was still dangerous; too many roads were not meeting fixed obligations and there was nothing on the economic horizon to indicate any change. Commodity Credit Corporation loans had ceased to be luxuries and had become necessities for most farmers.

Jones also worried about the mortgage markets. Since 1929, mortgage lending had gone the same way as commercial lending—down and down as building and loan associations,

[17] Henry Morgenthau Diaries, December 6 and 10, 1934, Morgenthau Papers; *New York Times*, November 20, 24, and 27, 1934.

[18] "Transcripts of Board Notes," September 10, 1934, NA, RG 234, RFC, Secretarial Division.

banks, mortgage loan companies, and insurance companies converted mortgage money into government bonds. Between 1932 and 1935 the RFC had loaned more than $144 million to open and closed building and loan associations, $380 million to mortgage loan companies, and $136 million to insurance companies. The Farm Credit Administration and Home Owners' Loan Corporation refinanced urban and rural mortgages, and the Federal Housing Administration was insuring loans for residential repair and construction. But it was not enough. Between 1929 and 1934 the total volume of mortgage debt in the United States had declined by more than 50 percent.[19] Jones wanted a new RFC agency to underwrite mortgages. He decided to use the RFC extension in January 1935 as an opportunity to address all these questions as well as the criticism of the Hardy-Viner report. Jones put Tommy Corcoran with Benjamin Cohen to draft the legislation. The bill was finished in mid-December and Jones gave it to the president for his approval on the eighteenth. It called for a three-year extension of RFC authority; the right to make loans up to a maximum of ten years; removal of the $500,000 limitation on industrial loans so the RFC could consider making fixed capital equity investments; the right of the RFC to purchase first mortgage railroad bonds to assist railroad reorganizations; and the authority to establish an RFC mortgage bank to buttress the mortgage markets and finance new construction.[20]

The bill went before the Senate and House Banking and Currency Committees early in January 1935 and encountered little opposition. It had the backing of the president and Jesse Jones as well as the support of business-oriented Republicans.

[19] RFC, *Reconstruction Finance Corporation. Summary of the Activities of the Reconstruction Finance Corporation*, p. 5; Carl F. Behrens, *Commercial Bank Activities in Urban Mortgage Financing* (New York, 1952), p. 33; American Bankers' Association, *Changes in Bank Earning Assets*, p. 33; American Bankers' Association, *Government Lending Agencies*, p. 1003; Frederic Taber Diary, October 9, 1934, Taber Papers.

[20] Jesse Jones to Franklin D. Roosevelt, December 18, 1934, FDRPL, OF 643, RFC; Niznik, "Thomas G. Corcoran," pp. 68–69; RFC, *Circular No. 13* (Washington, D.C., February, 1935), pp. 1–2.

The only real change came in the Senate when a limit of $1 million was put on any single RFC industrial loan and the extension was limited to two years. Other than those changes the RFC gained the right to make industrial loans of up to $1 million for up to ten years, allow those loans to be used for a variety of business purposes, purchase the first maturity bonds of railroads, extend the life of the Commodity Credit Corporation and Export-Import Bank, purchase the preferred stock of mortgage loan companies, and, if necessary, establish a government corporation to invest in mortgages. President Roosevelt signed the measure into law on January 31, 1935.[21]

The RFC extension confirmed the changing direction of the New Deal. Throughout 1933 and early 1934, the New Deal had tinkered with centralized planning without ever investing the power or resources necessary to really implement it. The RFC had loaned billions to a host of financial institutions, invested heavily in the preferred stock of banks, trust companies, and insurance companies, and was prepared to invest in the mortgage bonds of railroads. But commercial lending was stillborn. The administration never embraced Berle's vision of the RFC controlling capital flow in the economy, and Jones had made the RFC an astute and powerful, if conservative, government bank out to liquefy the money markets without compromising its own assets. The RFC extension in 1935 gave the business loan program a new lease on life, but it was destined to fall victim to economic reality and the changing political fortunes of the New Deal. Faith in centralized planning was giving way to more traditional beliefs in balanced budgets and antitrust campaigns.

Even with liberalized regulations and more statutory authority, the RFC's business loan program never got off the ground. During 1935 and 1936, the RFC disbursed only $78 million in business loans, and banks took participations in only $8 million of them. The RFC received only 6,214 appli-

<hr>

[21] *New York Times*, January 2, 8, 11, 15, 22, and 31, 1935, and February 1, 1935; U.S. Congress, House, Committee on Banking and Currency, *Hearings on H.R. 4240. A Bill to Extend the Functions of the R.F.C.*, 74th Cong., 1st Sess., 1935, pp. 4–5.

cations for business loans, hardly the volume they anticipated, and approved only 2,286 of those applications. The others were rejected as poor credit risks.[22] Although it had become a much more powerful agency under Roosevelt, the RFC philosophy of recovery had changed very little. Its direct loans had been hampered by lack of demand and the marginal condition of so many applicants. The RFC was far more successful as a discounting agency for banks than as a bank itself. Between the fall of 1933 and the end of 1936, the RFC had made less than $80 million in business loans while extending more than $2 billion to banks and $600 million to railroads.[23]

The commercial loans of the Export-Import Bank were no more impressive. Despite an active program soliciting business loans and bank participations in 1935 and 1936, the Export-Import Bank encountered the same problems as the RFC Business Loan Division: less demand than they had expected and only marginally worthy borrowers. The EIB made a series of loans to assist businesses in getting their money out of frozen foreign exchanges, but commercial loans were few. To encourage borrowing the bank dropped its interest rate from 5 to 4 percent in mid-1936, but the change made little difference. By early 1937, the Export-Import Bank had loaned only $35 million to finance foreign sales of American-made products, hardly enough to affect recovery.[24]

Nor were RFC efforts to buttress the real estate mortgage markets any different. Late in 1934, Jones let the RFC subscribe to the preferred stock of any mortgage loan company where private investors would match the government money. It had worked for banks, at least in terms of making them more sol-

[22] RFC, "Direct Loans to Industry as of January 27, 1937," unpublished manuscript, NA, RG 234, RFC, Statistical Division.

[23] Frederic Taber Diary, February 7, 1935, Taber Papers; *New York Times*, September 28, 1935; U.S. Congress, House, Committee on Banking and Currency, *Hearings on H.R. 4240*, pp. 4–5; speech by Jesse Jones to the National Democratic Club, February 9, 1935, NA, RG 234, RFC, Speeches of Key Personnel.

[24] Export-Import Bank of Washington, *Annual Report for 1936*, pp. 1–5.

vent, and he hoped the mortgage loan companies, infused with new capital, would make more loans. Jones's faith that expansion in the money supply would automatically lead to more consumer spending was still intact. The RFC extension had given the RFC the authority to make those investments. Proceeds from the sale of preferred stock could be used to finance new construction, refinance existing mortgages, or relieve distressed holders of mortgage bonds and certificates. Wanting to make sure the companies did not compete with existing institutions in the private sector, Jones set interest rates at 6 percent.[25]

Demand for the loans was just not there and it was next to impossible to get matching funds from private investors. Direct loans seemed inevitable. Since the Home Owners' Loan Corporation, Farm Credit Administration, and Federal Housing Administration assisted rural and urban homeowners, Jones decided to supplement their work and create, if possible, an active mortgage market for urban revenue property—primarily apartments, office buildings, hotels, warehouses, theaters, stores, and factories. In March 1935, the RFC organized the RFC Mortgage Company with $10 million in capital.[26]

The RFC owned the RFC Mortgage Company and was prepared to loan it as much money as it could use. Applicants had to prove an inability to get loans from other mortgage sources, and the RFC Mortgage Company loan rate was 5 percent. The RFC Mortgage Company planned on reestablishing a market for mortgages on urban, income-producing property by loaning on new construction and by refinancing existing urban

[25] Jesse Jones to John Dockweiler, November 29, 1933, FDRPL, OF 643, RFC; speech by Jesse Jones to the American Bankers' Association, October 18, 1934, NA, RG 234, RFC, Speeches by Key Personnel; "Minutes of the Committee on Operations," June 1, 1936, NA, RG 234, RFC; RFC, *Circular No. 13*, pp. 1–4.

[26] RFC, Minutes, 25 (February 17, 1934), 3139; U.S. Congress, Senate, Committee on Banking and Currency, *Hearings on S. 1175. Bill to Extend the Functions of the* RFC, 74th Cong., 1st Sess., 1935, pp. 29–30; *New York Times*, February 3, 1935; Clarence Cannon to Franklin D. Roosevelt, August 23, 1933, FDRPL, OF 706, Credit.

mortgages. Jones, as usual, considered the RFC Mortgage Company only a temporary agency until private lenders returned to the markets.[27] The RFC insisted on the same cooperative arrangements established by its own Business Loan Division and the Export-Import Bank, permitting private lenders to participate in or to purchase loans. Increasing the volume of mortgage loans was the primary objective. Once that process was under way, Jones intended to liquidate the RFC Mortgage Company.[28]

The RFC Mortgage Company, however, never lived up to his expectations. Significant demand for loans did not materialize. Private capital to organize mortgage loan companies or national mortgage associations, or to invest in existing ones, was not available. Late in 1935 the RFC Mortgage Company began buying and selling FHA-insured mortgages to create a secondary market for them. It hoped to resell the mortgages.[29] Finding the financial worthiness of prospective borrowers impaired, the RFC Mortgage Company approved only 10 percent of the applications. Generally it would not loan on property held by mortgage loan companies unless they had substantial equity in it. The Mortgage Bankers' Association insisted that the private sector was meeting legitimate demand and that the RFC Mortgage Company was superfluous. By the end of 1936, the RFC Mortgage Company had approved 8,898 loans, but

[27] Jesse Jones to Franklin D. Roosevelt, March 12, 1935, FDRPL, OF 643, RFC; Transcripts of Board Notes, April 4, 1935, NA, RG 234, RFC; *New York Times*, March 12 and April 5, 1935; "Historical Summary, 1935-1939," unpublished manuscript, NA, RG 234, RFC, Records of the RFC Mortgage Company, pp. 1–2; RFC Mortgage Company, *Bulletin No. 1* (Washington, D.C., 1935), p. 1.

[28] Transcripts of Board Notes, April 4 and 29, 1935, NA, RG 234, RFC; *Washington Post*, March 12, 1935; *New York Times*, March 14-15, 1935.

[29] "Historical Summary, 1935–1939," p. 5; *New York Times*, August 2 and 28, 1935; Jesse Jones to Stewart McDonald, August 27, 1935, FDRPL, OF 643, RFC; Jesse Jones to all bankers, February 12, 1936, NA, RG 234, RFC, Records of the RFC Mortgage Company; "Minutes of the Committee on Operations," June 1, 1936, NA, RG 234, RFC; *Washington Post*, February 28, 1936; Jesse Jones to Franklin D. Roosevelt, July 8, 1936, NA, RG 234, RFC, White House Correspondence.

nearly 7,200 of them were purchases of FHA mortgages. It had loaned nearly $23 million for refinancing existing mortgages and only $1.8 million for new construction.[30]

The direct lending programs of the RFC Business Loan Division, the Export-Import Bank, and the RFC Mortgage Company had been less than successful, at least in terms of the expectations of those who believed a huge, unsatisfied demand for credit existed throughout the country. After two years of loans, all three had loaned only $140 million, a far cry from the RFC estimate in 1934 that a shortage of at least $700 million in credit would cripple the NRA. Demand for business, export, and mortgage loans was nowhere near that figure and bank participations were disappointingly small. In July 1936 Jones tried to stimulate all three programs by lowering government interest a full point, from 5 to 4 percent, but it did little to bring in more applications. The fundamental nature of the depression was not what conventional economic wisdom had assumed.[31]

The lack of demand for government business loans as well as the conclusion of the Hardy-Viner report that policymakers had exaggerated the volume of unsatisfied credit needs introduced doubts in the minds of several New Deal officials about the need for the RFC. Inside the RFC, suspicions that bankers had been right all along in claiming that business demand for working capital loans was depressed grew stronger. For more than three years Jesse Jones had criticized and cajoled bankers, telling them to increase the volume of commercial and working capital loans or the country would stay mired in the depression indefinitely. But when the RFC started making those loans, Jones found himself agreeing with them: the number of applications was low and the credit worthiness of prospective borrowers left much to be desired. Small businesses were the exception, and by the end of 1936 few people doubted that their

[30] J. W. Slacks to Charles Henderson, February 9, 1938; "Biweekly Report of the RFC Mortgage Company," December 31, 1936; "Monthly Statement of Condition," December 31, 1936; James Dougherty to Jesse Jones, October 12, 1936, all in NA, RG 234, RFC, Records of the RFC Mortgage Company.

[31] RFC, *Press Release No. 1271* (Washington, D.C., 1936), pp. 1–2.

credit needs were special. Jones was frustrated that bankers were not being more cooperative. In a speech to the American Bankers' Association at the end of 1935 he remarked: "I think you are a swell lot of guys. Some of you are afraid of your own shadows, and wouldn't lend more than ten dollars on a twenty dollar bill." But Jones was also coming around to the conviction that simply expanding the money supply and making more credit available, whether from the banks or the federal government, was having little effect on the economy.[32]

In fact, New Deal policymakers had done about all they could do with monetary policy. The Federal Reserve Board had lowered interest rates and reserve requirements, and its Open Market Committee had bought bonds on the open market, creating billions of dollars of excess reserves; the Banking Act of 1935 had consolidated Federal Reserve Board power and given banks the authority to make real estate loans; the Gold Reserve Act and Silver Purchase Act of 1934 had devalued the dollar and inflated the money supply; and the RFC's programs—the gold buying episode, preferred stock plan, railroad loans, and credit expansion of the Commodity Credit Corporation, Export-Import Bank, Electric Home and Farm Authority, the RFC Mortgage Company, and the other New Deal credit agencies—had restored liquidity to the money markets. But they had not brought about the long-awaited revival of commercial credit. The economy had improved by 1936. Employment was up and so were commodity and security prices. But the economic expansion did not seem connected to bank credit in any discernible way. Loans for member banks of the Federal Reserve system had gone from $23.2 billion in

[32] Discussion Notes, August 16, 1934, Harrison Papers; *New York Times*, August 5, 22, 28, 31, and September 7 and 13, 1934, and April 15, 1935; Frederic Taber Diary, February 7, 1935, and April 23 and 27, 1938, Taber Papers; "Report of the National Industrial Conference Board," unpublished manuscript, fall 1938, Box 86, Hopkins Papers; speech by Jesse Jones over Mutual Broadcasting System, May 1, 1938, FDRPL, OF 643, RFC; Henry Morgenthau Diaries, April 21, 1938, Morgenthau Papers; Franklin D. Roosevelt to Jesse Jones, November 12, 1935, and speech of Jesse Jones to the American Bankers' Association, FDRPL, PPF 756, American Bankers' Association.

December 1929 to $11.3 billion in June 1933, and $10.5 billion in December 1934. By the end of 1936 those loans had started up again, to $11.6 billion. Administration officials were encouraged by the trend, but it had a long way to go before it reached pre-depression levels.[33]

Classical economic theory held that central bankers, in dealing with unemployment, simply had to implement expansive policies; increasing the money supply would lower interest rates, and reduced interest rates would lead automatically to increases in investment demand, employment, and consumption. But by 1933 interest rates had fallen below 2.5 percent, and what Keynes described as the "liquidity trap" had gone into effect. Bankers preferred to hold the additional money in the form of idle reserves; with deflation actually forcing prices down, the real value of those funds was increasing anyway. The RFC policy of pegging interest rates above prevailing levels was particularly ineffective. With general rates below 2.5 percent, RFC rates of 5 to 6 percent had little appeal to prospective borrowers. Even the July 1936 reductions—from 4 to 3 percent for banks, 5 to 4 percent for industry, and 5 to 4 percent for the RFC Mortgage Company—had little effect. Large corporations had accumulated liquid reserves during the early 1930s to finance expansion, and other businessmen were not prepared to increase production until they had seen demand materializing among consumers.[34] The RFC had helped restore liquidity to the money markets but it had not brought about any substantial increase in bank credit or consumer demand.

Growing doubts about the RFC lending program and the extent of business demand for money, as well as the demise of the National Recovery Administration, gave the upper hand for a time to the budget balancers in the Treasury Department, where Henry Morgenthau's insistence on cuts in federal spending and increases in reserve requirements was gaining support. Morgenthau was convinced that significant business

---

[33] *Federal Reserve Bulletin*, 23 (September 1937), 923; Franklin D. Roosevelt to John R. Hylan, July 23, 1935, FDRPL, OF 706, Credit.

[34] RFC, *Press Release No. 1271*, pp. 1–2.

demand for credit did not exist, but he saw the lack of demand as a question of confidence. The Securities Act of 1933 had demoralized the capital markets, and the consistent budget deficits, as well as the gold buying program of late 1933, had sapped business confidence. With serious doubts about the future of the economy and government fiscal policies, businessmen had no intention of going into debt to finance new production. Morgenthau also worried that excess reserves would be used to fuel an inflationary spiral once a recovery was underway. A balanced federal budget would go a long way toward restoring business confidence and stimulating new investment and production.[35]

Jesse Jones had been fighting the budget battle with Morgenthau for a long time. In January 1934 Roosevelt had asked him to hold down RFC spending and not use more than $500 million from the Treasury in fiscal 1935, but he had to rescind the order six months later because the preferred stock plan and railroads still needed attention.[36] Later in the year the pressure was on again. Jones readily admitted that the bank reconstruction program was in its final stages. Morgenthau was looking forward to the 1936 fiscal year and wanted to keep the deficit under $3 billion. That would be difficult because the president had decided to ask Congress for $4 billion in new relief money. The money had to come from somewhere, and on December 26, 1934, Roosevelt instructed all agency heads to not spend unobligated funds, save money, and not expect new appropriations. Morgenthau especially wanted to put the lid on the RFC. He got Roosevelt to approve transfers of RFC funds to the Civil Works Administration and Public Works Administration. If the RFC ceased making loans altogether in fiscal 1936, the Treasury expected repayments to exceed $1.2 billion.[37]

[35] Henry Morgenthau Diaries, October 23 and 28, and November 12, 1935, Morgenthau Papers.

[36] Franklin D. Roosevelt to Jesse Jones, January 20, 1934, and Jesse Jones to Franklin D. Roosevelt, June 29, 1934, NA, RG 234, RFC, White House Correspondence.

[37] Franklin D. Roosevelt to all agency heads, December 26, 1934, FDRPL, OF 643, RFC; New York Times, September 14, 1934, and February 7, 1936;

Morgenthau had favored extension of RFC lending authority in January 1935 if it did not require new appropriations. The secretary of the treasury began advocating liquidation of the Home Owner's Loan Corporation, redemption of RFC preferred stock, and sale of the PWA bonds the RFC had purchased. All three steps would bring in new revenues, reduce the deficit, and eliminate the need for a tax increase. The RFC should also stop buying PWA bonds and preferred stock. Jones fought an intense battle with Morgenthau throughout 1935, but the end of bank failures and the lack of success of the RFC Mortgage Company, Export-Import Bank, and direct loan program weakened his argument. The Supreme Court decision in May 1935 outlawing the NRA further undermined Jones's position.[38]

Roosevelt and Morgenthau were adamant about reducing the budget deficit, and on July 15, 1935, the RFC stopped accepting applications for preferred stock and capital note purchases. On November 12, 1935, in a speech to the American Bankers' Association, Jones announced that the bank emergency was over. Although the RFC still had much work to do in the area of farm commodity loans, railroad reorganization, and the secondary mortgage market, its work as a discounting agency for troubled banks was over. By the end of 1935, the RFC had already loaned out $10,616,833,860, making it the largest government agency in American history.[39]

Although Jones did not want banks to retire their preferred stock immediately, those entering the program reluctantly back in 1933 began to bail out in 1935. By the end of the year

Blum, *From the Morgenthau Diaries*, vol. I, pp. 238–39, 244; Harry L. Hopkins to Henry Morgenthau, September 27, 1934; Henry Morgenthau to Franklin D. Roosevelt, October 23, 1934; Jesse Jones to Franklin D. Roosevelt, November 26, 1934; and Henry Morgenthau to Franklin D. Roosevelt, December 21, 1934, all in FDRPL, OF 444, Federal Emergency Relief Administration.

[38] Henry Morgenthau Diaries, April 22 and November 18–19, 1935, Morgenthau Papers; Blum, *From the Morgenthau Diaries*, vol. I, pp. 283–85.

[39] *New York Times*, June 6 and November 2, 1935; speech by Jesse Jones to the American Bankers' Association, November 11, 1935, FDRPL, PPF 756, American Bankers' Association.

the RFC had sold back nearly $100 million in preferred stock or capital notes and early in 1936 most of the largest banks did the same, including the First National Bank of Chicago, Manufacturers Trust Company, Chase National Bank, Continental Illinois Bank and Trust Company, and the National City Bank. By July 1936 more than 25 percent of all outstanding preferred stock and capital notes had been retired. In October the RFC even began providing interest rate incentives to banks retiring their stock early.[40] At the same time its bank loans were also declining. In 1936 the RFC loaned only $65 million to banks and trust companies, after loaning only $108 million in 1935. Compared to the totals of $426 million in 1934, $846 million in 1933, and $948 million in 1932, it was a pittance. Roosevelt had urged all loan agency heads to save money in fiscal 1936, and he was delighted when the RFC provided a net credit of $239 million that year. He then requested another credit of $275 million for fiscal 1937. Jones resisted, arguing that the RFC still had important tasks facing it, but Roosevelt was insistent. He wanted a budget more in line with Morgenthau's expectations, knew that a tax increase was out in 1936 because of the election, and decided to cut $660 million from the budgets of the RFC and its affiliates.[41]

Jones agreed that the RFC could probably save more than $700 million in fiscal 1937 by slowing down the pace of its loans and not providing funds to other government agencies, most of which were becoming increasingly unnecessary. But when Morgenthau and Daniel Bell, acting budget director, tried to reduce RFC lending by legislative mandate, Jones resisted. Bell and Morgenthau wanted to limit RFC authority to make loans to the Federal Deposit Insurance Corporation, Farm Credit Administration, and Public Works Administra-

[40] *New York Times*, April 8, May 16, 22, and 27, June 18–19, July 1 and 7, October 5, and November 19–20, 1936.

[41] Blum, *From the Morgenthau Diaries*, vol. I, pp. 262–65; Jesse Jones to Franklin D. Roosevelt, March 6 and July 12, 1936; Franklin D. Roosevelt to Jesse Jones, July 10, 1936, both in FDRPL, OF 643, RFC; Henry Morgenthau to Marvin McIntyre, February 13, 1936, FDRPL, OF 21, Treasury; RFC, *Quarterly Report for October 1 to December 31, 1938* (Washington, D.C., 1939), pp. 4–5.

tion, but Jones saw it for what it really was: a preliminary attempt to end RFC authority altogether. He held the line for a while in 1936 and early 1937, and Roosevelt went along, but the RFC's days seemed clearly numbered, at least as long as Morgenthau's Treasury group was on top.[42]

During 1937 the RFC continued its lending operations, but on the reduced scale Roosevelt and Morgenthau wanted. Between the end of 1935 and the late summer of 1937, the RFC made another $250 million in railroad loans, with more than $125 million going to purchases of railroad bonds and equipment trust certificates. Bank loans in 1937 were less than $43 million. Applications for RFC loans averaged fewer than fifty a month throughout the year. The Business Loan Division disbursed only $27 million in 1937, bringing its total between 1935 and 1937 to $106 million. Mortgage work, however, increased. The RFC made loans totaling more than $100 million to mortgage loan companies in 1936 and 1937, and the RFC Mortgage Company authorized loans of more than $150 million. Of that total, $41 million went to finance new construction and $68 million to buy FHA mortgages.[43]

The administrative flexibility of the RFC, however, still appealed to Roosevelt. On May 11, 1935, the president created the Rural Electrification Administration by executive order. Rural dwellers organized local cooperatives and then built electric transmission lines with low-interest REA loans. The Reconstruction Finance Corporation supplied the REA with its loan money. By 1940 the RFC had provided the REA with $246 million.[44]

[42] Jesse Jones to Franklin D. Roosevelt, March 6, 1936; Franklin D. Roosevelt to Jesse Jones, March 8, 1936; Jesse Jones to Franklin D. Roosevelt, July 2 and 22, 1937; Jesse Jones to Daniel Bell, March 5, 1936, and January 5, 1937, all in FDRPL, OF 643, RFC; Franklin D. Roosevelt to Jesse Jones, June 29, 1937, NA, RG 234, RFC, White House Correspondence.

[43] RFC Mortgage Company, *Monthly State of Condition for December 1937* (Washington, D.C., 1938), pp. 1–3; Jesse Jones, *Reconstruction Finance Corporation Seven Year Report* (Washington, D.C., 1939), pp. 1–10; RFC, *Press Release No. 1394* (Washington, D.C., 1938), pp. 1–2; *New York Times*, December 3, 1935, and October 11, 1936.

[44] For the best study of the REA, see D. Clayton Brown, *Electricity for Rural*

Roosevelt also turned to the RFC for government disaster aid programs. When a devastating earthquake struck southern California in 1933, Congress authorized the RFC to make low-interest loans to property owners for reconstruction. On a number of other occasions between 1933 and 1936—an earthquake in Montana, flooding in New York, Connecticut, and southern California—Congress made similar authorizations, and by the end of 1936 the RFC had extended nearly $17 million in such loans. The laws required, however, that RFC disaster loans be channeled through local, nonprofit corporations, a cumbersome requirement when people needed money quickly to rebuild homes and businesses.[45] In 1937, the flooding of the Ohio River was severe enough that Jesse Jones wanted to scrap the intermediary corporation requirement, and Congress authorized him to establish an RFC subsidiary, the Disaster Loan Corporation, to handle reconstruction loans. Formed on February 11, 1937, with $40 million in RFC capital, the Disaster Loan Corporation quickly made nearly 8,000 loans totaling $8.8 million, and assisted timber and home owners after a severe forest fire in Oregon.[46] In September 1938 a hurricane destroyed homes, businesses, and forests throughout Long Island and New England, and the Disaster Loan Corporation made more than $6 million in rehabilitation loans. By 1940, the Disaster Loan Corporation had made loans totaling $55 million in thirty-four states.[47]

America: The Fight for the REA (Westport, Conn., 1980). Also see Jones, *Fifty Billion Dollars*, pp. 200–202; Daniel Bell to Franklin D. Roosevelt, March 4, 1936; Jesse Jones to Franklin D. Roosevelt, March 3, 1936; Franklin D. Roosevelt to Jesse Jones, all in FDRPL, OF 643, RFC.

[45] William Simpson to Franklin D. Roosevelt, March 11, 1933, and Jesse Jones to Franklin D. Roosevelt, June 22, 1933, FDRPL, OF 643, RFC; Frederic Taber Diary, March 19, 1936, Taber Papers; William Gibbs McAdoo to Franklin D. Roosevelt, March 18, 1933, and November 5, 1934, FDRPL, OF 83, Disasters; Minutes of the Committee on Operations, June 1, 1936, NA, RG 234, RFC, Secretarial File.

[46] *New York Times*, February 12 and June 9, 1937; RFC, *Press Release No. 1325* (Washington, D.C., 1937), p. 1.

[47] Jesse Jones to Franklin D. Roosevelt, November 3, 1939, FDRPL, OF 3720, Federal Loan Agency; Disaster Loan Corporation, Minutes, 1 (February

Despite the work of the Rural Electrification Adminstration and the Disaster Loan Corporation, however, the RFC was only a shell of its former self. Morgenthau wanted it dissolved. Certain that Jones would do all he could to keep the RFC alive, either through the Commodity Credit Corporation, railroad loans, or now the Disaster Loan Corporation, Morgenthau believed the balanced budget goal rested squarely on dismantling the Jesse Jones empire.[48] The economy appeared to be steadily improving. Because of relief expenditures, the release of veterans' bonuses, and a rise in industrial orders, a modest economic expansion had occurred in 1936, with unemployment dropping to six million people, down from its 1933 high of thirteen million, and industrial production reaching and even moving beyond 1929 levels. National income also approached within 10 percent of its 1929 level.[49]

The good news was just what Morgenthau had been waiting for. With the economy obviously improving, the time had come to reduce the federal establishment, balance the budget, tighten the money supply, and restore business confidence. Between August 1936 and May 1937, the Federal Reserve Board doubled reserve requirements in order to prevent any inflationary spiral in the wake of recovery. The Treasury's gold sterilization program between December 1936 and the spring of 1938 grew out of the same fear. By 1936, as the economy began to stabilize and the United States balance of payments improved, gold imports increased and Secretary of the Treasury Henry Morgenthau worried that they would fuel a rapid increase in the money supply and an inflationary spiral. To prevent that, he convinced President Roosevelt to implement the gold sterilization program, which placed the incoming gold into an inactive Treasury account which banks could not use to expand credit. It eventually contributed to the economic

---

16, 1937), 9; 5 (July 13, 1937), 870; 5 (July 16, 1937), 1161; 16 (September 23, 1938), 591; 26 (September 8, 1939), 326; 27 (November 8, 1939), 315.

[48] Charles E. Stewart to Marvin McIntyre, October 28, 1937, FDRPL, OF 971, Export-Import Bank; Henry Morgenthau Diaries, October 22–27, 1937, Morgenthau Papers; *New York Times*, April 21 and October 19, 1937.

[49] Conkin, *The New Deal*, pp. 96-97.

contraction of 1937 and 1938, just as did the cuts in federal spending and doubling of Federal Reserve requirements. And in October 1937 Roosevelt informed Jesse Jones that the RFC was finished—no new loans and quick work toward dissolution. Henry Morgenthau wrote Jones with the same message, secretly delighted with his victory. The intensity of his belief in balanced budgets was matched only by his jealousy of Jesse Jones. Bank credit was nowhere near its pre-depression level, but the crisis seemed over, and so, in the minds of Roosevelt and Morgenthau, was the need for the RFC. The early New Deal, with its faith in a cooperative business commonwealth characterized by government-business planning, had breathed its last.[50]

[50] Henry Morgenthau Diaries, January 30, October 22 and 27, 1937, Morgenthau Papers; Henry Morgenthau to Jesse Jones, October 28, 1937, FDRPL, OF 643, RFC; speech of Jesse Jones to the National Association of Supervisors of State Banks, October 8, 1937, NA, RG 234, RFC, Speeches of Key Personnel; Berle and Jacobs, *Navigating the Rapids*, p. 142.

Revival

THE DREAMS of 1937 were shattered by the winter of 1938. The encouraging prosperity of 1936 and early 1937 was an aberration, an unintentional by-product of federal spending. In 1936, because of Works Progress Administration relief expenditures, the release of veterans bonuses, and the accumulated value of other federal programs, the net government contribution to national income exceeded $4.1 billion. Recovery came in the wake of federal spending. Certain that the country was finally coming out of the depression, Henry Morgenthau and the budget balancers convinced President Roosevelt to implement the spending cuts they had been demanding since 1933. Between August 1936 and May 1937, the Federal Reserve Board, afraid of runaway inflation developing because of excess reserves, doubled reserve requirements, creating a credit contraction, exactly what Jesse Jones and the RFC had been fighting for five years. Because of severe cuts in relief spending at the end of 1937 and the deflationary impact of new social security taxes, the net federal contribution to national income in 1937 was only $800 million, compared to $4.1 billion in 1936. The consequences were immediate.

Hopes for retrenchment, balanced budgets, and business confidence collided head-on with the most serious economic decline since 1933. In October 1937, even while Roosevelt was telling Jesse Jones the RFC's days were numbered, the country was slipping into the recession of 1937–1938. Between October 1937 and May 1938, industrial production fell more than a third, durable goods production more than a half, and business profits more than three-quarters. National income was down by 13 percent, employment by 20 percent, payrolls by 35 percent, and industrial stock averages by 50 percent. After all the public rhetoric in 1936 and 1937 predicting the end of the Great Depression, the recession was a political disaster, especially with the congressional elections of 1938 looming on the horizon.[1]

Roosevelt found himself presiding over a complicated economic debate. Although Henry Morgenthau, Jr., continued to advocate spending cuts and balanced budgets, and business groups like the U.S. Chamber of Commerce and National Association of Manufacturers remained convinced that the government relief and reform programs were undermining confidence, that point of view had no more credibility in 1938 than it had in 1933. They claimed that if the administration waited out the decline, the economy would recover quickly and be healthier in the long run. But as British economist John Maynard Keynes had said, "In the long-run, we are all dead." That was especially true in politics. The sharp dip in the economy, coming so quickly on the heels of the 1937 budget cuts, was not a coincidence, and with the elections coming up Roosevelt had to act.

He had two policy choices. Antimonopolists, led by Harvard professor Felix Frankfurter, former NRA economist Leon Henderson, Solicitor General Robert Jackson, RFC special counsel Thomas Corcoran, and legislative draftsman Benjamin Cohen, were convinced that corporate monopolies had destroyed the American economy by engaging in a "sit-down strike" of capital. What the country needed was less economic planning and more "trust-busting." Economic concentration stifled entrepreneurial initiative, squeezed small business, and crushed labor unions. By breaking up large monopolies, the federal government could restore competition and let the free market allocate resources. Prices would stabilize, production rise, and unemployment drop. The "New Freedom" of Woodrow Wilson and Louis Brandeis was alive and well in 1937 and 1938.

Advocates of deficit spending gave Roosevelt another option. For several years economists taking their cue from Keynes had called for the federal government to spend its way

[1] Patrick D. Reagan, "Recession of 1937-1938," in Olson, *Historical Dictionary of the New Deal*, pp. 408–10.

out of the depression. Increased costs and rising prices had combined with lagging private investment to cut deeply into consumer purchasing power. Just when the federal government should have been increasing its net contribution to national income, Roosevelt had cut the RFC and WPA, the Federal Reserve Board had raised reserve requirements, and social security taxes had gone into effect. The result was the recession of 1937–1938. The only answer was spending, not the hit-and-miss public works programs of the early 1930s but a conscious effort to restore national income to a level sufficient to create full employment. Harvard economist Alvin Hansen was the most prominent academic exponent of Keynesian values, and in the administration he was joined by Federal Reserve Board Governor Marriner Eccles, Secretary of the Interior Harold Ickes, Secretary of Commerce Harry Hopkins, and Federal Reserve economist Lauchlin Currie, among others.[2]

Between November 1937 and April 1938 both groups defended the New Deal publicly and tried to convince Roosevelt privately. They wanted Roosevelt to adopt compensatory government spending and launch an extended antitrust drive. Characteristically, Roosevelt went along with both groups, and post-1937 New Deal economic policy reflected the values of antitrusters and Keynesians. The later New Deal was an amalgam of both, although Roosevelt made a full commitment to neither. Right up to the outbreak of World War II, New Deal economic policy remained as confused as ever. The RFC was caught in the middle of the debate.

Roosevelt appeased the antitrusters in 1938 by beefing up the Antitrust Division of the Department of Justice, calling for the Temporary National Economic Committee, and convening a small business conference. In March 1938, law professor Thurman Arnold left Yale to take over the Antitrust Division. An advocate of consumer protection and consumer purchas-

---

[2] For general discussions of the New Deal recovery debates, see Robert Lekachman, *The Age of Keynes* (New York, 1966); J. Ronnie Davis, *The New Economics and the Old Economists* (New York, 1971); and Theodore Rosenhof, *Dogma, Depression, and the New Deal. The Debate of Political Leaders over Economic Recovery* (New York, 1975).

ing power, Arnold used the "rule of reason" in dealing with large corporations, avoiding antitrust suits for their own sake and concentrating on industries where abuses were flagrant. He increased the attorneys and investigators in the Antitrust Division from 40 to nearly 300 and filed 230 suits for restraint of trade by 1943. His leadership of the Antitrust Division contrasted sharply with its low profile earlier in the New Deal and appeased antimonopolists in Congress and the administration.[3]

In a monopoly message to Congress on April 29, 1938, Roosevelt called for an investigation of antitrust enforcement, and in response Congress created a Temporary National Economic Committee. Thomas Corcoran and Benjamin Cohen had lobbied intensely for the president to deliver the message, and he agreed out of personal loyalty to them as well as a concern about the political atmosphere. Senator Joseph O'Mahoney of Wyoming, a confirmed antitruster, led the investigation. Composed of three senators, three congressmen, and representatives of the Securities and Exchange Commission, the Federal Trade Commission, and the Departments of Justice, Treasury, Commerce, and Labor, the TNEC held fifteen hearings between 1938 and 1941. Although the TNEC issued forty-three technical reports, it was more of a political tool than one of serious reform, reflecting the confusion and variety of opinion about economic recovery among New Dealers. Proponents of industrial self-government, antitrust, and compensatory spending all testified before the TNEC, and although its bias was along Frankfurter-Brandeisian lines, it had little impact upon public policy, except to mollify those who insisted that a competitive economy could be restored.[4]

In addition to strengthening the Antitrust Division and establishing the TNEC, Roosevelt convened a small business conference in early February 1938. Secretary of Commerce Daniel Roper had been planning the meeting for a long time, but the

[3] Hawley, *The New Deal and the Problem of Monopoly*, pp. 420–42.

[4] Dwight MacDonald, "The Monopoly Committee: A Study in Frustration," *The American Scholar* 8 (Summer 1939), 295–308.

political pressure now made the meeting imperative. Small business had been complaining for years about difficulty in getting working capital from banks, discrimination by large wholesalers, and government policies benefiting large corporations. On February 2 and 3, 1938, more than 1,000 small businessmen came to the White House, where they complained bitterly about the dictatorial power of big business, Wall Street, and the federal government. They charged that the National Recovery Administration had actually made things worse and that the RFC had ignored them.[5]

The bad publicity of the conference and frustration of small businessmen forced Roosevelt to act. Roper founded the National Small Business Men's Association to serve as the collective voice of small businessmen, and the Department of Commerce conducted a nationwide credit survey. The study concluded that small businesses paid excessive interest rates when they could get loans, were often unable to get working capital loans using receivables or reputation as collateral, and had no access to long-term equity capital. The small business conference rekindled the debate about the availability of credit and the nature of economic recovery. Most bankers said worthy businesses had no difficulty with credit or blamed federal bank examiners for severe criteria in classifying loans. Small businessmen claimed they were being discriminated against by the conservatism of big banks.[6]

The demands of small businessmen for more credit, especially direct federal government loans, the severity of the recession, and the demands of the spending group forced Roosevelt to revive the RFC and several other major spending programs. In the fall of 1937, when Roosevelt ordered the RFC to be dis-

[5] Ernest Draper to Franklin Roosevelt, January 25, 1938, and Margaret Rauber to Margaret Durand, January 28, 1938, FDRPL, OF 172-A, Business; *New York Times*, January 21 and February 29, 1938; "Final Report on the Conference of Representatives of Small Business," unpublished manuscript, Department of Commerce, FDRPL, OF 172-A, Business; Henry Morgenthau Diaries, April 25, 1938, Morgenthau Papers.

[6] Alexander Dye to Ernest G. Draper, February 23, 1938, FDRPL, OF 172-A, Business.

mantled, Jones had requested special legislation canceling the agency's obligation to the Treasury for the nearly $2 billion it had extended to the Federal Emergency Relief Administration, Civil Works Administration, and Works Progress Administration in 1933, 1934, and 1935. Senator Harry Byrd of Virginia was criticizing the RFC for "huge losses," and Jones wanted to prove that, except for the relief loans mandated by federal legislation, the agency was certain to recover all the government's investment, probably with interest. Roosevelt had approved the legislation, and it passed Congress in mid-February.[7] No sooner had the debt been wiped out than Roosevelt authorized more RFC spending.

The president's decision to resume heavy spending was not, however, really contradictory to the antitrust program. At several critical points in 1937 and 1938, the views of the spenders and the trustbusters converged. Antitrusters were convinced that the concentration of business power had caused the depression. By seeking price stabilization, monopolies warped natural economic forces. When demand was down, they reduced production rather than prices, forcing people out of work. Fixed prices combined with lower production costs and technological progress to divert real purchasing power from mass consumers to the privileged few, producing excess savings and rising inventories. Businessmen cut production even more, making the problem worse. The return of competition would automatically reduce prices, enhance purchasing power, and stimulate the economy.[8]

By late 1937, most antitrusters—including Brandeis, Frankfurter, Corcoran, and Cohen—were beginning to fuse the compensatory spending and antitrust philosophies. Federal spending would increase competition by putting more purchasing power in consumers' pockets and creating new opportunities

[7] *New York Times*, October 17, 1937, and February 9, 16, and 17, 1938; Jesse Jones to Carter Glass, February 4, 1938, Glass Papers; U.S. Congress, House, Committee on Banking and Currency, *Hearings on H.R. 9379. Reconstructon Finance Corporation Relief Obligations*, 75th Cong., 3d. Sess., 1938, pp. 3–4.

[8] Hawley, *The New Deal and the Problem of Monopoly*, pp. 299–300.

for entrepreneurial initiative. A combination of spending and antitrust activity would provide new outlets for private investment and help break the monopolies' stranglehold on the economy. Inelastic prices, industrial concentration, poor distribution of income, and excess savings all seemed related, and vigorous antitrust activity and deficit spending would rectify each one of them.[9]

Marriner Eccles, Lauchlin Currie, Harry Hopkins, and Harold Ickes were delighted. English economist John Maynard Keynes had written Roosevelt early in February 1938, arguing that the economic revival in 1936 had come from RFC stabilization of the money markets, unemployment relief, and public works spending. Increases in the supply of goods or credit would not generate adequate demand by themselves. The revival of consumer demand was the prerequisite for recovery, and the 1937 cuts in federal spending had the opposite effect. Revival of government spending was the answer.[10] Morgenthau and the budget balancers opposed the spending revival, but the recession had undermined them. The connection between spending cuts and economic decline seemed obvious, even to casual observers. Political imperatives in 1938 only made the revival of spending even more likely. On February 18, 1938, Roosevelt told Jones to revive the RFC.[11]

The resurrection of the RFC was a preliminary to a comprehensive legislative program to stimulate the economy by increasing the spending power of the Works Progress Administration, Farm Security Administration, U.S. Housing Authority, and the Reconstruction Finance Corporation by $4.5 billion. Of that $4.5 billion, Jones and the RFC had responsibility for $1.5 billion, to be extended in direct loans to business, railroads, and public works construction. Jones had the RFC board reduced to five members, eliminating the secre-

[9] Ibid., pp. 300–301.

[10] John Maynard Keynes to Franklin D. Roosevelt, February 1, 1938, FDRPL, PPF 5235, John Maynard Keynes; Marriner Eccles to Arthur Vandenberg, June 14, 1938, Henry Morgenthau Diaries, Morgenthau Papers; Berle and Jacobs, *Navigating the Rapids*, pp. 141–42.

[11] Blum, *From the Morgenthau Diaries*, vol. I, pp. 405, 417–18.

tary of the treasury as an ex-officio member. Morgenthau and the budget balancers were out, at least as far as recovery policy was concerned. Jones immediately wrote to all bankers informing them that the RFC was in business again, urging them to participate in its business loans as often as possible.[12]

The revival of the RFC in 1938 changed the philosophical rationale it had been operating under since 1932. Ever since Herbert Hoover first asked Congress to establish the RFC, agency leaders had insisted it was a temporary organization with a limited future. Once the financial emergency was over the RFC would be liquidated, just as the WFC before it. But by 1938 many people were convinced that the economic crisis might not be temporary and that government economic intervention might be a new fact of life. Within the RFC, that sentiment had taken over. Early in 1938 Jesse Jones began discarding the notion that the RFC's future might be limited and cautiously suggested that the federal credit establishment might exist indefinitely.[13]

The RFC had to deal with continuing problems in agriculture, the mortgage markets, railroad finance, and commercial credit, and to boost employment the president wanted to resume the public works construction projects it had abandoned to the PWA in 1933. The Agricultural Adjustment Act of 1933 and then the Soil Conservation and Domestic Allotment Act of 1936 had failed to reduce farm surpluses because too few farmers were voluntarily limiting production. The cotton crop in 1936 reached an unprecedented 18 million bales, driving prices down, and wheat, corn, and tobacco farmers were in similar straits. Farm bloc lobbyists wanted higher subsidies, fewer production restrictions, and export dumping. In the

[12] Franklin D. Roosevelt to Jesse Jones, February 18, 1938; Jesse Jones to Emil Schram, February 19, 1938; Franklin D. Roosevelt to Jesse Jones, January 20, 1938; Jesse Jones to all bankers, February 26, 1938, all in FDRPL, OF 643, RFC.

[13] Jesse Jones to Franklin D. Roosevelt, February 15, 1938, NA, RG 234, RFC, White House Correspondence; U.S. Congress, Senate, Committee on Banking and Currency, *Hearings on S. 1102. A Bill to Extend the Functions of the R.F.C.*, 76th Cong., 1st Sess., 1939, pp. 10–13.

summer of 1937 the House Committee on Agriculture held hearings throughout the country and Congress debated an administration farm bill between December 1937 and February 1938. Roosevelt signed a new Agricultural Adjustment Act on February 16, 1938. Among other provisions, the bill strengthened the Commodity Credit Corporation. It would make loans on surplus crops at prices just below the parity levels of 1909–1914. If market prices went above the value of the loan, the farmer could sell his produce at a profit and repay the government. If prices fell below the value of the loan, the farmer surrendered the crop to the Commodity Credit Corporation, which would absorb the loss. Commodity Credit Corporation lending authority went up to $900 million.[14]

Although the RFC Mortgage Company helped the secondary mortgage market by purchasing mortgages on old homes and self-liquidating urban property, and making new loans, banks and building and loan associations were reluctant to make construction loans because they could not market the mortgages. The National Housing Act of 1934 authorized the creation of national mortgage associations, and the RFC had offered to purchase preferred stock in them. But by 1938 no national mortgage associations had been formed because of investor fears about the mortgage markets. The construction industry between 1934 and 1937 was hardly the best of investments. Most mortgages accepted for insurance by the Federal Housing Administration had been renewals of existing obligations instead of new construction. Banks just did not want to participate.[15]

When the economy collapsed in 1937, Roosevelt asked Jones to consider establishing a national mortgage association

[14] Olson, *Historical Dictionary of the New Deal*, pp. 7–12, 92–93.

[15] Jones, *Fifty Billion Dollars*, p. 151; Jesse Jones to Franklin D. Roosevelt, July 8, 1936; speech by Charles Henderson to National Association of Life Underwriters, August 27, 1937, NA, RG 234, RFC, White House Correspondence and Speeches of Key Personnel; *New York Times*, February 17, 1936; *Washington Post*, February 28, 1936; Jesse Jones to Stewart McDonald, July 24, 1935, "Policy, Procedures, and Legal Opinions," Records of the RFC Mortgage Company, NA, RG 234, RFC.

to purchase FHA mortgages on new homes. Jones considered the proposal and agreed the RFC could manage such an agency. On February 7, 1938, Roosevelt asked Jones to move ahead, and on February 10 Jones did so, paying up $40 million in its capital stock. Jones named Charles Henderson and Emil Schram of the RFC board to direct the new Federal National Mortgage Association, or "Fannie Mae," along with RFC general counsel Claude Hamilton and board assistant William Costello. Fannie Mae was responsible for purchasing FHA mortgages on new construction, and Jones confined the RFC Mortgage Company to old loans.[16]

In addition to problems in the mortgage markets, railroad finances were still perilous. Congress allowed the position of federal coordinator of transportation to lapse in 1936 because Joseph Eastman had been unable to overcome the opposition of railroad management and the railway labor unions to consolidation. All the basic problems were still there. Freight revenues continued to decline as the railroads lost business to trucks, aircraft, and automobiles. Not once in the 1930s did net revenue recover to 1929 levels, and bankruptcies or judicial reorganizations were common. Of the fifteen largest railroads receiving RFC loans in the 1930s, ten were bankrupt by early 1938. Railroad miles in receivership rose from 22,545 in 1932 to 77,013 at the end of 1938.[17] Railroad bonds had risen from a composite average of 26 early in 1933 to 79.4 in 1935 and 94.7 in 1936, but the recession had sent them into another tailspin, dropping to 73.7 in December 1937 and 54.6 in March 1938.[18]

The decline in the railroad bond market was not as serious as it had been early in the 1930s because so many money market institutions had been shedding railroad assets, replacing them with more liquid government securities. Life insurance

[16] James Dougherty to Jesse Jones, January 31, 1938, NA, RG 234, RFC, Federal National Mortgage Association, "Articles of Association"; *New York Times*, November 20, 1937; Franklin D. Roosevelt to Jesse Jones, February 7, 1938, and Jesse Jones to James Roosevelt, May 20, 1938, FDRPL, OF 643, RFC.

[17] Ari and Olive Hoogenboom, *A History of the ICC*, pp. 120–21.

[18] *Federal Reserve Bulletin* 24 (January 1938), 39; (April 1938), 309; (August 1938), 717; and (December 1938), 1071.

companies, for example, had reduced their holdings of railroad bonds from 26.5 percent of assets in 1919 to only 9.2 percent in 1939, and mutual savings banks had got rid of more than 70 percent of their railroad bonds between 1930 and 1940.[19] By mid-1937, just before the economic decline set in, banks and trust companies had repaid $1.8 billion of the $1.9 billion they had borrowed from the RFC; mortgage loan companies $248 million of $368 million; building and loan associations $115 million of $117 million; and life insurance companies $86 million of $90 million. Railroads, however, had repaid only $177 million of the $532 million they had borrowed. But with the banking system stabilized and the percentage of railroad bonds as assets substantially reduced, the money markets were not as vulnerable to problems in the railroad industry.[20]

But the administration was still concerned about the economic impact of a sick railroad industry. RFC director Emil Schram remarked in March 1938 that the RFC could "continue to make loans to railroads but this alone will never solve the problem. Nor can it be solved in its entirety by merely raising railroad rates which if too high will drive traffic to cheaper unregulated forms of transportation."[21] In mid-March Roosevelt convened a special meeting with representatives of the ICC, RFC, SEC, and the Departments of Agriculture, Commerce, and Treasury, as well as labor and management representatives, to consider the question of railroad relief and consolidation. Roosevelt picked a committee composed of ICC commissioners Joseph Eastman, Walter Splawn, and Charles Mahaffie to report on the conference. The committee recommended RFC loans for equipment purchases, RFC loans to pay fixed charges without ICC approval, and congressional relief of existing bankruptcy regulations.[22]

[19] The Commission on Money and Credit, *Life Insurance Companies as Financial Institutions*, p. 48; Welfling, *Mutual Savings Banks*, p. 89.

[20] Spero, *Reconstruction Finance Corporation Loans to Railroads*, p. 33.

[21] Speech by Emil Schram to Jefferson College, March 25, 1938, NA, RG 234, RFC, Speeches of Key Personnel.

[22] Ari and Olive Hoogenboom, *A History of the ICC*, pp. 134–35; Henry Morgenthau Diaries, March 28, 1938, Morgenthau Papers.

Jesse Jones estimated that only a handful of railroads were relatively safe from bankruptcy, but existing ICC regulations prohibited RFC loans to insolvent lines. He concurred with the recommendation of the Splawn committee. In April 1938 Jones had a meeting with Senators Burton K. Wheeler of Montana and Harry S Truman of Missouri, Congressman Clarence Lea of California, chairman of the House Interstate Commerce Committee, Charles Mahaffie of the ICC, and representatives of the railway brotherhoods and the Association of American Railroads. They jointly recommended that the RFC make loans for the purchase of railway equipment, taking the equipment as security; work loans to replace people furloughed since October 1937; and loans for fixed payments to troubled roads without ICC approval. Adolf Berle was still trying to get the administration to acknowledge the fact that eventually the federal government would have to mandate railroad consolidation, but Roosevelt never concurred with him.[23]

Senator Harry S Truman and Congressman Henry Steagall of Alabama sponsored the legislation in May 1932. Although the bill had administration backing, Roosevelt did not fight openly for it. The ICC did not want to lose its power of prior approval of RFC railroad loans because Joseph Eastman feared the RFC would only perpetuate a structurally weak industry. A few well-orchestrated bankruptcies and reorganizations could accomplish at least some of the consolidation the Emergency Railroad Transportation Act of 1933 had failed to implement. Worse for the bill, a number of progressive Republicans in the Senate, led by Robert La Follette, Jr., of Wisconsin, opposed the bill as a bailout of the railroad industry and its Wall Street financiers, voicing much the same hostility they had been expressing about RFC railroad loans since 1932. The bill died in committee in May and June of 1938. RFC railroad loans still

[23] Jesse Jones to Franklin D. Roosevelt, April 26, 1938, FDRPL, PPF 703, Jesse Jones; Jesse Jones to Franklin D. Roosevelt, April 5, 1938, NA, RG 234, RFC, White House Correspondence; Jesse Jones, *Fifty Billion Dollars*, pp. 118-19; U.S. Congress, House, Committee on Banking and Currency, *Hearings on H.R. 10608. Loans to Railroads by the RFC*, 75th Cong., 3d Sess., 1938, pp. 1-3.

needed the approval of the Interstate Commerce Commission, and its powers remained as they had been since the RFC Extension Act of 1935 permitting the corporation to make loans to railroads for payment of fixed obligations, with ICC approval and purchases of railroad securities, including equipment trust certificates.[24]

In addition to the establishment of Fannie Mae and the resumption of RFC railroad loans, Roosevelt called for the revival of direct commercial lending. The fact that the RFC had more than $1.5 billion in disposable funds ready for investment and loans made it especially attractive.[25] The president wrote Jones in December asking him to have the RFC begin making industrial loans again, especially if the loans would increase employment, and Thomas Corcoran and Benjamin Cohen prepared legislation to make it easier to do. The RFC resumed its direct commercial loans in February.[26]

After meetings in March between Jesse Jones, Franklin D. Roosevelt, Henry Morgenthau, and a number of congressmen, Senator Carter Glass of Virginia agreed to sponsor the legislation. Corcoran and Cohen drafted a bill allowing the RFC to make loans on self-liquidating construction projects, as it had done in 1932 and 1933 before the PWA was created; lifting the ten-year maturity period on RFC loans, allowing the corporation to finance a greater variety of business projects; and eliminating the strict requirements on security for all RFC loans. The bill received the support of Harold Ickes, Harry Hopkins, Henry Morgenthau, Adolf Berle, and Secretary of Commerce Daniel Roper. It passed the Senate on April 2 and the House on April 5. Roosevelt signed it five days later.[27]

[24] *New York Times*, May 17, 1938; U.S. Congress, Senate, Committee on Banking and Currency, *Hearings on S. 3948. A Bill to Amend So Much of the R.F.C. Act, As Amended, As Relates to Railroads*, 75th Cong., 3d Sess., 1938, pp. 1–10.

[25] Berle and Jacobs, *Navigating the Rapids*, pp. 141–42; *New York Times*, November 10 and December 17, 1937.

[26] Franklin D. Roosevelt to Jesse Jones, December 21, 1937, and February 18, 1938, FDRPL, OF 643, RFC; Niznik, "Thomas G. Corcoran," pp. 336–37.

[27] *New York Times*, March 26–27 and 30, April 2, 5, 7, and 10, 1938; Jesse Jones to Carter Glass, March 21, 1938, Glass Papers; Jesse Jones to Franklin

As part of the resumption of RFC lending, the administration changed bank examination regulations for the FDIC and the comptroller of the currency. Bankers had been claiming ever since 1933 that federal examiners contributed to the financial crisis by classifying as "slow" all loans carrying maturities of more than six months or which had collateral worth less than the full value of the loan. Jesse Jones had been fighting with FDIC head Leo Crowley and Comptroller J.F.T. O'Connor about the issue since 1934. Relaxing bank examination regulations would give bankers more freedom to make long-term loans to needy businesses, reviving commercial credit and stimulating the economy. Jones wanted bank examiners to look carefully at the real quality of the loan and save the "slow" classification for those loans which were probably losses. Crowley and O'Connor refused to acknowledge that bank examination policies had prolonged the depression, but late in the spring of 1938 they nevertheless agreed to change examination policies. Instead of the "slow," "doubtful," and "loss" classifications, the FDIC and comptroller agreed to a numerical system. Class I was for sound loans assured of repayment. Class II was for risky loans from businesses lacking enough collateral or burdened with a low net worth. Class III meant the loan was weak and would probably yield a net loss. Class IV was for guaranteed losses. In computing bank capital, 50 percent of all Class III loans and all of Class IV loans would be subtracted from total assets. Roosevelt supported the changes because he felt it would relieve bankers of their fear of federal criticism of loans and encourage a revival of commercial credit.[28]

D. Roosevelt, March 28, 1938, FDRPL, OF 643, RFC; Jesse Jones, unpublished memorandum to Franklin D. Roosevelt describing a March 24, 1938, meeting to discuss emergency credit needs, NA, RG 234, RFC, White House Correspondence; Henry Morgenthau Diaries, April 27, 1938, Morgenthau Papers.

[28] Henry Morgenthau Diaries, April 12, 21, and 28, May 3–4, and June 21, 1938, Morgenthau Papers; RFC, *Press Release No. 1424* (Washington, D.C., 1938), p. 1; "Report of the Resolutions Committee of the American Bankers' Association, September 28, 1939," FDRPL, PPF 756, American Bankers' Association; Gurden Edwards, *How Banks Lend* (New York, 1939), pp. 7–8; Federal Reserve Bank of New York, *Annual Report for 1938* (Washington,

After signing the Glass bill, Roosevelt outlined his recovery package. It was a three point program aimed at "stopping the downward spiral." To expand the money supply, he desterilized $1.4 billion in Treasury gold and reduced total reserve requirements in the Federal Reserve system by $750 million. But he also recognized that "by themselves, monetary measures are insufficient to bring a sustained upward movement." To boost purchasing power, Roosevelt provided $1.25 billion to the Works Progress Administration, $175 million to the Farm Security Administration, $75 million to the National Youth Authority, $300 million to the U.S. Housing Authority, and $50 million to the Civilian Conservation Corps. Finally, he wanted the RFC to provide $1.5 billion in direct loans to business and self-liquidating loans to political subdivisions for public works construction. Morgenthau and the budget balancing crowd were hardly enthusiastic about the revival of the deficits, but they had no choice.[29]

Jones appreciated having the RFC back in business, but he was no more enthusiastic about making industrial loans than he had been in 1934. Most applications were marginal and he did not want to throw good government money after bad. Nearly one-fourth of all the business loans the RFC had made since 1934 were in default, a record almost as bad as the railroad money, and far worse than any of the money market institutions. Jones was willing to tolerate the railroad losses because they had been necessary to prop up banks, insurance companies, and building and loan associations. But he did not feel the same about the business loans.[30] He also still had doubts about the extent of legitimate demand for credit. A new round of credit surveys were under way by the National In-

D.C., 1939), pp. 22–23; Alva Adams to J.F.T. O'Connor, November 22, 1934, O'Connor Papers.

[29] Henry Morgenthau Diaries, April 12 and 14, 1938, Morgenthau Papers; Jesse Jones to James Roosevelt, May 20, 1938, FDRPL, OF 643, RFC; *New York Times*, April 19, 1938; George Harrison to Marriner Eccles, May 20, 1938, and Marriner Eccles to George Harrison, May 26, 1938, Harrison Papers.

[30] *New York Times*, February 19, 1938; Frederic Taber Diary, April 23 and 27, and November 11, 1938, Taber Papers.

dustrial Conference Board, American Bankers' Association, and the Investment Bankers' Association, and they all concluded that most legitimate demand by worthy borrowers was being satisfied, and that if any problem existed, it was the inability of small businesses to secure long-term credit.[31] In his speeches and press conferences in April and May of 1938, Jones frequently expressed doubt about the extent of business demand, but nevertheless urged bankers to loan more aggressively and promised the RFC would do the same. He wanted banks to participate with the RFC in industrial loans, set RFC loan rates at 5 percent, and agreed to accept as collateral for a loan first mortgages on real estate, warehouse receipts, and current receivables, all of which were more liberal than previous RFC requirements.[32]

During the rest of 1938 the RFC picked up the pace of its loans. The RFC Mortgage Company purchased $36 million in existing mortgages; the Federal National Mortgage Association bought $38 million in new FHA mortgages; and the RFC disbursed $88 million to railroads for debt refinancing and equipment purchases, $130 million to mortgage loan companies for construction loans, and $52 million to businesses for working capital and long-term financing. The Export-Import Bank loaned $20 million in 1938 to finance export sales. Loans to political subdivisions for self-liquidating construction loans totaled only $33 million in 1938.[33] But compared to

[31] Henry Morgenthau Diaries, April 21, 1938, Morgenthau Papers; American Bankers' Association, *The Rise in Bank Lending Activity* (New York, 1940), pp. 3–4; "Report of the National Industrial Conference Board, Fall, 1938"; Grosvener Jones to N. H. Engle, June 21, 1939, and E. E. Anderson to Stuart Guthrie, May 4, 1939, Hopkins Papers, Box 86; Discussion Notes, June 6, 1940, Harrison Papers.

[32] See the speech by Jesse Jones over the Mutual Broadcasting System, May 1, 1938, and to the U.S. Chamber of Commerce, May 4, 1938, NA, RG 234, RFC, Speeches of Key Personnel; *New York Times*, April 19 and 28, May 2, and July 19, 1938; speech by James H. Perkins, Chairman of the Board of National City Bank of New York, over the Mutual Broadcasting System, May 1, 1938, FDRPL, OF 643, RFC.

[33] RFC, *Quarterly Report for October 1 to December 31, 1937* (Washington, D.C., 1938), Table 1; RFC, *Quarterly Report for October 1 to December 31, 1938* (Washington, D.C., 1939), Table 1; Jesse Jones to Henry Steagall,

Roosevelt's initial hope of having the RFC disburse up to $1.5 billion, the results were marginal at best, and criticism of the RFC started up again. Although the RFC had authorized 4,825 loans for $837 million since February 1938, less than half the money had been disbursed.[34]

In August 1938 Roosevelt wrote Emil Schram asking if the RFC could speed up its railroad equipment loans, reduce interest rates from 4 to 3 percent, and make loans up to 100 percent rather than 90 percent of the value of the equipment. Criticism of the RFC Mortgage Company, Fannie Mae, and the Export-Import Bank surfaced as well. The charge was an old one: the RFC and its subsidiaries were more concerned with their own liquidity than with the credit needs of the country.[35] Jones responded by "circling the wagons," as he had done in the past. He castigated banks for reducing commercial credit during the recession, from a total of $22.5 billion in mid-1937 to only $21 billion in September 1938. The RFC was declining most loan applications for the same old reasons: either the loan was going to be used to retire existing indebtedness, or the company's prospects for repayment were poor. Jones also expressed disappointment that banks had not joined the RFC in its business loans, participating in only 15 percent of them. Ironically, Jones was also delighted with a random sampling of RFC business loans conducted by Secretary of Commerce Harry Hopkins early in 1939. Hopkins randomly selected 300 rejected RFC loan applications and found 236 of them to be completely unsatisfactory because of poor financial condition, inadequate collateral, weak earning potential, and intention to use the money for speculation or indebtedness. Hopkins concluded there would be no big increase in RFC business loans unless the corporation was prepared to accept major losses.[36]

February 20, 1939, NA, RG 234, RFC, RFC, *Press Release No. 1474* (Washington, D.C., 1939).

[34] *New York Times*, December 9, 1938.

[35] Franklin D. Roosevelt to Emil Schram, August 17, 1938, FDRPL, OF 643, RFC; Basil O'Connor to Franklin D. Roosevelt, December 8, 1938, FDRPL, OF 971, Export-Import Bank.

[36] Speech of Charles Henderson to the Botany Worsted Mills, May 11, 1939, NA, RG 234, RFC, Speeches of Key Personnel; "Agency Review Commit-

The conservatism of the RFC came as no surprise to many insiders in Washington, particularly those enthusiastic about vigorous antitrust action and heavy spending. Marriner Eccles and Harold Ickes had not even wanted Jesse Jones and the RFC involved in the resumption of spending because they were convinced Jones would sabotage the effort. He had had no faith in the business loan idea since its inception in 1934, and things had changed very little. Jones would not risk government money on bad loans.[37] Antitrusters like Thomas Corcoran were also disappointed because small businesses had not benefited much from RFC loans. The hearings of the Temporary National Economic Committee made it abundantly clear that small businesses were having terrible problems securing equity capital and short-term loans from banks. They were unable to get fixed capital by issuing securities because the expenses charged by underwriters for small issues were prohibitive. Because the survival rate for small businesses was so low, and because the depression had seriously depleted their resources, banks and the RFC had been reluctant to advance them credit. The rise of personal and business finance companies during the 1930s was proof that traditional institutions were not extending enough money to small business.[38]

Jones believed that most of the demand for credit by small businessmen came from very weak companies. The RFC's loan experience between 1934 and 1937 confirmed his position. Of the 6,000 applications the RFC had received, more than 4,000 were rejected. Less than 7 percent of the RFC business loan money had gone out in amounts of less than $25,000, while more than 60 percent exceeded $200,000. Larger loans to larger businesses had been infinitely safer than smaller loans to

tee of the Atlanta Loan Agency," January-October 1940, NA, RG 234, RFC, Transcripts of Board Notes; U.S. Senate, Committee on Banking and Currency, *Hearings on S. 1482. A Bill to Provide for Insurance Loans to Business*, 76th Cong., 1st Sess., 1939, pp. 405–7.

[37] Berle and Jacobs, *Navigating the Rapids*, p. 168.

[38] Temporary National Economic Committee, *Problems of Small Business* (Washington, D.C., 1941), pp. 239–43; Jerome Frank to Harry Hopkins, June 9, 1939, Hopkins Papers.

smaller businesses. The records of RFC participation with private banks revealed a similar trend. The willingness of banks to participate with the RFC in loans had been directly proportional to the size of the loan, with banks least willing to go in on loans of less than $5,000 and far more willing on loans exceeding $500,000.[39]

The increasingly loud demands for government attention on the part of small businessmen, the revelations about monopoly coming from the Temporary National Economic Committee, the faith of the antitrusters, disappointment with RFC loan policies, and the demands of the spending group led to a resurrection of the proposal for an Industrial Credit Corporation and pushed Jesse Jones out of the RFC in 1939. Congress agreed to extend the life of the RFC in January 1939, but there was an outspoken cry for administrative reform—for some way of meeting the credits of small businesses. Although the RFC continued making loans in 1939, Jones at the same time fought a rearguard action to prevent any legislative transformation of the corporation. Business loans had left him with his most significant losses in his seven years with the RFC, and he had no intention of magnifying them to satisfy critics.[40]

A variety of proposals to provide government loans or government loan insurance to private business went to Congress in 1939. Even after the 1935 legislation giving the RFC greater authority in the commercial lending, a few people kept calling for a broader program. Congressman Herman Koppelman submitted a bill to Congress in mid-1935 establishing an Intermediate Industrial Credit Corporation to provide federal loans, but the proposal had no chance for success because of the similar powers held by the RFC and the Federal Reserve sys-

[39] "Business Loans," April 18, 1938; "Size of Business Loans," November 13, 1939; and "Direct Loans to Industry," October 15, 1937, all in NA, RG 234, RFC, Statistical and Economic Division, Reports; RFC, *Press Release No. 1387* (Washington, D.C., 1938), p. 1; RFC, *Press Release No. 1426* (Washington, D.C., 1938), p. 1.

[40] *New York Times*, January 30, 1939; Franklin D. Roosevelt to Jesse Jones, January 25, 1939, FDRPL, OF 643, RFC.

tem.[41] Adolf Berle continued to campaign between 1936 and 1939 for an ambitious government capital lending program. He urged Roosevelt to create a government railroad equipment corporation to order, finance, and purchase equipment for railroads in trouble, and to force consolidation of weak roads. At the same time he was advocating a series of capital credit banks to provide long-term equity financing to needy businesses; a bill to insure bank loans to small businesses; and a Public Works Finance Corporation to rediscount and purchase the bonds of self-liquidating public construction projects.[42] Senator Claude Pepper submitted a bill providing for $12 billion to capitalize a series of twelve regional industrial banks; Congressman Wright Patman wanted twelve regional federal loan banks to be controlled by associations of local businessmen and farmers; and Senator James Mead submitted two measures to Congress allowing the RFC to insure small business loans and to provide for twenty-year Federal Reserve industrial loans. Marriner Eccles, governor of the Federal Reserve Board, was calling for creation of a Federal Reserve Industrial Loan Corporation.[43]

None of the proposals succeeded. Berle's call for federal capital banks, a railway equipment corporation, and forced railroad consolidation was out of touch with the temper of the times. The planning formula of the brain trust had already had its day, and the prevailing antitrust mood was not really sympathetic to any large-scale government intervention in the money markets. Claude Pepper's proposal for $12 billion in

[41] Herman Koppelmann to Marvin McIntyre, June 26, 1935, FDRPL, OF 706, Credit; Frank R. Wilson to Daniel C. Roper, October 10, 1938, NA, RG 234, RFC, White House Correspondence.

[42] Berle and Jacobs, *Navigating the Rapids*, p. 168; Adolf Berle, "A Banking System for Capital and Credit," unpublished memorandum for the Temporary National Economic Committee, May 29, 1939, Berle Papers, Box 71.

[43] Grosvenor Jones to Harry Hopkins, March 27, 1939, Hopkins Papers, Box 86; U.S. Congress, Senate, Committee on Banking and Currency, *Hearings on S. 3420. A Bill to Provide the Insurance by the RFC of Loans by Banks to Business Enterprise*, 75th Cong., 2d Sess., 1938, pp. 1–5; Allen Sproul to Edmund Day, July 21, 1939, and Allen Sproul to Marriner Eccles, July 21, 1939, Harrison Papers, Box 12.

capital was far too ambitious, and Wright Patman's plan left too much power over government money in local hands. There was also little support for the flow of any government money to large businesses. That too smacked of the early New Deal's cooperative business commonwealth philosophy. The only consensus emerging concerned the credit plight of small businesses, and even then many people felt such loans fell more into the category of venture capital than working capital because of the risks.[44]

The small business conference in February 1938 had dramatized the issue, but throughout 1938 and 1939 a series of studies, some by the Temporary National Economic Committee and others by government and private agencies, documented money market changes which had left small business outside the flow of credit. Before the depression small businesses financed expansion by reinvesting profits, support from local business investors, working capital loans from banks, and the sale of securities. But by the late 1930s, all four sources had dried up. Profits to reinvest were limited; local investors and commercial banks were reluctant to make loans because of liquidity fears; and the capital markets had all but collapsed. Even the RFC and Federal Reserve loans had discriminated against small business for the same reasons bankers had refused to loan: poor credit risks, weak assets, and inadequate collateral. When small businesses got credit, it was usually short-term, ninety days or less, or subject to immediate recall. Equity was difficult to secure because of the costs of floating small securities issues. The real place for government to fill in the credit gap was in small business financing.[45]

[44] Federal Reserve Bank of Philadelphia, "Direct Loans of Reserve Banks to Industry," unpublished manuscript, 1940, Harrison Papers.

[45] J. L. Nicholson, "The Fallacy of Easy Money for the Small Business," *Harvard Business Review*, 16 (Autumn 1938), 31–32; Rudolph L. Weissman, *Small Business and Venture Capital* (New York, 1945), pp. 39–44, 51–52, 68–74; John H. Cove, *Problems of Small Business* (Washington, D.C., 1941), pp. 208–30; "Interim Report of the Committee on the Credit Needs of Small Business," Department of Commerce, March 2, 1939, and Grosvenor Jones to Harry Hopkins, March 27, 1939, Hopkins Papers, Box 86.

The two financing proposals receiving the greatest consideration in 1939 were the Eccles proposal for a Federal Reserve Industrial Loan Corporation and the Mead proposals for RFC insurance of business loans. Bankers opposed both bills as unnecessary. Legitimate credit demands were being met by private institutions, and the dismal loan record of the RFC and Federal Reserve banks was proof that most applications for small business loans were poor risks. Department of Commerce studies of those loans confirmed banking opinion. Indeed, between 1934 and the end of 1938, the Federal Reserve Bank of New York had received 4,937 inquiries about loans, which resulted in 1,387 applications. Only 358 of those applications were approved. Because of the lackluster performance of the Federal Reserve banks over the previous four years, Eccles's proposal for a Federal Reserve Industrial Loan Corporation fell on deaf ears. According to the Department of Commerce, the Federal Reserve banks needed to be prepared to sustain heavy losses if they entered the small business credit field with any aggressiveness.[46]

The Mead bills encountered the same opposition from bankers arguing government insurance was unnecessary. One Mead bill had the RFC insure commercial banks against losses on business loans smaller than $200,000 and amortized at 4 percent over seven years. The other bill authorized the RFC to insure any loss in excess of 10 percent of the principal, for loans not exceeding $1 million, over a ten-year period. Bankers did not want to see the government so deeply engaged in private economic affairs, especially since it was not really necessary. Opposition came from other sources as well. Jesse Jones and the RFC criticized the Mead bills as potential disasters for banks and the government if they loaned too much money to weak, marginal firms. He wanted nothing to do with them. His attitude affected others in the New Deal. Those who wanted some type of government loans to small business—like

[46] Willard L. Thorpe to E. J. Noble, May 15, 1939; Grosvenor Jones to Harry Hopkins, March 27, 1939; Henry E. Hermann to Harry Hopkins, June 5, 1939, all in Hopkins Papers, Box 86; *New York Times*, June 18, 1939.

Marriner Eccles, Adolf Berle, Thomas Corcoran, and Benjamin Cohen—had little faith that Jesse Jones was the person to be administering it. His own misgivings about direct business loans were so long-standing, and confirmed so clearly by the RFC's lack of enthusiasm, that even if the Mead bills passed they would probably have little effect. Also, many people were convinced that banks would have little to do with the insurance program because they would have to absorb the first 10 percent loss themselves. Eccles and Berle were also concerned that the Mead bills provided no equity financing for small businesses, which was exactly what so many of them needed. Although small business groups enthusiastically supported the bills, Roosevelt was concerned about the diversity of opposition to Mead's proposals. The president did not exert any real effort on their behalf and they died a quiet death. Citing Jones's behind-the-scenes opposition to the measures, Mead withdrew them at the end of July.[47]

Even though the proposals for government insurance of loans had failed, the need for small business loans still appeared to exist, and some administration officials began taking another approach. People like Benjamin Cohen and Thomas Corcoran felt that the RFC already had the authority to loan aggressively to small business, and that only Jesse Jones stood in the way. In a letter to Secretary of Commerce Harry Hopkins, Cohen argued that

> while a liberal construction of the statute . . . might theoretically make it possible for the RFC under existing law to do most of the things provided in the Mead bill, that will not practically be possible without a thorough revision of RFC

[47] James M. Mead to Franklin D. Roosevelt, July 22, 1939, FDRPL, OF 3732, James M. Mead; Discussion Notes, June 15, 1939, and "The Mead Bill and Chairman Eccles's Suggestion of a Federal Reserve Industrial Loan Corporation," Harrison Papers, Box 12; Morgenthau Diaries, June 7, 1939, Morgenthau Papers; Marriner Eccles to Harry Hopkins, June 7, 1939; Charles Guthrie to Benjamin Cohen, May 5, 1939; and Jerome Frank to Harry Hopkins, June 9, 1939, all in Hopkins Papers, Box 86; U.S. Congress, Senate, *Hearings on S. 1482*, pp. 3–4, 34, 51–60, 75, 85–90, 117–118, 130, 155–57, and 235; *New York Times*, July 2, 17, and 18, 1939.

policy and without an aggressive campaign which will not only bring home to the banks what RFC will do but will bring home to small business men what their local banks can do.[48]

Jones, Schram, and other RFC directors argued back that the RFC was not a commercial bank, that it occupied a middle ground between government and private banking, urging bankers to loan more enthusiastically and at the same time picking up the credit slack when they refused. To do what Cohen, Corcoran, Mead, and other antitrusters wanted would transform the RFC into a commercial bank, something Jones had been resisting ever since the Hoover administration.[49]

For a while the administration hoped the Reorganization Act of 1939 would solve their problem with Jesse Jones. Government reorganization for better management and efficiency was a major issue in Roosevelt's second administration. He had appointed the President's Committee on Administrative Management, headed by political scientist Louis Brownlow, to study government reorganization, and their published report in 1937 recommended major changes in the executive branch. Intense political debate raged over the reorganization proposal in 1938, but a modified version passed Congress late in March 1939 and Roosevelt signed the act on April 3. Among a number of other changes, the act created a Federal Loan Agency to coordinate the Reconstruction Finance Corporation, Export-Import Bank, Federal Housing Administration, Home Owners' Loan Corporation, RFC Mortgage Company, Disaster Loan Corporation, Federal National Mortgage Association, and the Electric Home and Farm Authority. At Tommy Corcoran's suggestion, Roosevelt removed Jones as head of the

[48] Benjamin Cohen to Harry Hopkins, April (?), 1939, Hopkins Papers, Box 86. Also see Benjamin Cohen to Harry Hopkins, June 23, 1939, and Benjamin Cohen, "Memorandum for the Insurance of Loans to Business," March 3, 1939, unpublished manuscript, Hopkins Papers, Box 86.

[49] Jesse Jones speech over NBC Radio, April 9, 1939; Emil Schram speech over NBC Radio, November 20, 1939, and December 10, 1939, NA, RG 234, RFC, Speeches of Key Personnel; Jesse Jones to all bankers, March 23, 1939, FDRPL, OF 643, RFC; Henry Morgenthau Diaries, February 6, 1940, Morgenthau Papers; U.S. Congress, Senate, *Hearings on S. 1102*, pp. 4–13.

RFC and made him the new federal loan administrator. The change came at a White House press conference, where Jones heard about it for the first time. Jones resigned from the RFC and Roosevelt replaced him with Emil Schram, a longtime RFC director.[50]

Getting Jones out of the RFC, however, had little impact on its activities because as federal loan administrator Jones ruled the federal credit establishment with an iron hand. Emil Schram, his successor at the RFC, was a loyal devotee of Jones who viewed the credit czar as his mentor and a man of unparalleled business and financial acuity. Schram also ran the Electric Home and Farm Authority. Lynn Talley, head of the Commodity Credit Corporation, viewed Jones in the same way, grateful to him for career boosts Jones had provided a decade before. Warren Lee Pierson, president of the Export-Import Bank, had gotten his start in Washington as special counsel in the RFC. Jones had liked him immediately and had sponsored his appointment to the EIB. Sam Husbands, a member of the RFC since 1932 and a director since 1936, headed the Federal National Mortgage Association, managed the affairs of the RFC Mortgage Company, and looked to Jones for leadership. Finally, Jones had selected Stewart McDonald, head of the Federal Housing Administration, as his second in command at the Federal Loan Agency. Whatever hopes Cohen, Corcoran, and Roosevelt had for limiting Jones's influence by "promoting" him out of the RFC were quickly shattered.

Removing Jones from the RFC and replacing him with someone more willing to enter the business credit field with enthusiasm was another option, but Jones's reputation inside and outside Congress was too strong for any casual dismissal. When Secretary of the Navy Claude Swanson died in July 1939, during the congressional debate over the Mead bills,

---

[50] For studies of government reorganization, see Barry D. Karl, *Executive Reorganization and Reform in the New Deal. The Genesis of Administrative Management, 1900–1939* (Cambridge, Mass., 1963), and Richard Polenberg, *Reorganizing Roosevelt's Government. The Controversy Over Executive Reorganization, 1936–1939* (Cambridge, Mass., 1966). Also see Jones, *Fifty Billion Dollars*, pp. 530–31.

Roosevelt asked Jones to join the cabinet as the new secretary of the navy, but Jones had more sense than that. He was not going to give up RFC for the navy post. Early in 1940 the president then asked Jones to replace Harry Hopkins as secretary of commerce. Jones immediately asked if he would be able to continue as federal loan administrator. When Roosevelt said no, Jones refused the appointment. The president ended up getting a joint congressional resolution passed allowing Jones to become secretary of commerce while remaining federal loan administrator.[51] The political power Jones had exercised since 1933 was still intact.

During the next year, between the summer of 1939 and the spring of 1940, Jones walked that tightrope between a government agency and a commercial bank, trying to respond to the criticisms of the antitrusters without compromising RFC solvency. The interest rate on RFC and Export-Import Bank business loans was reduced from 5 to 4 percent late in April 1939, FHA rates from 5 to 4.5 percent, and HOLC loans from 5 to 4 percent. Jones also tried to make more loans to smaller businesses. Between 1934 and early 1938, 32 percent of RFC business loans had been for less than $10,000 and 50 percent for less than $25,000. But between the resumption of RFC lending in February 1938 and the end of 1939, more than 52 percent of all loans were in amounts of $10,000 or less, and 71 percent were under $25,000.[52] He also tried to make sure that more loan applications were approved, and that stronger loan applications were received. In the fall of 1937, when Roosevelt ordered the RFC shut down, its loan record in terms of approvals and denials was essentially the same as the loan record of the Federal Reserve banks. By the end of 1939 the RFC had approved about 60 percent of the applications it had received, but Federal Reserve banks had approved less than 30 percent. By the end of 1939 the Federal Reserve banks had authorized

[51] Jones, *Fifty Billion Dollars*, pp. 256–57.
[52] "Size of Business Loans," November 13, 1939, NA, RG 234, RFC, Statistical Division; RFC, *Press Release No. 1482* (Washington, D.C., 1939), p. 1; RFC, *Press Release No. 1394* (Washington, D.C., 1938), p. 1.

$188 million in industrial loans, but by that same time the RFC had authorized business loans totaling nearly $370 million.[53]

The rest of the RFC programs were also moving ahead at Jones's pace, somewhat faster than he was really comfortable with but slower than many people in the administration wanted. By the end of 1940 the RFC Mortgage Company had disbursed a total of $170 million, nearly 60 percent of it in purchases of FHA mortgages, and Fannie Mae had bought $223 million in new FHA mortgages. Loans to mortgage loan companies stood at nearly $600 million by the end of 1940, up more than $100 million since the end of 1938. The RFC had authorized $911 million to eighty-six railroads, including $144 million to purchase railroad bonds and equipment trust certificates. A total of $786 million had actually been disbursed to railroads. To provide construction work on self-liquidating public projects, the RFC bought $214 million in bonds between 1938 and 1940. By the end of 1940 its business loan authorizations totaled $446 million to 7,917 businesses, with more than $240 million of that disbursed. Export-Import Bank loans accelerated in 1939, with loans exceeding $16 million each going to Norway, Sweden, Spain, and Chile.[54]

But even while Jones was trying, modestly of course, to satisfy his antitrust and Keynesian critics, he encountered trouble late in 1939 and early in 1940 from an old nemesis—Henry Morgenthau and the budget balancers were at work again. The recovery debate plaguing the New Deal ever since 1933 was still going on. Part of the problem was success. From its lows in the spring of 1938, the economy had staged a modest

[53] "Number of Loans and Participations to Business Enterprises From February 19, 1938 to April 15, 1939," NA, RG 234, RFC, Statistical Division; *Federal Reserve Bulletin*, 26 (November 1940), 1193; Jesse Jones to John F. Fahey and Steward McDonald, July 22, 1939, FDRPL, OF 3720, Federal Loan Agency.

[54] RFC Mortgage Company, "Monthly Statement of Condition," December 31, 1940, NA, RG 234, RFC, Records of the RFC Mortgage Company; Federal National Mortgage Association, "Monthly Statement of Condition," December 31, 1940, NA, RG 234, RFC, Records of the Federal National Mortgage Association; RFC, *Quarterly Report for September 30, 1940 to December 31, 1940* (Washington, D.C., 1941), pp. 2–4.

but important recovery. Average prices for common stocks had risen from 64 in March 1938 to 95 in October 1939. The industrial production index had jumped from 75 to 124 in the same period, and the index of factory employment had risen from 82 to 103.[55] With the economy coming out of its recent malaise, Morgenthau and the Treasury group once again thought it was time to restore business confidence by cutting government spending and balancing the budget. Keynesianism had few converts at Treasury.

During late 1939 and early 1940 the RFC was caught in the middle of an intense debate within the administration about future economic policies. The Wall Street crowd, their allies in the Federal Reserve Bank of New York, and Henry Morgenthau's Treasury group all advocated reductions in government spending, balanced budgets, and transferral of funds from the major government corporations to eliminate the deficits. In their view, that was the only "long-term solution" to the country's economic problems.[56] Opposed to them were antitrusters like Tommy Corcoran, Benjamin Cohen, and Felix Frankfurter, and spenders like Harry Hopkins, Harold Ickes, and Marriner Eccles. Weekly meetings of the Fiscal and Monetary Committee were usually attended by Morgenthau, Eccles, federal budget director Harold Smith, Under Secretary of the Treasury Daniel Bell, Federal Reserve economist Lauchlin Currie, and at various times Jesse Jones, Secretary of Agriculture Henry Wallace, and John Carmody, head of the Federal Works Agency. Eccles and Currie campaigned for massive federal spending, while Morgenthau, Smith, and Bell wanted a balanced budget. Late in 1939 Roosevelt began urging economies on the RFC, and early in 1940 proposals to begin taking money from the federal loan agencies to balance the budget began to gather steam. Morgenthau's ancient jealousy of Jesse Jones had not abated, and cutting the government corporations was one major step toward eliminating the deficits. For

[55] *Federal Reserve Bulletin*, 26 (January 1940), 40, 45, and 48.

[56] George Harrison to Marriner Eccles, March 4, 1939, Harrison Papers; Daily Memoranda, May 23, 1939, Harold Smith Papers.

Eccles and Currie, the RFC budget was also a convenient target, primarily because of its cash reserves and unused balances. If Morgenthau had to have a balanced budget, let him get the money from the RFC, where it might otherwise sit indefinitely. Jones opposed those proposals, seeing them as preoccupations with "bookkeeping, nothing more," but it all looked like a curtain call on the RFC experience in 1936 and 1937—the beginning of another series of restrictions on RFC authority. Then the German invasion of France and the Low Countries in May 1940 changed everything.[57]

[57] Franklin D. Roosevelt to Henry Wallace, December 27, 1939, FDRPL, OF 285; Daily Memoranda, May 23, June 14, 28, 30, and December 13 and 23, 1939, January 17, February 15 and 27, March 12, 25, and 29, 1940, Smith Papers.

CHAPTER X

War and Transformation

A S EARLY AS 1938 Jesse Jones had become concerned about the possibility of war and financing critical industries, especially electrical utilities, and Roosevelt asked him to consider making loans to increase production.[1] But not until the Nazi invasion of France in the spring of 1940 did the administration put the economy on a war footing. All the debates about economic recovery disappeared and the RFC was transformed into the most powerful agency in the country. The RFC had become so ubiquitous to the New Deal that journals were referring to it as the "fourth branch of government" or the "fourth estate," but its activities in the 1930s were barely a shadow of its power during the war. World War II lifted all the restrictions and most of the fears concerning the RFC. Recovery gave way to defense.

Antitrusters, Keynesians, and even budget balancers realized that national security required substantial boosts in government spending, and that business demand for credit, stimulated by billions of dollars of defense contracts, would be enormous. Private capital would be inadequate, as it had been during World War I, and the RFC would have to fill the void.[2] Late in May Benjamin Cohen and Tommy Corcoran drafted legislation liberalizing RFC loan requirements so the RFC could flexibly negotiate interest rates, maturities, amounts, and collateral. No longer was the RFC a slave to collateral, security, and repayment considerations. Congress approved the legislation on June 25, 1940, and Roosevelt signed it immediately. The legislation allowed the RFC to make loans or purchase

---

[1] *New York Times*, November 3, 1938; RFC, *Press Release No. 1474* (Washington, D.C., 1939), p. 1; Franklin D. Roosevelt to Marvin McIntyre, August 15, 1938, FDRPL, OF 643, RFC.

[2] Jerome Frank to Franklin D. Roosevelt, May 18, 1940, FDRPL, OF 643, RFC.

stock in any corporation for the transportation or production of critical materials; for plant construction, expansion, equipment, and working capital in a defense related business; and for the acquisition or production of strategic materials and weapons.[3]

Jones immediately began to change direction for the RFC. The Electric Home and Farm Authority closed early in 1942; its program of increasing the domestic consumption of electricity ran head-on into the demands of war production and conservation. The RFC Mortgage Company stopped financing new construction loans and joined the Federal National Mortgage Association in purchasing new FHA-insured mortgages and underwriting the secondary market. Soon the RFC ceased to be a recovery agency and came to resemble its ancestor, the War Finance Corporation. Although a variety of recovery theories had appeared during the 1930s, the essence of the New Deal had been state capitalism. When the outbreak of World War II removed most restraints on federal government activity, state capitalism was unleashed with a vengeance. Jones created a host of new RFC subsidiaries.

On June 28, 1940, after meeting with representatives of Goodyear, Firestone, B. F. Goodrich, General Tire, and United States Rubber, he created the Rubber Reserve Company with Howard J. Klossner, an RFC director, as president. At first the company worked to accumulate a supply of rubber and end American dependency on Japanese-controlled supplies in Southeast Asia. It was a fortuitous decision. The Rubber Reserve Company quickly became the sole importer of crude rubber in the United States, stockpiling reserves and selling them as needed, at cost plus carrying charges, to the major rubber corporations. By the end of 1941 the Rubber Reserve Company stockpile had reached 630,356 tons, enough to supply the war machine for a year, but the string of Japanese victories in southern Asia early in 1942 sealed off that source. Jones

[3] Jesse Jones to Franklin D. Roosevelt, June 19, 1940, FDRPL, OF 643, RFC; Niznik, "Thomas G. Corcoran," p. 480; RFC, *Circular No. 23* (Washington, D.C., 1940), pp. 1–2.

then launched a government-owned synthetic rubber industry. By 1945 the RFC investment in synthetic rubber had reached $677 million and the government was managing fifty-one plants producing 760,000 tons of synthetic rubber a year.[4]

On the same day he established the Rubber Reserve Company, Jones also set up the Metals Reserve Company to stockpile such strategic materials as aluminum, chrome, copper, manganese, tin, nickel, mica, tungsten, platinum, and quartz crystals. He selected Charles Henderson, an RFC director, as president of the Metals Reserve Company. During the next four years the Metals Reserve Company spent $2.75 billion acquiring fifty separate minerals and metals, as well as another $1 billion in subsidies and premium price payments to finance marginal production of strategic metals. In doing so it established cooperative partnerships with the major corporations in the extraction industries, including Anaconda Copper and Phelps-Dodge. The Metals Reserve Company also worked closely with another RFC subsidiary, the United States Commercial Company, which Jesse Jones established on March 26, 1942, to enter neutral markets and purchase raw materials, regardless of price, which the Axis powers needed. By the end of the war the United States Commercial Company had spent nearly $2 billion.[5]

On August 20, 1940, Jones set up the Defense Plant Corporation to take over some of the work of the RFC Business Loan Division and finance new plant construction for war industries, and a week later he established the Defense Supplies Corporation to acquire critical industrial materials—aviation gasoline, industrial alcohol, sugar, molasses, sodium nitrate, wool, cotton, diamond dies, silk, quinine, and timber. In June 1942 Jones established the Smaller War Plants Corporation to finance plant construction in small industries. The RFC also continued making small business loans, primarily for working capital to companies with government contracts. By 1945 the Defense Plant Corporation had invested $9.2 billion, the De-

[4] Jones, *Fifty Billion Dollars*, pp. 396–434.
[5] Ibid., pp. 387–94, 434–50.

fense Supplies Corporation $9.3 billion, the RFC $4.4 billion, and the Smaller War Plants Corporation $200 million. The Defense Plant Corporation constructed 2,300 factories and equipped them with tools and machinery. Usually the plant was leased to private corporations for a nominal fee, with the government agreeing to share modestly in any profits but to assume all losses. Those companies doing business with the government were among the largest in the world, including the Aluminum Company of America, General Motors, United States Steel, Curtis-Wright, Republic Steel, Chrysler, Ford Motor, Anaconda Copper, Dow Chemical, United Aircraft, General Electric, Union Carbide, Standard Oil, Bendix Aviation, Goodyear, Studebaker, Packard Motor, B. F. Goodrich, E. I. du Pont, and Sperry. When the war ended, the Defense Plant Corporation disposed of its plants by selling them to private companies, usually those already leasing the facilities, at an average of less than 50 percent of appraised value. State capitalism proved to be a windfall to corporate America.[6]

There were other RFC subsidiaries as well. On October 23, 1940, he established the Defense Homes Corporation to loan money for the construction of new homes for workers coming into the defense plants. Congressional legislation in September 1940 lifted the loan limit of $20 million on the Export-Import Bank and permitted loans for the sale of war supplies and direct loans to foreign governments. The EIB's borrowing capacity went up to $700 million.[7] One week after Pearl Harbor Jones established the War Damage Corporation to assist insurance companies in underwriting business property against enemy attack. The Petroleum Reserve Company was established

---

[6] Ibid., pp. 315–86. For a history of the Defense Plant Corporation, see Gerald T. White, *Billions for Defense. Government Financing by the Defense Plant Corporation during World War II* (University, Ala., 1980).

[7] Jesse Jones to Franklin D. Roosevelt, May 7, 1941, FDRPL, OF 643, RFC; Jesse Jones to Congress, July 21, 1940, FDRPL, OF 971, Export-Import Bank; Jesse Jones speech over NBC Radio, October 7, 1940, NA, RG 234, RFC, Speeches of Key Personnel; Jesse Jones to Franklin D. Roosevelt, December 2, 1940, FDRPL, OF 3720, Federal Loan Agency; Jesse Jones, *Fifty Billion Dollars*, pp. 387–95, 451–55.

in 1943 to stockpile oil and gasoline. Ten months after the German invasion of France in 1940, the RFC, its subsidiaries, and the Export-Import Bank had loaned out more than $2.5 billion, and over the next four years they handed out $37 billion more. Massive federal spending ended the Great Depression.[8]

THE CIRCLE was complete. The War Finance Corporation had first appeared in 1918, and business demand absorbed its resources. The WFC was active in agricultural finance through the Federal Intermediate Credit Bank system until 1924, when it was gradually dissolved. But just when the WFC was finishing up its last paperwork in 1931, Herbert Hoover used it as a model in establishing the RFC. Throughout the 1930s the RFC was a barometer of the New Deal, playing a central role in the appearance of state capitalism in the federal markets and the discrediting of monetary policy which preceded the national conversion to Keynes.

Classical economists, whose discipline emerged during the capital-scarce decades of the nineteenth century, had traditionally assumed that increases in the money supply and the volume of credit automatically resulted in economic growth. Businessmen and entrepreneurs were limited only by the amount of money available for expansion. Demand was always there; capital was not. When the money supply went up businessmen immediately put it to use. In the early years of the twentieth century, when the Federal Reserve system began to exercise some control over the money supply, economists used interest rates and reserve requirements to stimulate production and employment or, conversely, to restrain prices. World War

---

[8] Jesse Jones to Congress, July 21, 1940, and "Statement of Loans and Commitments," March 3, 1941, FDRPL, OF 971, Export-Import Bank; speech by Jesse Jones over NBC Radio, October 7, 1940, NA, RG 234, RFC, Speeches of Key Personnel; Emil Schram to Franklin D. Roosevelt, December 31, 1940, FDRPL, OF 42-B, Electric Home and Farm Authority; RFC Mortgage Company, "Monthly Statement of Condition," December 31, 1941, NA, RG 234, RFC, Records of the RFC Mortgage Company; Federal National Mortgage Association, "Monthly Statement of Condition," December 31, 1941, NA, RG 234, RFC, Records of the Federal National Mortgage Association.

I proved their point. Demand for credit outpaced capital, and without federal intervention a bottleneck would have put a cap on productive capacity. The WFC entered the breach and the capital it funneled into the economy made up the difference.

When the economy slid into the depression after 1929, and then refused to come out of it, economists were looking for culprits, some telltale sign of what was going wrong. They were used to the boom and bust cycle but expected the economy to find its "equilibrium" once again. It did not, and many economists focused on the volume of commercial credit. Between the end of 1929 and mid-1933, total loans of Federal Reserve member banks had dropped from $23 billion to $11 billion, in spite of very low interest rates and reserve requirements.[9] According to theory, idle bank reserves should have been put to use, absorbed by optimistic businessmen anxious to expand. Instead banks began accumulating excess reserves at Federal Reserve banks—$43 million in 1929 to $250 million in 1932.[10]

Assuming that the liquidity crisis in 1931 had unduly frightened bankers and made them far too cautious, Hoover established the RFC to do what the WFC had done in 1918—help meet the demand for capital. Through short-term loans, the RFC would relieve liquidity fears and allow bankers to start lending again. Abundant credit would lift the country out of the depression. In 1932 the real purpose of the RFC was to liquefy money market assets and encourage more lending. Between 1932 and 1937 the RFC loaned billions to banks, but excess reserves mounted even more, from $528 million in 1933 to $2.5 billion in 1935. Congress authorized the RFC to make direct business loans, but to Jones's surprise the demand he expected did not materialize. The RFC received thousands of requests for money, but most came from badly managed businesses with little collateral and poor prospects for survival. Excess reserves dropped temporarily to $1.2 billion and member bank loans rose temporarily to $12.6 billion in 1937, but

[9] *Federal Reserve Bulletin*, 23 (September 1937), 923.
[10] Board of Governors of the Federal Reserve System, *Banking and Monetary Statistics* (Washington, D.C., 1943), pp. 34–35, 368.

neither increase had anything to do with a change of heart among bankers. Relief spending and veterans' bonuses stimulated the economy and created fresh business demand for credit. When the economy turned down again late in 1937, excess reserves began climbing again, to $2.5 billion in 1938, $4.4 billion in 1939, and $6.3 billion in 1940. Not until 1941, with war production up, did excess reserves drop and bank loans rise.[11]

In focusing on the volume of commercial credit as a key to recovery, the Hoover and Roosevelt administrations were employing a faulty assumption. Classical economic theory was not prepared for the depression, the collapse of consumer demand and business investment which John Maynard Keynes described as the liquidity trap. Although shortages of capital had limited economic growth in the nineteenth century, there was no shortage of capital during the 1930s. The only shortage was consumer demand. The two most successful RFC direct loan programs—the Electric Home and Farm Authority and the Commodity Credit Corporation—boomed because there was enormous demand for the credit from worthy borrowers.

The decline in commercial credit, which the RFC struggled against through both administrations, had started back in the 1920s. Between 1923 and 1929, commercial loans as a portion of bank assets declined from 45 to 36 percent. After 1929, businessmen liquidated inventories and reduced receivables to get the money they needed to eliminate bank debt and finance operating losses. The total volume of business loans dropped after 1929 because of bank losses from bad debts and the suspension of more than 9,000 banks between 1930 and 1933. Bankers were cautious about loaning money in the 1930s, preferring the security of government bonds, but the RFC assumption that the decline in commercial loans resulted from banker fear was incorrect. Sound businesses were just as cautious about borrowing as bankers were about lending.[12]

[11] Ibid.
[12] Benjamin H. Beckhart, ed., *Business Loans of American Commercial Banks* (New York, 1959), pp. 9–12.

The failure of the RFC business loan program to stimulate a general recovery was part of a larger pattern of economic debate during the 1930s. Hoover's initial belief in the "rhetoric of confidence" had died quickly when confronted by massive, continuing unemployment. Cordell Hull's faith in the export panacea, implemented in the Reciprocal Trade Agreements Act of 1934, brought no miraculous industrial expansion. The wishful thinking of the institutional economists and business planners that the NRA would bring about a coordinated economy evaporated in a flood of cumbersome regulations, small business opposition, and Supreme Court hostility. The budget balancers, led by people like Secretaries of the Treasury Andrew Mellon in the 1920s, and Ogden Mills and Henry Morgenthau in the 1930s, waged a losing battle, especially when the recession of 1937–1938 followed so quickly on the heels of the 1937 cuts in federal spending. Although the budget balancers began to reassert themselves in 1940, the war in Europe crushed their plans.

The recovery debate continued between two groups. One group, led by Herbert Hoover, William Woodin, Jesse Jones, and others, concentrated on the supply of credit as the key to recovery, while another group, including people like Harry Hopkins, Lauchlin Currie, Marriner Eccles, and Harold Ickes, focused on consumer demand as the prerequisite for expansion. Throughout the 1930s, the "monetarists" tried to "push the monetary string" to expand credit and production. The Federal Reserve had lowered interest rates and reserve requirements; the Open Market Committee had bought government securities and consolidated its power with the Banking Act of 1935; and the Gold Reserve and Silver Purchase Acts of 1934 had devalued the currency and artificially tried to inflate prices. The most important New Deal agency in the monetary assault on the Great Depression had been the RFC, but all of its efforts—the bank loan program, preferred stock program, gold buying, industrial loan program, RFC Mortgage Company, Export-Import Bank, Electric Home and Farm Authority, Federal National Mortgage Association, and Commodity Credit Corporation—had not revived commercial credit or brought an industrial recovery. Even at the end of World War II bank loans had not reached their levels of the mid-1920s.

Historians have studied the "Keynesian revolution," looking to the 1937–1938 recession when reductions in federal spending triggered a serious economic decline and bankrupted the budget balancers. The 1938 increases in federal spending and the accompanying improvement in the general economy gave Keynesians more credibility. Ultimately, massive government spending during World War II convinced most Americans that manipulating consumer demand through taxation and spending was the magic cure for unemployment and inflation. But years of monetary experimentation preceded the conversion. Between 1931 and 1938, the government ran the gamut of monetary solutions using the RFC and the Federal Reserve system, but gradually, as the money supply theories faltered, fiscal theories reached a wider audience and gained credibility. Not until World War II did Keynesian economics triumph, but the frustrations and setbacks of the RFC business loan program during the 1930s prepared the way for the intellectual breakthrough demand management achieved between 1938 and 1945.

For the RFC, World War II represented the fulfillment of its 1930s' expectations. Suddenly there was a scarcity of capital and unprecedented demand for credit. Bankers began increasing the volume of their loans, from just over $21 billion in 1938 to more than $40 billion in 1945. For the first time the RFC found itself facing a huge demand for loans from sound companies. During the next four years, the RFC approved nearly $40 billion in loans to tens of thousands of businesses. Defense spending created an insatiable need for RFC resources, and excess reserves were soaked up by hungry businesses. The liquidity trap was broken. Deficit spending became enshrined as the backbone of postwar economic policy.

Between 1933 and 1940, Jesse Jones and the RFC walked carefully along the twisting path of New Deal public policy, passing through the bank reconstruction and cooperative planning phase of the NRA in 1933 and 1934, the direct loan phase of 1934 and 1935, the budget balancing phase of 1936 and 1937, and the antitrust and spending phases of 1938 and 1939. Through it all the RFC staked out a middle ground, avoiding the extremes of the political left and right, trying to find an accommodation between the needs of business and the demands of government. While insisting that the RFC avoid bailing out bad Wall Street loans, Jones also refused to use the agency in any populistic crusade, digging in, for example, on the proposal that the RFC pay off the depositors in closed banks. Although he allowed the RFC to buy preferred stock in thousands of banks, he would not let common stockholders off the hook, insisting that they match the government investment before he would proceed. Jones refused to have the RFC follow the lead of Adolf Berle and Rexford Tugwell in becoming a massive agency controlling the flow of capital in the economy, but he also realized that the age of laissez-faire, if it had ever existed, was thoroughly dead by the 1930s. Jones wanted the RFC to liquefy the money markets, but he did not want the federal government to assume ownership or even control of them. He successfully resisted making bad loans to the clamoring hordes of small businessmen, but had no problem with the RFC enthusiastically creating a secondary market for FHA mortgages or permanently entering the banking field with the Commodity Credit Corporation.

If the RFC loan program had failed to bring commercial credit back to its 1920s levels, its accomplishments during the 1930s were nevertheless impressive and, in many instances, permanent. The bank reconstruction and preferred stock investment program had rebuilt the money markets, and along with the rest of the New Deal credit establishment, the RFC had provided a financial liquidity which prevented a total collapse of the economy and set the stage for recovery. Although RFC railroad loans and investments had not restored solvency to the transportation system, they had postponed bankruptcies and permitted reorganizations, buying time for insurance companies and mutual savings banks to reduce their holdings of railroad bonds. Fannie Mae and the RFC Mortgage Company did not revive the construction industry, but provided a valuable secondary market for FHA mortgages. From the vantage point of a 1939 interview, Jesse Jones described the philosophy which governed the RFC:

> The day has gone forever when business men can expect to go merrily on their way, conducting their affairs as they see fit, without any interference from government. The public has such a big stake in the continuing functioning of the economic machine and is so greatly affected by a breakdown that its government must apply the brakes when the speed limits are exceeded.
>
> But that doesn't mean that the Federal government should have a representative on the board of directors of every American corporation. It doesn't mean that the government has license to dictate to business or crucify business men, big or little, whenever it seems convenient to do so because conditions are not as good as they might be or because some program may not be going along as smoothly as it might.
>
> It is as important for government and its representatives to realize the essential nature of business enterprise in this country as it is for business men to get it through their heads that government is in business to stay. Both must realize that neither can get along without the other, and that more is to be gained through cooperation and restraint than by keeping constantly at each other's throats.[13]

By the end of World War II, public policy in the United States bore little resemblance to its 1920 counterpart. The federal government emerged out of the Great Depression and World War II with direct responsibility for regulating the business cycle. State capitalism had become the norm. The federal credit establishment was permanently underwriting the money markets, and Keynesian economics had become the panacea for achieving full employment and stable prices. The foundation for state capitalism had been laid during the 1930s, and dozens of government agencies had appeared to support the private economy. The Reconstruction Finance Corporation had been directly involved with most of them: the Federal

---

[13] *New York Times*, July 2, 1939.

Emergency Relief Administration, Public Works Administration, Works Progress Administration, Civil Works Administration, Federal Home Loan banks, Federal Deposit Insurance Corporation, Tennessee Valley Authority, Electric Home and Farm Authority, Disaster Loan Corporation, Home Owners' Loan Corporation, Farm Credit Administration, Regional Agricultural Credit Corporations, Federal Intermediate Credit banks, Federal Land banks, Federal Farm Loan Commissioner, Federal Farm Mortgage Corporation, Federal Housing Administration, Rural Electrification Administration, Resettlement Administration, RFC Mortgage Company, Export-Import Bank, Commodity Credit Corporation, National Recovery Administration, Federal National Mortgage Association, and the Agricultural Adjustment Administration. Conservative but not ideological, pragmatic but not experimental, the RFC avoided political extremes while wholeheartedly accepting its responsibility for saving capitalism. It was, quintessentially, a product of the American mainstream. Along with the National Recovery Administration and the Agricultural Adjustment Administration, the Reconstruction Finance Corporation was a major recovery agency and, as the only one to survive intact throughout the 1930s and World War II, the most symbolic of the New Deal and the state capitalism it fostered.

Selected Bibliography

Manuscript Collections

Bernard Baruch Papers, Princeton University.

Adolf Berle Papers, Franklin D. Roosevelt Presidential Library.

Comptroller of the Currency Papers, Records Group 101, National Archives.

James Couzens Papers, Library of Congress.

Fred Croxton Papers, Herbert Hoover Presidential Library, West Branch, Iowa.

Charles Dawes Papers, Northwestern University.

Department of Commerce Papers, Records Group 40, National Archives.

Department of the Treasury Papers, Records Group 56, National Archives.

Federal Reserve Board Papers, Federal Reserve Board, Washington, D.C.

Carter Glass Papers, University of Virginia.

E. A. Goldenweisar Papers, Library of Congress.

Charles Hamlin Papers, Library of Congress.

George Harrison Papers, Columbia University.

Leon Henderson Papers, Franklin D. Roosevelt Presidential Library.

Herbert Hoover Papers, Herbert Hoover Presidential Library.

Harry Hopkins Papers, Franklin D. Roosevelt Presidential Library.

Jesse Jones Papers, Library of Congress.

Ogden Mills Papers, Library of Congress.

Henry Morgenthau Papers, Franklin D. Roosevelt Presidential Library.

William Myers Papers, Princeton University.

J.F.T. O'Connor Papers, University of California, Berkeley.

Gifford Pinchot Papers, Library of Congress.

Atlee Pomerene Papers, Kent State University.

Reconstruction Finance Corporation Papers, Records Group 234, National Archives. Records Group 234 also includes the records of the Federal National Mortgage Association, the RFC Mortgage Company, the Electric Home and Farm Authority, the Disaster Loan Corporation, and the Commodity Credit Corporation.

Franklin D. Roosevelt Papers, Franklin D. Roosevelt Presidential Library.

Harold Smith Papers, Franklin D. Roosevelt Presidential Library.
Henry Stimson Papers, Yale University.
Frederic Taber Papers, Records Group 234, National Archives.
Robert Wagner Papers, Georgetown University.

ORAL HISTORIES

New York. Columbia University Oral History Research Office
    (COHR)
    Adolf Berle   Chester Morrill
    Henry Bruere   Jackson Reynolds
    William Clayton   Rexford Tugwell
    Clifford Durr   James Warburg
    Jerome Frank   Walter Wyatt
    Eugene Meyer
West Branch, Iowa. Herbert Hoover Presidential Library
    James H. Douglas, Jr.   Bradley Nash
    Raymond Moley   Stanley Reed

NEWSPAPERS

    Baltimore Sun   *Nashville Tennessean*
    Chicago Tribune   *Nevada State Journal*
    Commercial & Financial   *New Orleans Times-Picayune*
        Chronicle   *New York Herald Tribune*
    Des Moines Tribune   *New York Times*
    Detroit Free Press   *Wall Street Journal*
    Detroit News   *Washington Post*
    Idaho Daily Statesman

CONGRESSIONAL PUBLICATIONS

House. Committee on Banking and Currency. *Hearings on H.R.
    5060 and H.R. 5116: Creation of a Reconstruction Finance Cor-
    poration.* 72d Cong., 1st Sess., 1932.
House. Committee on Banking and Currency. *Hearings on H.R.
    4240: A Bill to Extend the Functions of the R.F.C.* 74th Cong.,
    1st Sess., 1935.
House. Committee on Banking and Currency. *Hearings on H.R.
    5357: Banking Act of 1935.* 74th Cong., 1st Sess., 1935.

230

House. Committee on Banking and Currency. *Hearings on H.R. 11104: The Commodity Credit Corporation.* 74th Cong., 2d Sess., 1936.

House. Committee on Banking and Currency. *Hearings on H.R. 9379: Reconstruction Finance Corporation Relief Obligations.* 75th Cong., 3d Sess., 1938.

House. Committee on Banking and Currency. *Hearings on H.R. 10608: Loans to Railroads by the RFC.* 75th Cong., 3d Sess., 1938.

House. *Document No. 449: Summary of the Activities of the Commodity Credit Corporation through June 30, 1939.* 76th Cong., 1st Sess., 1939.

Senate. Committee on Banking and Currency. *Hearings on S. 1: Creation of a Reconstruction Finance Corporation.* 72d Cong., 1st Sess., 1932.

Senate. Committee on Banking and Currency. *Hearings on S. 4115: A Bill to Provide for the Safe and More Effective Use of Assets of Federal Banks and National Banking Associations.* 72d Cong., 1st Sess., 1932.

Senate. Committee on Banking and Currency. *Hearings on S. 4632, S. 4727, and S. 4822: Bills Relating to Federal Loans to Aid Unemployment.* 72d Cong., 1st Sess., 1932.

Senate. Subcommittee of the Committee on Manufactures. *Hearings on S. 4592: Federal Cooperation in Unemployment Relief.* 72d Cong., 1st Sess., 1932.

Senate. Committee on Manufactures. *Hearings on S. 5125: Federal Aid for Unemployment Relief.* 72d Cong., 2d Sess., 1933.

Senate. Committee on Banking and Currency. *Hearings on S. 5336: Further Unemployment Relief through the RFC.* 72d Cong., 2d Sess., 1933.

Senate. Committee on Banking and Currency. *Hearings on S.J. Res. 245: Joint Resolution to Suspend the Making of Loans to Railroads by the RFC.* 72d Cong., 2d Sess., 1933.

Senate. Committee on Banking and Currency. *Hearings on S. 509: Bill to Amend the Emergency Relief and Construction Act of 1932.* 73d Cong., 1st Sess., 1933.

Senate. Committee on Banking and Currency. *Hearings on S. 1094: Purchase of Preferred Stock of Insurance Companies by R.F.C.* 73d Cong., 1st Sess., 1934.

Senate. Committee on Interstate Commerce. *Hearings on S. 1580: A*

Bill to Relieve the Existing National Emergency to Interstate Railroad Transportation. 73d Cong., 1st Sess., 1933.

Senate. Committee on Banking and Currency. *Hearings on S.J. Res. 84 and S. Res. 56 and 97: Stock Exchange Practices.* 73d Cong., 2d Sess., 1934.

Senate. Committee on Banking and Currency. *Report No. 529: Financing of Exports and Imports by the R.F.C.* 73d Cong., 2d Sess., 1934.

Senate. Committee on Banking and Currency. *Hearings on S. 1175: Bill to Extend the Functions of the RFC.* 74th Cong., 1st Sess., 1935.

Senate. Committee on Banking and Currency. *Hearings on S. 3420: A Bill to Provide the Insurance by the RFC of Loans by Banks to Business Enterprise.* 75th Cong., 2d Sess., 1938.

Senate. Committee on Banking and Currency. *Hearings on S. 3948: A Bill to Amend So Much of the R.F.C. Act, As Amended, As Relates to Railroads.* 75th Cong., 3d Sess., 1938.

Senate. Committee on Banking and Currency. *Hearings on S. 1102: A Bill to Extend the Functions of the R.F.C.* 76th Cong., 1st Sess., 1939.

Senate. *Hearings on S. 1084: A Bill to Continue the Functions of the Commodity Credit Corporation and Export-Import Bank of Washington.* 76th Cong., 1st Sess., 1939.

Senate. Committee on Banking and Currency. *Hearings on S. 1482: A Bill to Provide for Insurance Loans to Business.* 76th Cong., 1st Sess., 1939.

GOVERNMENT DOCUMENTS

Electric Home and Farm Authority.
Annual Reports, 1935–1942.
Federal Reserve Board.
Annual Reports, 1930–1937.
Federal Reserve Bulletin, 1930–1940.
Minutes of the Meetings of the Federal Reserve Board, 1932–1935.
Interstate Commerce Commission.
Annual Reports, 1930–1938.
Reconstruction Finance Corporation.
Circulars, 1932–1935.
Custodian Bulletins, 1932–1933.
Emergency Relief Bulletins, 1932–1933.

Loan Agency Bulletins, 1932–1933.
Minutes of the Meetings of the Board of Directors, 1932–1940.
Press Releases, 1932–1940.
Quarterly Reports, 1932–1940.
Regional Agricultural Credit Corporation Bulletins, 1932–1933.
Special Loan Agency Bulletins, 1932–1933.
Secretary of the Treasury.
Annual Reports, 1919–1921, 1931–1935.
War Finance Corporation.
Annual Reports, 1918–1929.

Books and Articles

Adams, Henry H. *Harry Hopkins*. New York: 1977.
American Bankers' Association. *Banking After the Crisis*. New York: 1934.
———. *Changes in Bank Earning Assets*. New York: 1936.
———. *Government Lending Agencies*. New York: 1936.
———. *The Earning Power of Banks*. New York: 1939.
———. *The Rise in Bank Lending Activity*. New York: 1940.
Anderson, Clay J. *A Half-Century of Federal Reserve Policymaking, 1914–1964*. Philadelphia: 1965.
Arey, Hawthorne. *History of the Export-Import Bank of Washington*. Washington, D.C.: 1953.
Awalt, Francis G. "Recollections of the Banking Crisis of 1933." *Business History Review* 43 (Autumn 1969), 347–371.
Ballantine, Arthur. "When All the Banks Closed." *Harvard Business Review* 26 (Autumn 1948), 129–143.
Beckhart, Benjamin H., ed. *Business Loans of American Commercial Banks*. New York: 1959.
———. *The New York Money Market*, vol. 3. *Uses of Funds*. New York: 1932.
Beckhart, Benjamin, James G. Smith, and William Brown. *The New York Money Market*, vol. 3. *External and Internal Relations*. New York: 1932.
Behrens, Carl F. *Commercial Bank Activities in Urban Mortgage Financing*. New York: 1952.
Bellush, Bernard. *The Failure of the NRA*. New York: 1975.
Berle, Beatrice Bishop and Travis Beal Jacobs, eds. *Navigating the Rapids 1918–1971. From the Papers of Adolf A. Berle*. New York: 1973.

Blackorby, Edward B. *Prairie Rebel. The Public Life of William Lemke*. New Brunswick: 1963.

Blum, John Morton. *From the Morgenthau Diaries*, vol. I. *Years of Crisis, 1928–1938*. Boston: 1959.

Brennan, John A. *Silver and the First New Deal*. Reno, Nev.: 1969.

Brown, D. Clayton. *Electricity for Rural America. The Fight for the REA*. Westport, Conn.: 1980.

Bullock, Hugh. *The Story of Investment Companies*. New York: 1959.

Burns, Arthur E. and Donald S. Watson. *Government Spending and Economic Expansion*. Washington, D.C.: 1940.

Burns, Helen M. *The American Banking Community and the New Deal Banking Reforms, 1933–1935*. New York: 1974.

Caro, Robert A. *The Years of Lyndon Johnson. The Path to Power*. New York: 1982.

Chandler, Lester V. *American Monetary Policy, 1928–1941*. New York: 1971.

Clough, Shephard. *A Century of American Life Insurance*. New York: 1946.

Collins, Charles. *Rural Banking Reform*. New York: 1931.

Conkin, Paul. *The New Deal*. New York: 1967.

Cove, John H. *Problems of Small Business*. Washington, D.C.: 1941.

Cowing, Cedric B. *Populists, Plungers, and Progressives. A Social History of Stock and Commodity Speculation, 1890–1936*. Princeton: 1965.

Davis, J. Ronnie. *The New Economics and the Old Economists*. New York: 1971.

Dublin, Jack. *Credit Unions. Theory and Practice*. Detroit: 1966.

Eccles, Marriner S. *Beckoning Frontiers*. New York: 1951.

Edwards, Gurden. *How Banks Lend*. New York: 1939.

Ewalt, Josephine. *The Savings and Loan Story, 1930–1960*. Chicago: 1962.

Fischer, Gerald. *The American Banking Structure*. New York: 1968.

Friedman, Milton S. and Anna Jacobsen Schwartz. *The Great Contraction, 1929–1933*. Princeton: 1967.

Galbraith, John Kenneth. *The Great Crash, 1929*. Boston: 1954.

Goldenweisar, E. A. *Federal Reserve System in Operation*. New York: 1925.

Hardy, C. O. and Jacob Viner. *Report on the Availability of Bank*

Credit in the Seventh Federal Reserve District. Washington, D.C.: 1935.

Hawley, Ellis W. *The New Deal and the Problem of Monopoly*. Princeton: 1966.

Hawtrey, Ralph G. *The Art of Central Banking*. London: 1932.

Himmelberg, Robert F. *The Origins of the National Recovery Administration. Business, Government, and the Trade Association Issue, 1921–1933*. New York: 1976.

Hoag, W. Gifford. *The Farm Credit System. A History of Financial Self-Help*. New York: 1976.

Hoogenboom, Ari and Olive. *A History of the ICC. From Panacea to Palliative*. New York: 1976.

Hoover, Herbert. *The Memoirs of Herbert Hoover*. New York: 1952.

Jacoby, Neil and Raymond Saulnier. *Business Finance and Banking*. New York: 1947.

———. *Term Lending to Business*. Washington, D.C.: 1942.

Jones, Jesse H. *Fifty Billion Dollars*. New York: 1951.

Karl, Barry D. *Executive Reorganization and Reform in the New Deal. The Genesis of Administrative Management, 1900–1939*. Cambridge, Mass.: 1963.

Kennedy, Susan Estabrook. *The Banking Crisis of 1933*. Lexington, Ky.: 1973.

Keynes, John Maynard. *A Treatise on Money*. London: 1930.

Latham, Earl. *The Politics of Railroad Coordination, 1933–1936*. Cambridge, Mass.: 1959.

Lekachman, Robert. *The Age of Keynes*. New York: 1966.

Leuchtenburg, William E. *Franklin D. Roosevelt and the New Deal, 1932–1940*. New York: 1963.

Lintner, John. *Mutual Savings Banks in the Savings and Mortgage Markets*. Boston: 1948.

McDonald, Dwight. "The Monopoly Committee: A Study in Frustration." *The American Scholar* 8 (Summer 1939), 295–308.

Maney, Patrick J. *"Young Bob" La Follete. A Biography of Robert M. La Follette, Jr., 1895–1953*. Columbia: 1978.

Margold, Stella. *Export Credit Insurance in Europe Today*. Washington, D.C.: 1934.

Marvell, Thomas B. *The Federal Home Loan Bank Board*. New York: 1969.

Moley, Raymond. *The First New Deal*. New York: 1966.

Moody, J. Carroll and Gilbert C. Fite. *The Credit Union Movement. Origins and Development, 1850–1970.* Lincoln, Nebr.: 1971.

Morgenthau, Henry, Jr. *Farm Loans and Mortgage Refinancing through the Federal Land Bank System.* Washington, D.C.: 1933.

Muchmore, Lynn. "The Banking Crisis of 1933: Some Iowa Evidence." *Journal of Economic History* 30 (September 1970), 627–40.

Myers, Margaret. *Financial History of the United States.* New York: 1970.

Myers, William S., ed. *The State Papers and Other Public Writings of Herbert Hoover.* New York: 1934.

Nadler, Marcus, Sipa Heller, and Samuel Shipman. *The Money Market and Its Institutions.* New York: 1955.

O'Connor, J.F.T. *The Banking Crisis and Recovery under the Roosevelt Administration.* Chicago: 1935.

Olson, James S. "The Boise Banking Panic of 1932." *Idaho Yesterdays* 18 (Winter 1974–1975), 25–28.

———. "Herbert Hoover and the National Credit Corporation." *Annals of Iowa* 41 (Fall 1972), 1104–13.

———. *Herbert Hoover and the Reconstruction Finance Corporation, 1931–1933.* Ames, Iowa: 1977.

———. "Rehearsal for Disaster: Hoover, the RFC, and the Banking Crisis in Nevada, 1932–1933." *The Western Historical Quarterly* 6 (April 1975), 149–62.

Orren, Karen. *Corporate Power and Social Change. The Politics of the Life Insurance Industry.* Baltimore: 1974.

Oser, Jacob. *The Evolution of Economic Thought.* New York: 1963.

Pearson, James C. *The Reciprocal Trade Agreements Program. The Policy of the United States and Its Effectiveness.* New York: 1942.

Perkins, Van L. *Crisis in Agriculture. The Agricultural Adjustment Administration and the New Deal, 1933.* Berkeley: 1969.

Polenberg, Richard. *Reorganizing Roosevelt's Government. The Controversy Over Executive Reorganization, 1936–1939.* Cambridge, Mass.: 1966.

Reeve, Joseph. *Monetary Reform Movements.* Washington, D.C.: 1943.

Roos, Charles F. *NRA Economic Planning.* New York: 1937.

Rosen, Elliott A. *Hoover, Roosevelt, and the Brains Trust. From Depression to New Deal.* New York: 1977.

Rosenhof, Theodore. *Dogma, Depression, and the New Deal. The Debate of Political Leaders over Economic Recovery*. New York: 1975.

Rosenman, Samuel I., ed. *The Public Papers and Addresses of Franklin D. Roosevelt*, vol. II. *The Year of Crisis, 1933*. New York: 1938.

Sargent, James E. "FDR and Lewis Douglas: Budget Balancing and the Early New Deal." *Prologue* 6 (Spring 1974), 33–44.

Saulnier, Raymond J. *Industrial Banking Companies and Their Credit Practices*. New York: 1940.

———. *Urban Mortgage Lending by Life Insurance Companies*. New York: 1950.

Schlesinger, Arthur M. *The Age of Roosevelt*, vol. II. *The Coming of the New Deal*. Boston: 1958.

Shaterian, William S. *Export-Import Banking*. New York: 1956.

Sobel, Robert. *The Great Bull Market. Wall Street in the 1920s*. New York: 1968.

Solmon, Lewis C. *Economics*. New York: 1972.

Soule, George. *Prosperity Decade. From War to Depression, 1917–1929*. New York: 1947.

Spero, Herbert. *Reconstruction Finance Corporation Loans to Railroads, 1932–1937*. New York: 1939.

Sternsher, Bernard. *Rexford Tugwell and the New Deal*. New York: 1964.

Stokes, W. N., Jr. *Credit to Farmers. The Story of the Federal Intermediate Credit Banks and Production Credit Associations*. New York: 1973.

Timmons, Bascom N. *Jesse H. Jones: The Man and the Statesman*. New York: 1956.

Trescott, Paul. *Financing American Enterprise. The Story of Commercial Banking*. New York: 1963.

Upham, Cyril B. and Edwin Lamke. *Closed and Distressed Banks*. Washington, D.C.: 1934.

Wehle, Louis B. *Hidden Threads of History*. New York: 1953.

Weissman, Rudolph L. *Small Business and Venture Capital*. New York: 1945.

Welfling, Weldon. *Mutual Savings Banks. The Evolution of a Financial Intermediary*. Cleveland: 1968.

Wicker, Elmus R. *Federal Reserve Monetary Policy, 1917–1933*. New York: 1966.

Wilson, Winston P. *Harvey Couch*. Nashville: 1947.

DISSERTATIONS

Bee, Clair. "The Reconstruction Finance Corporation." Master's thesis. Rutgers—The State University. 1933.

Carter, John. "The Recovery Program of the Hoover Administration." Master's thesis. University of California at Berkeley. 1936.

Cho, Hyo Won. "The Evolution of the R.F.C." Ph.D. dissertation. Ohio State University. 1953.

Hildebrandt, Donald. "The Reconstruction Finance Corporation." M.B.A. thesis. Ohio State University. 1951.

Neville, Howard R. "An Historical Study of the Collapse of Banking in Detroit." Ph.D. dissertation. Michigan State University. 1956.

Niznik, Monica Lynne. "Thomas G. Corcoran: The Public Service of Franklin Roosevelt's 'Tommy the Cork.' " Ph.D. dissertation. University of Notre Dame. 1981.

Index

LIBRARY OF CONGRESS CATALOGING-IN-PUBLICATION DATA

Olson, James Stuart, 1946–
Saving capitalism.

Bibliography: p.
Includes index.
1. Reconstruction Finance Corporation—History. 2. New Deal, 1933–
1939. 3. United States—Economic policy—1933–1945. I. Title.
HG3729.U5O47 1988 353.0082′5′09 87-7275
ISBN 0–691–04749–9 (alk. paper)